Syndicates and Societies

When you work on the streets of Dhaka, crime is part of everyday life. Rackets are ubiquitous, political muscle widespread and territory often fought over. Locals refer to the syndicate that lie behind the façade of the city, controlling who works where, how services are delivered and who profits. Based on years of research, *Syndicates and Societies* reveals how syndicates shape life in Kawran Bazaar, the largest marketplace in Bangladesh, and offers a new approach to understanding the nexus of crime and politics. The book traces the bazaar's history from a heartland of gangsters to being dominated by ruling party leaders and state officials. It follows a group of labourers as they seek a place in this world, aligning themselves to leaders, orchestrating bombings and fighting off rivals. *Syndicates and Societies* thus explores the relationship between crime and order, revealing a world of extortionists and informers, political muscle and union leaders.

David Jackman is a Leverhulme Early Career Fellow at the University of Oxford. He studies the political economy of crime and violence in South Asia with a focus on Bangladesh and West Bengal. He is co-editor of the volume *Controlling the Capital: Political Dominance in the Urbanizing World* (2023).

SOUTH ASIA IN THE SOCIAL SCIENCES

South Asia has become a laboratory for devising new institutions and practices of modern social life. Forms of capitalist enterprise, providing welfare and social services, the public role of religion, the management of ethnic conflict, popular culture and mass democracy in the countries of the region have shown a marked divergence from known patterns in other parts of the world. South Asia is now being studied for its relevance to the general theoretical understanding of modernity itself.

South Asia in the Social Sciences features books that offer innovative research on contemporary South Asia. It focuses on the place of the region in the various global disciplines of the social sciences and highlights research that uses unconventional sources of information and novel research methods. While recognising that most current research is focused on the larger countries, the series attempts to showcase research on the smaller countries of the region.

General Editor
Partha Chatterjee
Columbia University

Editorial Board
Stuart Corbridge
Durham University

Satish Deshpande
University of Delhi (retired)

Christophe Jaffrelot
Centre d'etudes et de recherches internationales, Paris

Nivedita Menon
Jawaharlal Nehru University

Books in the series:

Government as Practice: Democratic Left in a Transforming India
Dwaipayan Bhattacharyya

Courting the People: Public Interest Litigation in Post-Emergency India
Anuj Bhuwania

Development after Statism: Industrial Firms and the Political Economy of South Asia
Adnan Naseemullah

Politics of the Poor: Negotiating Democracy in Contemporary India
Indrajit Roy

Nationalism, Development and Ethnic Conflict in Sri Lanka
Rajesh Venugopal

South Asian Governmentalities: Michel Foucault and the Question of Postcolonial Orderings
Stephen Legg and Deana Heath (eds.)

Adivasis and the State: Subalternity and Citizenship in India's Bhil Heartland
Alf Gunvald Nilsen

Maoist People's War and the Revolution of Everyday Life in Nepal
Ina Zharkevich

New Perspectives on Pakistan's Political Economy: State, Class and Social Change
Matthew McCartney and S. Akbar Zaidi (eds.)

Crafty Oligarchs, Savvy Voters: Democracy under Inequality in Rural Pakistan
Shandana Khan Mohmand

Dynamics of Caste and Law: Dalits, Oppression and Constitutional Democracy in India
Dag-Erik Berg

Simultaneous Identities: Language, Education and the Nepali Nation
Uma Pradhan

Deceptive Majority: Dalits, Hinduism, and Underground Religion
Joel Lee

Colossus: The Anatomy of Delhi
Sanjoy Chakravorty and Neelanjan Sircar (eds.)

When Ideas Matter: Democracy and Corruption in India
Bilal A. Baloch

In Search of Home: Citizenship, Law and the Politics of the Poor
Kaveri Haritas

Bureaucratic Archaeology: State, Science, and Past in Postcolonial India
Ashish Avikunthak

The Odds Revisited: Political Economy of the Development of Bangladesh
K. A. S. Murshid

An Uneasy Hegemony: Politics of State-building and Struggles for Justice in Sri Lanka
Shyamika Jayasundara-Smits

Founding Mothers of the Indian Republic: Gender Politics of the Framing of the Constitution
Achyut Chetan

Freedom in Captivity: Negotiations of Belonging along Kashmir's Frontier
Radhika Gupta

Memories in the Service of the Hindu Nation: The Afterlife of the Partition of India
Pranav Kohli

Sovereign Atonement: Citizenship, Territory, and the State at the Bangladesh-India Border
Md Azmeary Ferdoush

Legalizing the Revolution: India and the Constitution of the Postcolony
Sandipto Dasgupta

Performing Sovereign Aspirations: Tamil Insurgency and Postwar Transition in Sri Lanka
Bart Klem

Syndicates and Societies

Criminal Politics in Dhaka

David Jackman

Shaftesbury Road, Cambridge CB2 8EA, United Kingdom

One Liberty Plaza, 20th Floor, New York, NY 10006, USA

477 Williamstown Road, Port Melbourne, VIC 3207, Australia

314–321, 3rd Floor, Plot 3, Splendor Forum, Jasola District Centre, New Delhi – 110025, India

103 Penang Road, #05–06/07, Visioncrest Commercial, Singapore 238467

Cambridge University Press is part of Cambridge University Press & Assessment, a department of the University of Cambridge.

We share the University's mission to contribute to society through the pursuit of education, learning and research at the highest international levels of excellence.

www.cambridge.org
Information on this title: www.cambridge.org/9781009442305

© David Jackman 2024

This publication is in copyright. Subject to statutory exception and to the provisions of relevant collective licensing agreements, no reproduction of any part may take place without the written permission of Cambridge University Press & Assessment

First published 2024

Printed in India by Avantika Printers Pvt. Ltd.

A catalogue record for this publication is available from the British Library

ISBN 978-1-009-44230-5 Hardback

Cambridge University Press & Assessment has no responsibility for the persistence or accuracy of URLs for external or third-party internet websites referred to in this publication and does not guarantee that any content on such websites is, or will remain, accurate or appropriate.

Contents

Acknowledgements — ix
List of Abbreviations — xi

Introduction — 1
1. A Dhaka *Serai* — 22
2. The Years of Terror — 46
3. *Chanda(baji)* — 73
4. Labour Lords — 102
5. Fighting for Carrots — 129
6. (Not So) Friendly Societies — 150
7. When Crime Is Order — 166

Glossary — 185
Bibliography — 189
Index — 207

Acknowledgements

This book is the outcome of a long journey only possible with much privilege, support and guidance. Most of all I am indebted to the people in Dhaka who allowed me a glimpse into their lives, gave me valuable time, put up with my puzzling, often poorly phrased and intrusive questions and gave me endless cups of tea. In particular, I am grateful to the *'jhupri'* labourers at Karwan Bazaar. I still cannot fathom what they have seen and experienced growing up on the streets, and the gravity of the choices and challenges they continue to face. In Bangladesh I would also like to thank Anthony and Siddique, for their friendship, assistance and wise words. I am grateful to a number of NGOs, especially Aparajeyo Bangladesh and the Sajida Foundation for letting me into their worlds. I was fortunate to be affiliated with the Bangladesh Institute of Development Studies and would like to give particular thanks to Zulfiqar Ali for facilitating this and my stay in Bangladesh. None of the views expressed in this book should be taken as those of the people I acknowledge here.

Many other scholars of Bangladesh have guided and pushed me further with grace and wisdom. A thank you especially to my doctoral supervisors Joe Devine and Geof Wood, and to Mathilde Maitrot, David Lewis and Arild Engelsen Ruud. Thank you also to colleagues at the University of Manchester, the School of Oriental and African Studies and the University of Oxford for the fun and support. At Cambridge University Press I would like to thank Anwesha Rana and Priya Das for guiding me through the final steps of realising this project, as well as the insight of two anonymous reviewers. This research was only possible with the generous support of Economic and Social Research Council doctoral funding and a postdoctoral research fellowship, as well as an Early Career Research Fellowship from the Leverhulme Trust. Thank you also to the *European Journal of Development Research*, where some material from Chapter 5 was previously published as 'Intermediaries and Political Order in Bangladesh', *EJDR* 31 (2019): 705–723. Finally, love and thanks to my extraordinary parents Glenn and Irene, partner Mathilde, and children Evie and Colette.

Abbreviations

AL	Awami League
ASCA	Accumulating Savings and Credit Association
BAKSAL	Bangladesh Krishak Sramik Awami League
BNP	Bangladesh Nationalist Party
CEO	chief executive officer
CNG	compressed natural gas
DB	Detective Branch
DC	deputy commissioner
GDP	gross domestic product
ID	identity document
ILC	Indian Law Commission
ILO	International Labour Organization
INTUC	Indian National Trade Union Congress
JCD	Jatiobadi Chhatra Dal
JRB	Jatio Rakkhi Bahini
LGRD	Local Government and Rural Development
MFI	microfinance institution
MP	member of parliament
NGO	non-governmental organisation
NSDF	National Slum Dwellers Federation
OC	officer in-charge
RAB	Rapid Action Battalion
RCLI	Royal Commission on Labour in India
ROSCA	Rotating Savings and Credit Association
TV	television
VDP	Village Defence Party
WASA	Water Supply and Sewer

Introduction

Rubel[1] was only eight or nine when he came to Dhaka. He took a train alone from the north, arrived at a station in the centre of the city and walked to a nearby bazaar where he has worked ever since. Memories of his family and village have blurred over the years, and today he is married with two children and stays in a *basti* (slum) elsewhere in the city. For people who have grown up on the streets of Dhaka, such stories are common. Some recall odd details of their home but have forgotten the name of their village and even family. Some ran away from poverty and cruelty, and described a widowed mother, a resentful stepparent, a neglectful father, mental illness, abuse at school or the madrasah. For some, the story of their arrival is bound up with a precise moment of fear, such as losing a prized asset and not daring to return home or a particularly brutal argument. For others, the streets have always been their home, growing up in makeshift shacks formed from tarpaulin sheets that dot stretches of pavement, and where even today some babies are born.

Dhaka, the capital of Bangladesh, is one of the most densely populated cities on earth.[2] People here live in a sprawling mix of apartment blocks, a few upmarket neighbourhoods and large *basti*s. Others skirt the edges of these in bazaars, transport terminals and pavements. Despite being one of the most populous cities on earth, it is little known in the so-called Global North, so much so that foreigners often pronounce it 'Dakar' after the Senegalese capital. As a city it is rarely deemed beautiful by outside eyes, unlike its iconic cousin Kolkata, nor does it boast obvious distinctions to draw tourists or wider interest. When Dhaka does appear in the world's media, it is sometimes in reference to its violent politics, the garment factories which sit at its edges or its frequent designation as one of the least liveable cities in the world. The only Western film to feature Dhaka – a recent Netflix production concerning the abduction of an Indian drug lord's son and a white mercenary hero – was filmed in India and Thailand, and its earlier title of 'Dhaka' scrapped for the more marketable *Extraction*. Whatever outsiders make of it, Dhaka is projected to become the fourth largest city globally by 2050,[3] a rank some say it once exceeded almost 400 years ago.[4]

The children arriving here every day come from the sea-and-storm-ravaged south, the river-eroded north and everywhere in between, entering by rickety launches, rusty buses and atop trains. Some describe having been 'lost' from the family that accompanied them, while others arrive alone or with friends. The ports and stations are their gateways, where they first encounter city life. Buildings are taller than they have ever seen before, shops brighter and accents more diverse. Children quickly form small groups, those already familiar with urban life showing others the ways of the city. Many cluster around transport terminals, while others spread out, finding parks, markets and public spaces where they can beg, find odd jobs or more likely scour the city as scavengers, traipsing around with old cement sacks to collect discarded plastic bottles and paper.

Like many children, Rubel found Kawran Bazaar[5] – the largest wholesale market in the country, and a magnet for those in need of work. The bazaar is an incongruous sight: a large messy wholesale market of fish, fruit and vegetables, surrounded by hundreds of shops, all squeezed between commercial and government offices in the centre of Dhaka. The bazaar's arteries run past major media companies, including the leading Bengali daily *Prothom Alo*, as well as headquarters of important government corporations and departments. At night the doorsteps to these offices give way to large trucks, some imported from England long ago and now colourful beyond recognition, laden heavy with goods and unloaded by labourers into baskets and flat-backed rickshaw vans. Women and children hover nearby to scavenge loose vegetables and stow them away in old cement sacks, many later selling them at the side of the bazaar or beneath a nearby flyover at a street market named beggar's market (Fokinni Bazaar).

As a young child Rubel first found shelter here at a centre called Chinomul (rootless people) run by a non-governmental organisation (NGO), where he could occasionally rest, eat and get a basic education. But such centres opened and closed based on the flow of donor funding (as they still do today), passing children back to the streets, or if lucky, to another centre. In any case they were often closed at night. Rubel was hence raised by the bazaar, relying on the friendships he formed with other children, whom he describes as being like his family. From a young age, he was a leader among them, and together they survived at the edges of the bazaar before they were old and strong enough to labour. At night they roamed the alleys poaching vegetables, often running behind moving rickshaw vans, cutting small holes in sacks and making off with as many goods as they could carry without being caught. In the early hours of the morning, they used to crouch down at the side of the paths and sell the vegetables in small 10-taka piles.

Daily life at the bazaar, drifting between games of cricket at a nearby park, petty theft and NGO centres, was anchored by not only the friendships Rubel formed but also the figures of authority he looked up to. Such relationships are often spoken of through the language of fictive kinship, most commonly the idea of a *boro bhai*, or a big brother. A common refrain here is that 'you have to have a *boro bhai*'. When he was a thief, Rubel and his friends looked up to a big brother from the nearby *basti*, which until recently ran alongside the railway line and housed the city's largest illegal drug market. This *boro bhai* was a local dealer, with whom they would share their daily takings from selling vegetables and who would ostensibly protect them if a shop owner or the police caught them. This type of muscular, criminal and street-level figure had become more notable in the years just prior to Rubel's arrival in Dhaka. In 1991 Bangladesh had seen a return to parliamentary democracy and with it, politicians and parties sought to solidify control over their constituencies and compete with rivals by incorporating this type of muscle, grown from the streets upwards.

Although Kawran Bazaar is only a kilometre or so from Bangladesh's National Parliament (the Jatiya Shangshad), in Rubel's youth it was ruled not by political leaders or state authorities, but by *santrashi* (terrorist, gangster) or 'godfather', as they are termed, of whom the *boro bhai* Rubel described was a low-level affiliate. Through Rubel's youth, such gangsters grew to notoriety, imposing themselves on much of the city's political and economic life, often rising from humble beginnings to acquire wealth few of that class could have imagined. These figures were often affiliated to the country's major political parties (the Awami League and the Bangladesh Nationalist Party [BNP]) yet operated at arm's length. Navigating this landscape was crucial to the youth coming of age during these years, particularly for those with political ambitions, or outside of wealthy enclaves. It was a time when 'the godfather controlled everything … all the businesses paid them, and everyone was under them', as Rubel recalled about life at the bazaar in the 1990s and early 2000s. It was an era when you could be drinking tea at one moment, and the next moment a bomb would explode, 'one person losing a hand, another person a foot'.[6]

Much has changed in the years since. Rubel is today a labour leader in a lane of the bazaar named *jhupri* (shack) after the shelters that used to run down its side, where it is he who is now looked up to as a *boro bhai*. Bangladesh is currently lauded as a development success story, with high economic growth and the kudos of entering the ranks of middle-income nations.[7] The years of shifting political parties familiar to Rubel's generation have been stamped out by an entrenched and dominant Awami League government. The once infamous gangsters have been killed off, imprisoned or are in hiding abroad. Yet working at the bazaar is not straightforward. The crime and violence of Rubel's youth are far less overt, yet no less real. Twenty years ago, everyone looked to the godfathers as authorities, but today others sit in their place. 'David *bhai*, do you know who the biggest gangster [*santrashi*] in Bangladesh is today? The Awami League', Rubel put it to me on a number of occasions. At other times the biggest gangster was described as the police. In one of our early encounters at Kawran Bazaar, I explained to Rubel that I was there to study the lives of labourers and life at the bazaar. He replied with one line: 'If you want to understand Kawran Bazaar you must know that it is a syndicate. That's how things work here.'

Between Crime and Politics

The English word 'syndicate' is now commonplace in Bangladesh and much of South Asia. It sits alongside 'mafia', 'don' and 'godfather' as part of an everyday vocabulary of political life, evoking the discourse of Western organised crime. In Bangladesh, syndicates are seen lurking behind everything from government tenders to leaked exam papers. People speak of syndicates selling government jobs; controlling migrant labour; providing access to health care; selling fake passports; smuggling gold; supplying illegal gas, electricity and water in *basti*s; taking and defaulting on bank loans; grabbing land; running protection rackets among businesses and supply chains; and even controlling ambulances. A similar story can be found across the Indian border. In Jharkhand, syndicates are seen as controlling stolen coal,[8] in West Bengal they grab land[9] and limit access to the construction trade[10] and in Western Uttar Pradesh they control sand, operating as groups between ten to forty-five strong under the umbrella of a 'big mafia'.[11] In Arild Engelsen Ruud's analysis from Bangladesh, a syndicate is a network of 'businesspeople, politicians, criminals and the police' centring on political 'bosses' – the 'CEO-*netas*' – who illegally control local resources, such as lucrative government tenders.[12]

The usage of terms such as 'godfather', 'mafia' and 'syndicate' in part responds to a widespread sense across much of the subcontinent that politics, and indeed everyday life, has become criminalised. When Rubel was entering his teenage years, for example, Bangladesh was ranked by Transparency International as the most 'corrupt' country on earth. It maintained this ignominious title for five years (2001–2005).[13] Extortion, kidnapping, tender grabbing and political violence had become commonplace. Some commentators at the time explained this in terms of the 'criminalization of politics', pointing attention to the growing role of street 'thugs' or 'hoodlums' (*mastan*), used by both ruling and opposition parties in their attempts to control and disrupt.[14] Others took their analysis a step further and wrote of Bangladesh itself as having become a 'mastanocracy', with criminality so deeply permeating the country's politics as to define it.[15] Newspaper reports meanwhile highlighted the alleged crimes of politicians along with opaque figures in major cities, some designated as low-ranking party leaders, others as *top terror*, some as both. Although common, these reports were perhaps not as forthright as they would have been, had Bangladesh not also been ranked the most dangerous place for journalists in Asia.[16]

The place of crime in politics is crucial to understand far beyond Bangladesh. The United Nations' Global Study on Homicide from 2023 estimates that between 2019 and 2021 the annual global number of homicides was on average 440,000, the majority of which came from what they categorise as 'organized criminal groups/gangs'.[17] In fact, organised crime is often a greater source of violent deaths than 'conflict' and 'terrorism'. Yet the challenge posed is not simply the growth of organised criminal groups standing in opposition to states, but something rather more complex. Anthropologists Jean and John Comaroff, for example, argue that 'lawbreaking and law enforcement are so entangled as often to be impossible to set apart.'[18] Such metaphors are common. Rubel described the influence of local politicians in daily life as being like a 'tangle' (*pantch* or *patch*), the word conjuring images of an unwieldy knot or the thread of a screw, and a term often heard here to evoke the calculations and games that politics brings. In Italy the notion of *intreccio* (interweaving) refers to the collusion of crime and politics, and is apparently a term popular in Palermo, the traditional heartland of the mafia.[19]

A long-standing tendency has been to view the presence of crime in politics within the bracket of 'corruption', as we saw in the description of Bangladesh earlier in this section. This, in an obvious sense, is true. In Bangladesh such syndicates are at times referred to as corruption (*durniti*) and crime (*aparadh*) locally and they clearly break the letter of the law. Politicians and state officials themselves often publicly convey such views, as if to contain examples of criminality in politics or the state that reach the public eye as isolated cases of egregious politicians or officials, and therefore reflective not of a party or system, but a bad apple. It has been widely argued, however, that the challenge analytically with such characterisations is that they view these dynamics as aberrations from the systems of law and governance which are assumed to define states, regulate economies and be enshrined in constitutions.[20] As one scholar puts it, this view would portray racketeering as 'an intrusive pathology that contaminates an otherwise virtuous system of exchange'.[21]

The problem with claims of corruption then is that these dynamics are so widespread that there appears in many contexts to be a systematic relationship between political authority and criminal behaviour. This is rarely evidenced in official statistics and data. A glaring exception in the South Asian context is the long list of criminal cases against elected and candidate politicians in India. A number of scholars have highlighted through public data that the percentage of politicians with criminal cases elected to office is increasing. As of 2021, 43 per cent of members of parliament (MPs) elected to India's Lok Sabha had criminal cases against them, of which 29 per cent can be deemed 'serious'. For state assemblies, these figures stood at 40 and 26 per cent, respectively.[22] When the Awami League returned to power in Bangladesh in early 2009, almost 50 per cent of their MPs 'were accused of having a criminal past' and 18 MPs had faced murder charges.[23]

Such statistics have been brought to life over the past decade or so by literature within the fields of anthropology, development studies and political science, which has offered rich insights into the nexus of crime and politics in South Asia, exploring how a capacity for violence and crime is embodied in figures of authority, can serve as an electoral strength and shore up political parties.[24] In Bangladesh a growing body of literature has pointed to the coercive control that political leaders and those around them exert over the local economy and state resources.[25] The dynamics such work reveals are familiar in many contexts: politicians embroiled in crime, criminals protected by the police, security agencies complicit in unlawful violence and the boundaries between state, party and criminal often too opaque to discern. Public declarations conceal backroom and street-corner deals; public tenders are grabbed, rackets run and elections rigged. Where there should be confrontation and due process, we in fact find collusion. Purported enemies are often in fact allies.[26] Together such work suggests that the great conceptual frames used to understand society, state and law and order, are being undercut by a symbiosis. One recent volume succinctly articulates this as such: 'politics is systematically criminalised, and crime politicised'.[27]

Less insight, however, has been shed on how the nexus of crime and politics is experienced from below, and how such a lens in turn shapes our understanding of this nexus. How is this experienced in the lives of people like Rubel, and the labourers, traders and street vendors at places like Kawran Bazaar?[28] This book draws from hundreds of interviews in Dhaka and a year-long ethnography with the *jhupri* labourers, to study the nexus of crime and politics in everyday life. It develops an intimate portrait of how crime is deeply enmeshed in the political life of the streets, of how labourers find work and seek opportunities, how vendors ply their trade on pavements, of how political reputations are built and how careers are sustained. The notion of a syndicate is central to understanding this. As we noted earlier in this section, syndicates are widely spoken of in public life in Bangladesh. For the *jhupri* labourers, they are so significant that the whole of Kawran Bazaar warrants the label. Syndicates are also often noted in academic literature, yet they are little theorised. Basic questions remain underexplored: how can syndicates be conceptualised? What forms do they take? How do people form them? What roles do they play in society and politics at large?

The chapters to come argue that syndicates invisibly carve up Kawran Bazaar and Dhaka city. Unlike notions of organised crime framed in opposition to the state, syndicates refer to the illegal, organised and coercive accumulation of capital by groups in positions of political authority. A syndicate is both a noun and a verb (syndicate *kora*), and thus refers to both a group and an activity. Syndicates take many forms, yet a prominent way in which they are felt in everyday life is through the dependencies people sustain on local figures of authority, actors who can be conceptualised as intermediaries. Coercively mediating access to a resource, often known as racketeering, reflects a widespread form of syndicates. Though coercive, extractive and exploitative, syndicates are often in fact constitutive of how political order is produced. Syndicates are furthermore crucial to sustaining the strength of politicians and political parties, who need to nurture street muscle in order to dominate politically. As such, the organisation of syndicates in society reflects the political hierarchy. Though the discourse of 'syndicates' is relatively new, the hierarchies and forms of extraction they refer to appear far from it. These arguments are built empirically in the pages to come through the story of Kawran Bazaar and the struggles of labourers, set against the backdrop of Bangladesh's recent political history. They are contextualised and outlined in the rest of this chapter.

Everyday Syndicates

Syndicates are lambasted across Bangladesh as a source of unfair and coercive control over economic life. In the rolling hills and tea plantations of Sreemangal in the northeast of the country, trade union leaders have described to me how a syndicate of ruling party politicians led by the local MP limited the scope of workers to advocate for better wages. In the Sundarbans in the far south, fishermen described a syndicate controlling lucrative fishing territories around the remote Dubla Char, looking out at the Bay of Bengal. In Dhaka, the notion of a syndicate is used to describe the cause of many daily injustices, including the widespread protection rackets that control work and trade. Syndicates then are not something exceptional, but entirely ordinary, and routinely pointed to in newspaper articles and everyday conversations.

The ubiquity of syndicates reflects how political authority is configured. States typically project images of their authority as consolidated and extending effectively to all ends and depths of their territory. Liberal or Weberian ideals of the state emphasise such qualities as the essence of a modern nation, which should monopolise the means of violence and ensure bureaucratic and law-abiding modes of governance on this basis. In many contexts, however, we hear instead that authority in society is fragmented or diffuse, that sovereignty[29] or security[30] is 'decentralized' and that control of violence is 'dispersed'.[31] James Scott wrote of this as the 'localization of power'.[32] In South Asia it has been argued that 'de facto sovereignty' reflects 'a wide range of violent claimants to political rule',[33] and that democracy itself should be seen as locally embedded, subject to particularistic configurations of power, dominance and subordination.[34] A common argument then is that intertwined with formal political authority, we find that real authority in many contexts is held by a motley crowd of local figures, ranging from gangs, gangsters and the mafia to trade unions, associations, informal local leaders and many more. As Thomas Blom Hansen writes, '[t]he local "big man" is ubiquitous in everyday life and central to most relationships between authorities and ordinary people in urban India'.[35] Furthermore, the manner in which formal authority is gained and sustained often relies on coercion and clientelism.[36] We have already noted how a new set of vernacular terms drawing from the image of the mafia to denote this have been popularised in South Asia and become a commonplace way of referring to the entanglement of crime in politics. In academic work the broader notion of a 'violent entrepreneur' can be used to capture how varied actors use violence entrepreneurially to pursue economic goals.[37]

A long line of literature from across the social sciences has examined the dependencies that people maintain on figures of localised authority. The precise vocabulary deployed differs. Some write of intermediaries, brokers, middlemen and gatekeepers, others are concerned with village 'big men', neighbourhood bosses, mafia or gangs and a vast body of literature has focused on the figure of the patron and their followers or clients. Whilst not to deny that important differences can be discerned between many of these concepts, upon inspection the extent to which analytical differences in fact reflect empirical ones is often questionable. Characteristics are often held in common (charisma, muscle, connections) and the precise figures identified as powerful and as controlling resources in any given context often defy simple categorisation. Politicians differ from informers who differ from labour leaders, yet all can be intermediaries, local big men and patrons. Anthropologist Jeremy Boissevain made a similar point succinctly over fifty years ago when he wrote 'all patrons are also brokers, but not all brokers are patrons'.[38] This is not to deny that figures of de facto authority vary significantly in their roles or characteristics, but instead that more conceptual labels often overlap closely when applied to actual people.

The notion of an intermediary or broker (terms used here synonymously) has particularly wide traction in literature from South Asia. In India, for example, intermediaries have been portrayed as 'non-formal', 'personalized' and 'extra-legal' actors who exist 'in different forms in almost all segments of national life'.[39] The journalist Josy Joseph writes of how '[i]n every corner of this country there is a middleman. Almost every other big businessman or famous politician or consultant is a mere intermediary.'[40] The prevalence of intermediaries in South Asia has led some scholars to define both state and society in these terms, coining notions of 'intermediation societies'[41] and the 'mediated state'.[42] The variety of figures that can be denoted through this term is then enormous, ranging from an assistant on a hospital ward or a tout hovering outside a government office to a local gangster or politician. One definition of a broker is as a 'class of mediators in the broadest sense, referring to anyone who facilitates, or controls, other people's access to state institutions'.[43] Yet a striking feature of studies from across South Asia (and far beyond) is the sheer diversity of roles played by figures of de facto authority in local life. The state as it is formally defined need not be the locus of resources mediated. Access to jobs, other market opportunities, housing, private services and security might all be the resources controlled. This is then an entrepreneurial domain where people seek and 'recognise areas in which an appropriately placed valve might profitably mediate between resources'.[44]

For some, intermediaries thus play a productive role in society. Anirudh Krishna, for example, writes of how intermediaries 'help individuals and groups gain access to the agencies of the state', such that '[w]here these channels are weak, democracy itself is made feebler'.[45] This builds in part from the perception of intermediaries as filling a 'gap' between a centralised political authority, and local social, economic and political life. Eric Wolf long ago described brokers in Mexico as actors who 'stand guard over the crucial junctures or synapses of relationships which connect the local system to the larger whole'.[46] Similarly in South Asia a common narrative is that in the face of a weak bureaucracy and state, intermediaries are a means of closing the space between formal administrative structures and local communities.[47]

Others portray a darker picture of intermediaries.[48] Jonathan Pattenden argues that gatekeeping represents a form of accumulation, serving the dominant class at the expense of labour.[49] Very many actors can be seen as operating as intermediaries, but far fewer would be explicitly identified with such a concept. A typical translation of broker in much of South Asia is *dalal*, a pejorative term that people actively distance themselves from. Michael Levien argues that *dalals* are associated with the impoverishment of illiterate farmers, selling their land for lower prices or being flagrantly cheated. In his studied context some such *dalals* were local 'big men' and hence 'agents of social dissolution, violating the social norms and undermining the trust that would be necessary for collective action'.[50] Though not always deploying this terminology, a long history of rural ethnographies from Bangladesh resonate with this analysis, detailing the dependencies of the poor and labouring classes on local elites and the exploitation this entails.[51]

The chapters to come describe how at Kawran Bazaar people depend on a wide array of intermediaries, from labour leaders to toll collectors, association leaders, political leaders, activists and informers, all of which overlap as labels. These 'men in the middle',[52] as Nikita Sud puts it, are diverse yet colloquially often seen as *boro bhai*, and play the role of both broker and patron. To understand their roles, we need to appreciate that the legal framework which in theory is premised on the state's monopoly on violence rarely effectively regulates many relationships and transactions in society as it is designed to. Instead, figures of local authority mediate access to important resources, such as the ability in Kawran Bazaar to sell goods in a certain spot, unload vegetables, and even enter the bazaar and stay safe. Often it is only through dependencies on such figures that people are able to engage in key economic activities. To repeat the common refrain from the bazaar: 'you have to have a *boro bhai*'. Such figures in turn are always embedded within wider networks and groups, today associated with either a wing of the ruling party or a branch of the state. In a context where there are many competing and potential sources of authority, those operating as intermediaries are only able to do so by providing protection for that arrangement. At the same time, they themselves are often also a threat from which protection is required. Intermediaries then are usually coercive figures.[53] Thus the roles they in practice play are known in academic literature and Western popular culture as racketeering: the coercive extraction of tribute in exchange for some form of service.[54]

The argument here then is that the manner in which access to many everyday resources is mediated often constitutes a racket, and that a racket is synonymous with what in Bangladesh is often termed a syndicate. Not all intermediaries are racketeers, but all racketeers are intermediaries. Syndicates are not something people look at from afar but are embodied in individual figures of authority, and the networks and groups such actors sit within. Creating and controlling syndicates is a focus of local politics. They are thus part of everyday life, the subject of gossip, of tea stall chats, of whispered conversations, fights and struggles. In the pages to come we will see that syndicates are also not simply the preserve of political bosses, but even labourers and their leaders. The cast of characters at the helm of such petty syndicates is diverse: Rubel and his fellow *boro bhai*s of the *jhupri* labourers, a local street vendor moving into politics, locally infamous young men controlling trucks, and gangsters turned informers. There are many forms syndicates can take and many paths to building them. Prevalent at the grassroots is the formation of societies or associations (*samiti*) built around an ostensibly mutual and worthy goal and the collective accumulation of capital. In practice many such societies are a cover for syndicates, facilitating the extraction of capital by leaders on the basis of the access they mediate to resources. The title of this book thus points both towards the place of syndicates within society at large and the porous distinctions between syndicates and grassroots societies.

Order Making

The *boro bhai*s of serious standing at Kawran Bazaar, the ones with their images plastered on posters at the sides of the alleys and status in ruling-party bodies, are extremely powerful locally. Some hold court in nearby offices or shops at the bazaar surrounded by dozens of their followers dutifully waiting at their side, with younger or new affiliates nervous to speak. Such figures are accorded respect for good reason. They often have huge discretionary power within their domains, are close to local security officials and can pose serious threats to those who confront their interests. They run protection rackets of various kinds, they profit from tenders issued in nearby offices and are said to have a hand in the wider black economy such as the large drug market which until recently ran nearby. The big syndicates revolve around them. It is this type of authority which is reflected in the scholarly choice to use terms like 'bosses' and 'lords' to describe how such domains are almost mini fiefdoms. Yet these big brothers always look up to bigger brothers. These are not warlords or independent princely states, but towards the tail end of long chains that link lowly labourers to powerful ministers.[55]

The syndicates that invisibly carve up Kawran Bazaar are part of a bigger story about how political coalitions are organised in Bangladesh, and how political order itself is created. As argued in the previous sections, a basic characteristic of political authority in Bangladesh, and indeed many other places, is that de facto authority is associated with a capacity for violence, and this capacity is 'dispersed' throughout society. As such, political order cannot be understood as stemming from the monopoly on violence of a central state, as modern states are typically imagined. Instead, it appears to rest in part on those at the political centre drawing together an array of actors who can sufficiently dominate rivals to ensure a degree of stability and continuity.[56] In most contexts this typically revolves around a political party but incorporates a wide array of different actors. A simple form this takes in microcosm is the dependency of a politician on criminal actors and muscle to win elections.[57] The order created by such arrangements may of course still be violent. Laurent Gayer, for example, has described the 'ordered disorder' of Karachi's politics, marked by periodic escalations of violence and a 'complex ecology of violence co-produced by the city's belligerents'.[58] He argues such conflict reflects not that between 'ontological "enemies"' but the machinations of violent entrepreneurs and parties 'which have been, remain or could become again coalition partners'.[59] In a similar sense political order in Bangladesh must be understood as contingent on the formation of a political coalition, which in organisation weaves down to the streets. Syndicates, it will be argued, must be understood not as a deviation from how political coalitions and order are constructed, but as inherent to both.

For some, the roots of this entanglement of crime and violence in political life can be traced to recent history. Outside of Bangladesh some place blame at the feet of neoliberalism, and 'the uneven liberalization, deregulation, and deterritorialization' where the state has 'outsourced' or 'abdicated' responsibility.[60] Studies in various contexts testify to the impact that structural adjustment programmes have had, such as with the 'dons' of Kingston Jamaica,[61] and broader liberalisation such as in Russia[62] and China.[63] A contrasting (but not mutually exclusive) explanation is that crime and politics have become intertwined as a result of attempts by political elites to sustain control. Rachel Klenfield, for example, argues that such relationships stem from 'when politicians abdicate the monopoly of force and collude with violent groups to maintain power'.[64] There is similarly evidence for such dynamics in action, such as attempts in India by the Indian National Congress to consolidate power in the late 1960s and 1970s, where funding rules pushed parties and leaders to seek underground sources of cash to fund elections and office,[65] which arguably gave momentum to the place of criminality and criminals in the world's largest democracy.[66]

An assumption behind both explanations, however, is that the state had, or had more of, a monopoly on violence, which has been 'abdicated'. A challenge with this view is that while certain political arrangements do have more centralised forms of political authority, in many contexts, political regimes, at some level, have long incorporated a diverse array of actors into governance and politics. In other words, the formal state in many instances routinely and historically colluded with violent and other ostensibly non-state actors to maintain power. Meanwhile security agencies and officials regularly exercise authority in a distinctly unlawful manner. Charles Tilly's oft-quoted portrayal of the European state-making process describes how many 'shared the right to use violence'; rulers relied on an array of local lords and other strong men in a system of 'indirect rule' where 'a king's best source of armed supporter was sometimes the world of outlaws'.[67] Similarly colonial rule in South Asia has been characterised by a 'complex mix ... of what some have called overlapping, layered, residual, informal, shared, or quasi-"sovereignties"'.[68] An obvious historical example of this in the context of Bengal was the dependencies the East India Company and the British Raj had on *zamindars* and other powerholders for revenue and order, and the forms of local exploitation and coercion these entailed.

The account of Kawran Bazaar here sets syndicates within a broader historical context, thereby speaking to the ways and extent to which the 'entanglement' of crime and violence in political life is indeed new, and how it has changed over time. This then responds to calls to study Bangladeshi politics and the state in relation to its historical roots.[69] The opening vignette of Rubel has already hinted how the late 1980s to early 2000s was a period in which a distinct form of 'violent entrepreneur' rose to power across much of Dhaka. Much like the Italian Camorra, they were referred to through nicknames that sound odd to the foreign ear but sparked fear in the minds of locals. Picchi Hannan (tiny Hannan), Murgi Milon (chicken Milon) and Sweden Aslam (Sweden Aslam) are a few of the figures who feature in the bazaar's story. Both their groups and activities are described locally as syndicates. But today these men are legends, infamous names from the past who have little importance faced with the might of the state and ruling party.

In Bangladesh today, syndicates are not the preserve of the archetypal 'criminal' but of those with formal political power. The local figures of authority holding sway at the bazaar are part of complex chains that unite petty street vendors, labourers and street children to MPs and ministers. It is alleged that at times the money accrued from the lanes of the bazaar does reach such heights, but more commonly it is the spoils of low-level party activists and leaders across the multitude of different affiliate organisations built around the ruling Awami League. It is also the preserve of local officials and members of the security agencies, operating in a 'nexus' with party figures. These arrangements are extraordinarily widespread. They are so common that they serve as an incentive for political careers, for local party cadres to affiliate themselves with figures of note, attempt to ingratiate themselves and climb the ladder. This 'politicization of crime' helps understand the dominance and authoritarianism of the ruling Awami League today.

Though the characters in command change, in many crucial respects syndicates should not be seen as something structurally new to economic and political life in this region. An extremely common form of syndicate today, for example, revolves around informal and often concealed payments termed *chaada* or *chanda* (fee, subscription, tribute). Historically in Bengal *chanda* was a sum of money landlords demanded from their tenants on an auspicious occasion. Today *chandabaji* is protection racketeering, typically where access to an economic activity (the ability to set up shop on a pavement or bring goods into a bazaar, for example) is made conditional on such a payment.

These payments informally yet ubiquitously feed the political and state machinery at its lower echelons. In many regards this resembles the decentralised revenue farming arrangements long seen in this region and historically in much of the world, where local figures of coercive authority take a cut, provide order and make a payment upwards to more senior authorities. Previously a plethora of local headmen, tax farmers, officials and powerholders took such payments, and today it is the *boro bhai*, the 'lineman' (a street-level intermediary), labour leaders and others operating under higher forms of authority. The terminology may be new, but the structural arrangements described are far from it.

Together, the arguments built in the pages to come suggest that in certain contexts the 'entanglement' of 'violent entrepreneurs' in political life, and of crime and violence more broadly in politics, can counterintuitively reflect a way in which political order is being produced and sustained.[70] What precisely binds local figures of authority such as gangsters and criminal politicians to broader political coalitions is an open question, but it at least in part involves such actors accruing material resources to sustain their authority. It is argued here that syndicates are a key means through which those in power accrue such resources and that they are so prevalent and closely connected to party politics that they can be read as a basic building block of the Bangladeshi political economy. In this sense racketeering is an important resource base for those in power, and therefore a means through which the political order their rule creates is sustained. These arguments then suggest that syndicates are intimately tied to politics in contexts where political authority is both associated with a capacity for violence and dispersed, characteristics that differ markedly between (and indeed within) societies.

This Book

This book unfolds as follows. Chapter 1 introduces the people and places that ground this book. It describes the *jhupri* labourers and life at Kawran Bazaar and situates this within the history and growth of Dhaka city. It outlines politics in Bangladesh since 1971, the year of the country's formation, examining key periods of political history and the nature of the political coalitions seen. Chapters 2–6 then develop the core arguments and ethnography of the book, and progressively narrow in scale.

Chapter 2 examines the political history of Bangladesh over the past thirty years through the case of Kawran Bazaar and the rise and fall of the infamous gangster Picchi Hannan. It charts how he rose to power, how his syndicate was organised, the control it held locally and how this shaped everyday life at the bazaar. It examines the violence that ensued during this period, the rivalries with other locals and struggles by some to resist his group. Finally, it explains how Hannan and many others were eventually controlled or killed, and how this opened a new period in the politics of Dhaka city. It thereby details the so-called criminalisation of politics through the 1990s and early 2000s, as well as the start of what I term the 'politicisation of crime' seen subsequently. Chapter 3 continues the story following Hannan's death, detailing the rise in power of the Awami League. It does this through the lens of *chandabaji* and the widespread syndicates that invisibly carve up life at the bazaar. The chapter details how the authority of political leaders and security agencies is felt on the ground through an array of coercive intermediaries, ranging from *lineman* to informers and political activists. It argues that such arrangements provide order locally, and that though the discourse of 'syndicates' is new, the dynamics they refer to in fact closely resemble historical forms of tax intermediation seen in Dhaka and wider Bengal.

Chapters 4–6 examine labour hierarchies at the bazaar, the nature of leadership among the *jhupri* labourers and their struggles to find a place within this political landscape. The core ethnography comes from the contentious period of 2014–2015, though also drawing from research conducted over almost a decade (2013–2022). Chapter 4 examines how labour leaders are a key intermediary in the lives of labourers, not only in organising work but also crucially positioning workers in relation to political leaders and groups in an effort to seek opportunities and mitigate risks. It examines how the *boro bhai*s of the *jhupri* group such as Rubel sustain their authority on this basis and argues that labour leaders are often political entrepreneurs. It contextualises this within the history of labour intermediation on the subcontinent, arguing that such leaders have long been seen as coercive and extractive. Today, however, it is not the archetypal labour leader (*sardar*) who has the greatest power, but those organised as unions and associations or societies (*samiti*), bodies which in practice embody very similar hierarchies.

Chapter 5 continues the story of the *jhupri* labourers, examining their manoeuvrings for power in the politically unstable 2014–2015 period. The chapter centres on two struggles, the first for greater control over work to unload vegetable trucks, and the second on overt acts of political violence in support of the opposition BNP. It explores how the group fought a long-established labour leader to form a syndicate controlling the unloading of carrots at Kawran Bazaar, how they were fought off by a group of Chhatra League students (the student wing of the ruling Awami League) and faced police cases. It also examines how the group were aligned to a local BNP politician who used them to orchestrate local bombings in an effort to destabilise the ruling Awami League in the aftermath of the controversial 2014 general election. The chapter thus deepens our understanding of labour leaders as political entrepreneurs, illuminates the organisation of political violence and the place of labourers and street children within this. In essence it explores how the *boro bhai*s attempt to become bigger.

The final empirical chapter focuses on an individual labourer's discontent with the existing *boro bhai*s and wishing to usurp the hierarchy of the *jhupri* group and wider lane. We hence take one step further down the chain to how labourers envisage becoming *boro bhai*s. The chapter follows the attempts by an older labourer Liton to form a *samiti* to unify labourers around him and confront the group's leadership. Building on previous chapters it thus illuminates how grassroots associations can be explicitly political, violent and contentious bodies, operating in effect as syndicates. It builds this line of argument through the further case of a street vendor turned *samiti* president and Awami League leader from the south of the bazaar. Chapter 7 finally draws back to the key questions that animate this book, reflecting on the place of syndicates in societies.

Notes

1. Key details have been anonymised to protect the identity of individuals. The names of people at Kawran Bazaar have been anonymised, as well as other key details such as the name of the *jhupri* labour group. The only people not anonymised are some prominent politicians and other public figures of historical note (allegations about whom are already in the public domain).
2. Angel, Lamson-Hall and Blanco (2021); Demographia (2023).
3. Hoornweg and Pope (2017).
4. See the discussion in Chapter 1.
5. Note that the Bengali is anglicised either as 'Kawran' or 'Karwan'.
6. All unattributed quotes are based on personal interviews or conversations with *jhupri* labourers, NGO workers and journalists.
7. N. Hossain (2017).
8. Singh and Harriss-White (2019: 39).
9. Sissener (2019).

10. Sud (2014: 602).
11. Michelutti (2019: 179).
12. Ruud (2019: 266, 268).
13. See Transparency International's Corruption Perceptions Index, www.transparency.org/en/cpi (accessed 24 November 2023).
14. M. Chowdhury (2003: 274); Sobhan (2004).
15. I. Ahmed (2004).
16. Reporters Without Borders (2005).
17. United Nations Office on Drugs and Crime (2019).
18. Comaroff and Comaroff (2016: 34).
19. The term has been deployed in two prominent recent volumes from South Asia, namely, *Mafia Raj* and *The Wild East*. See Schneider (2018).
20. Goldstein and Arias (2010); North et al. (2012); Piliavsky (2014); Comaroff and Comaroff (2016).
21. Hirschfeld (2015: 6).
22. See Association for Democratic Reforms, 'National Election Watch', https://www.myneta.info/ (accessed 24 November 2023).
23. Alam and Teicher (2012: 866).
24. This literature has advanced notions of 'muscle politics' and 'bossism', studying processes of criminalisation and 'criminal political economies'. Gayer (2014); Vaishnav (2017); Michelutti et al. (2018); and Harriss-White and Michelutti (2019) are some prominent examples.
25. Ruud (2012, 2018, 2020); Suykens (2017, 2018); Jackman (2018, 2019); Jackman and Maitrot (2021, 2022); Kuttig (2019, 2020).
26. Jackman and Maitrot (2021).
27. Harriss-White and Michelutti (2019: 1).
28. Milan Vaishnav's *When Crime Pays* (2017), for example, focuses insightfully on ordinary people as voters or supplicants before criminal politicians. Lucia Michelutti et al.'s *Mafia Raj* (2018) offers a rich portrayal of 'bosses', ranging from MPs to political aspirants, all embodying a range of muscular, charismatic and other characteristics in their attempts to solidify and sustain authority. This book by contrast focuses further down the political hierarchy on the everyday lives of labourers and street traders, and how the world in which they work is shaped by the nexus of crime and politics. This then responds to the call for attention to move from studying the life of illegal goods to 'the study of the everyday criminal life of *legal* commodities' (Harriss-White and Michelutti 2019: 6).
29. Comaroff and Comaroff (2016: x).
30. Denyer (2015: 8).
31. North, Wallis and Weingast (2009: 14).

32. Scott (1972: 102).
33. Klem and Suykens (2018: 771).
34. Witsoe (2009: 66).
35. Hansen (2005: 184)
36. Such arguments also resonate with the now large body of work concerned with 'hybrid' governance (Meagher 2012; Colona and Jaffe 2016). In one articulation of this concept, the 'hybrid state' is seen as an 'emergent form of statehood in which different governmental actors – in this case, criminal organisations, politicians, police, and bureaucrats – are entangled in a relationship of collusion and divestment as they share control over urban spaces and populations' (Jaffe 2013: 735).
37. Blok (1974); Volkov (2002).
38. Boissevain (1969: 380).
39. Reddy and Haragopal (1985: 1159, 1150).
40. Joseph (2016: 29).
41. Wood (2010).
42. Berenschot (2010).
43. Witsoe (2012: 49).
44. Sanchez (2016: 73).
45. Krishna (2011: 99).
46. Wolf (1956: 1076).
47. Reddy and Haragopal, for example, write of the 'fixer' and 'middleman' who filled the gap between ambitious public policy and a poor administrative system. Such middlemen are understood by some as a 'traditional institution' that has 'stepped in to fill the institutional vacuum in the government's development strategy' (Reddy and Haragopal 1985: 1149). They can be seen as 'part of the landscape of imperfect, inaccessible states' (Sud 2014: 599). Similarly, where the state is filled with functionaries disembedded from the local socio-political hierarchy, intermediaries can be a means by which the 'gap' between the state and society locally is bridged (Witsoe 2012: 49).
48. Meehan and Dan (2022).
49. Pattenden (2011).
50. Levien (2015: 88).
51. Jahangir (1976); Arens and van Beurden (1978); Wood (1981); Bertocci (1982); BRAC (1983); Hartmann and Boyce (1983); White (1988); D. Lewis (1989); McGregor (1989); Devine (1999). Geof Wood, for example, conceptualises dependencies on such figures as a 'Faustian bargain' offering short-term security at the expense of long-term opportunities (Wood 2003).
52. Sud (2014).

53. Elsewhere I have conceptualised these as 'violent intermediaries' (Jackman 2019) and others have used the terms 'coercive mediator' (Wheeler 2014) and 'coercive broker' (Pope 2023).
54. In contrast with an individual act of extortion, protection racketeering can be seen as an 'institutionalised relationship' (Volkov 2002: 29). The basis on which protection is given differs widely. Varese (2013) argues that the mafia, for example, have been observed to offer 'protection against extortion, protection against theft and police harassment, protection of property rights, protection in relation to credit obtained informally and the retrieval of loans, protection of thieves, and the settlement of a variety of disputes.' A syndicate here then is understood as largely synonymous with a racket. It refers to the illegal and coercive appropriation or mediation of access to a resource by an actor, group or network enabling accumulation of wealth and/or power.
55. Hence Eisenstadt and Roniger (1984: 244) write of 'patron-brokerage' or 'organisational clientelistic brokerage', examining how patron–client relationships are often embedded within wider networks linked to 'central' political authorities. As such the authority and power of a 'patron' is contingent on their status relative to these wider networks. In other words, patrons often mediate the access their followers have to the market, state or positions of status, on the basis of their own position relative to wider networks of authority.
56. This is a key argument behind recent macro political-economy frameworks concerned with 'natural states' (North, Wallis and Weingast 2009) and 'political settlements' (M. Khan 2010).
57. A growing body of literature in diverse contexts is now explicitly examining the interdependencies found between state officials or politicians and criminal actors (when, indeed, they can be distinguished). This literature is attempting to dissect such relationships and schematically lay out their configurations (Moncada 2013; Cockayne 2016; Barnes 2017; Staniland 2017; Arias 2017). Who precisely matters within this work differs. All position themselves against the state but are concerned variably with 'warlords' (Malejacq 2016), 'criminal groups' (Barnes 2017), 'armed actors' (Staniland 2017) and 'community level armed groups' (Arias 2017). How and why these relationships vary also varies. For some it is the level of resources that matters (Malejacq 2016), for others the cooperative or conflictual nature of the relationship (Barnes 2017; Staniland 2017). In perhaps the most systematic analysis, Enrique Desmond Arias argues we should distinguish between the degree of consolidated power 'armed groups' hold, and the depth of their relationship with the state. Such schema are of course only illuminative if state and 'criminal' can be distinguished in the first place.
58. Gayer (2014: 12).

59. Ibid., 10.
60. Comaroff and Comaroff (2016: 31).
61. Jaffe (2013).
62. Volkov (2002).
63. Bakken and Wang (2021).
64. Klenfield (2018: 14).
65. Jha (2013), cited in Harriss-White and Michelutti (2019: 9).
66. Vaishnav (2017).
67. Tilly (1985: 173).
68. Gilmartin (2020: 6).
69. Lewis and van Schendel (2020).
70. Kaylvas, Shapiro and Masoud (2008); North, Wallis and Weingast (2009); North et al. (2013). You (2012: 315) summarises the argument of North, Wallis and Weingast well as the view that in most societies 'violence is contained by creating economic rents for powerful individuals and groups'.

1

A Dhaka *Serai*

Karon Shah was mad, he used to smoke lots of *gaza* [*ganja*; marijuana]. He started the business here with a small *arot* [wholesale market] … Kawran Bazaar is named after him.

—Liton, a labourer at Kawran Bazaar

I first met the *jhupri* labourers behind a row of parked buses. They were sprawled out on the backs of their rickshaw vans after a night of work: some were asleep, some smoking, some playing ludo. Rubel was seated on a van with others huddled around him. He wore a white *panjabi* (*kurta*) and a sparse beard, giving the impression he was both pious and not in fact a labourer. Unlike the rest of the group who were lean from carrying heavy sacks of vegetables, he was large, or 'short and fat' as others would later describe him. Foreigners were not an unfamiliar sight at the bazaar. Nearby offices and a five-star hotel meant visitors passed by on their way elsewhere. Some took photos of the colours and chaos. Foreign sisters from the Missionaries of Charity occasionally shopped here. An Italian priest had for decades visited weekly to help children with small ailments and injuries. Some of the group later claimed that 'bad foreigners' used the cheap hotels to meet sex workers, with Australians for some reason singled out as particularly guilty.

As the first foreigner to speak to the group there, Rubel saw it as an opportunity to preach. He gave a speech about Islam that I barely understood and the group found amusing. He then stated provocatively, 'We are all BNP here. Do you have a problem with that?' The claim of affiliation to the opposition BNP was an odd one. The election a few months previously in early 2014 had been highly controversial: the opposition had boycotted, the nation had seen widespread violence, and with the Awami League re-elected, public claims of loyalty to their rivals were risky. Whatever Rubel's motivations, the encounter was precisely the opportunity I had been looking for. For the past couple months I had been walking around the city, getting to know it better, looking for a route in to study local politics, somewhere to embed myself and normalise my presence on the pavements, in the *basti*s and bazaars of the city.[1] Scattered across Dhaka at the time were shelters run by local NGOs to support people living on the streets. Some offered a sliver of floor for the night, a locker to store valuables or a place to keep children when working. These gave me an entry point into the lives of people I would otherwise be too far removed from: a place where I could be, listen and chat without it being unusual. They also allowed me to meet people who begged, laboured, scavenged or sold sex in their workplaces: in the bazaars, stations, ports, pavements and parks. I began to build relationships, learn names and be a familiar sight. Kawran Bazaar slowly became a place I could go to, spend the day or evening, chat, smoke and drink tea. That late morning when I first met the *jhupri* labourers, I was being led by a field officer of a local NGO who was attempting unsuccessfully to involve labourers at the bazaar with the project's interventions. The research that has become this book truly began that morning.

Life in the *Jhupri* Lane

> You've grown up with you mother and father, right? They were the ones who fed you, made sure you were well. We're different. We didn't have our mothers or fathers, that's why we all live together here. This is like our family.
>
> —Shumon, *jhupri* labourer

The *jhupri* lane (*goli*) of Kawran Bazaar is much more than a lane. It is also a car park by day, where buses and other vehicles rest after shuttling workers to a nearby government office. It is a dormitory of sorts, where people sleep by night in the entrance ways of offices, and by day on the backs of rickshaw vans squeezed by the sides. It is a playground where children roam, playing with discarded bottles. It has branches of local banks, a convenience store and tea stalls. It is not the narrow lane of an archetypal bazaar but flanked by a thirty-storeyed building on one side and a thirteen-storeyed office on the other. Its local name originates apparently in the string of shacks that once stood by its sides, made of bamboo and jute sacks, with tin roofing to protect from the monsoon rain. These have now been knocked down to make way for more parking spaces, although the name persists. Others say the lane's appellation stems from the sight of people sleeping there covered with plastic tarpaulin.

It is here that by night eighty or so labourers unload trucks from across the country, supplying the city with cabbages, tomatoes and carrots, among other goods. This is one among several areas of the bazaar where goods arrive, each associated with a notable building or feature, and groups of labourers. There is also, for example, La Vinci (named after the adjacent hotel), WASA (named after the Water Supply and Sewerage Authority [WASA] headquarters), market (south of WASA), Sonargaon (the southern entrance to Kawran Bazaar, facing the five-star Sonargaon hotel) and the rail line (to the northeast). The bazaar is divided by what the labourers term a *bhag niyom* (a system of division), the basic principle of which is 'we can't take their goods [to unload], and they can't take ours', as one in the group put it.

People at Kawran Bazaar (Figure 1.1) are often bound together by their district of origin. The notion of an ancestral home (*bari*[2]) has deep resonance in Bangladesh as a way of making sense of who someone is, and often shapes their allegiances and how networks are built. Through the bazaar's history you can chart the prominence of districts, which leaders were in control and which wave of migration was most pronounced. Labourers in certain areas are dominated by certain districts. In the past, gangs were organised like this. The *jhupri* labourers,

Figure 1.1 A wet winter afternoon inside Kawran Bazaar
Source: Photograph by author.

by contrast, come from everywhere. Most have desperate stories of childhood trauma, running away from home or being abandoned, of coming to the city with their family who later died or suffered breakdowns and health crises. Rubel described how 'the best of us' in the *jhupri* lane came from NGO shelters at the bazaar, with 'batch' after 'batch' of young boys feeding the ranks of the group. In their younger years, most survived through a blend of scavenging and thievery. From a young age they have learnt that finding a place within this world requires positioning themselves hierarchically, or as it is more colloquially put, finding 'shelter', finding 'shade' or 'having' someone they can depend upon.[3] Today it is teenage boys at the cusp of being strong enough to labour who have to prove themselves to the *boro bhai*s of the group.

The *jhupri* labourers are one small part of a supply chain with many steps that feeds fresh goods into the bazaar and out again. One of the group's labourers, Hassan, once began explaining the market to me like this: 'Day and night are different worlds at Kawran Bazaar'. What he meant was that by day the market is busy with retailers selling goods, with small sellers dotting the pavements, with restaurants, customers and office workers. *Coolie*s work, mostly alone, carrying goods for individuals to nearby cars, restaurants or residences. But by night the bazaar is truly alive. The large adjacent road, Kazi Nazrul Islam Avenue, has back-to-back traffic as trucks pour in from across the country delivering goods.[4] Vegetables are brought by the *bepari*s (middlemen), who work with the *arotdar*s (wholesalers) to transport the goods from the trucks to the *arot*.[5] The *arotdar*s (wholesalers) are also known as 'commission agents' and are some of the bazaar's wealthiest businessmen. They have long been the object of local resentment. The *jhupri* labourers sometimes lambasted them as 'cheater[s]' and even 150 years ago, '*bepári*s complain[ed] bitterly' of their arrangements with them.[6]

Three types of labourers (*sramik*s) are typically involved in the delivery of fresh goods: *coolie*s (the labourers carrying goods in small baskets on their heads), the 'helpers' who support them (an entry point for boys in the labouring world), and rickshaw van drivers, such as the *jhupri* labourers (those unloading sacks of goods onto wooden flat-backed rickshaw vans). Van drivers have a particular reputation at the bazaar, in part on account of their vans, which hurtle through the bazaar without brakes or chains, and which the drivers themselves are often unable to stop. For some, the drivers are known as being addicted to *ganja* (marijuana) and the methamphetamine *yaba*, as having cut marks on their arms (from self-harm) and as thieves. A *coolie* in a nearby lane described them thus:

[T]he van drivers don't care about anyone. Their vans don't have a brake or a chain they just push through the crowd. You have to jump out of the way. They have strength. They have an organisation. They have someone to call when they are in trouble. They are the most oppressive. They don't even care about the MP. Even the *arotdar*s are afraid of them. The only people above them are the *hijra*s [third gender].

Much of my time with the group was spent by day at the side of the lane, looking out at the bazaar smoking, chatting and drinking tea. I spent a year across 2014–2015 researching here, and also short periods in 2013, 2017, 2018, 2019 and 2022. Often very little happened. When I would describe the group to friends outside the bazaar, key features of individuals I became close to stuck in my mind. Though somewhat arbitrary, they have stayed. Rubel became the proselytising *boro bhai* who does not smoke but used to sleep with prostitutes on the nearby water tank. Parvez was another *boro bhai*, wily, with a chipped tooth earned in a fight. Hassan was the joker, constantly mocking me in ways I barely understood; Shakib, the one everyone used to be scared of, once a phensedyl seller, good at throwing bombs and known in the past for having had two guns, one in each hand ('now he's gentle, but if you ask about it, he will get angry', another said of him); Shumon, the Muslim convert who was once mortified when I bumped into him at a Hindu festival in the south of the city; Salam, always jittery and often smoking marijuana. And then there was Liton, the odd one out: the one who spoke a smattering of basic English, wore jeans instead of a *lunghi* and was clearly down on his luck, a middle-class labourer who often referenced Stalin and Hitler.

After a night's work, the labourers send money back to family elsewhere through bKash (a mobile financial service), and then lie at the side of the bazaar, or in a shack nearby if they have one, many smoking marijuana to help them sleep amid the noise and heat. Days are spent resting, sleeping in stages, eating and hanging out. Shumon for a while owned a *khichuri* cart next to the WASA building. Those with their wives nearby are cooked for; women use makeshift spaces on the footpath, in the gutter or parking area to light small fires and bring pots stored nearby in wooden boxes and kept safe by padlock. The group often lay out ludo boards, engrossed in the game for hours. Mobile phones provide entertainment; people with touch screens ('touch mobile' as they were then known) buy memory cards that come pre-loaded with films and TV series (and swap them with others). Bollywood action films are unsurprisingly a favourite.

The group occasionally gambled, finding obscure corners or the back of a truck hidden from the main roads to play.[7] They also sometimes read horoscopes. In more recent years, they seem to keep themselves busy with Facebook.

Socially the group's numbers would swell during the day when nearby professionals joined them during their breaks. Journalists from major newspapers, bank workers and various contractors came to smoke marijuana which the group provided at the time (though this has since reduced due to the 'war on drugs' campaign that began in 2018). Shumon's role in this side hustle was to visit the nearby rail line *basti* and collect supplies. The group would then collectively cut bud and stem into 20- or 30-taka heaps wrapped in scrap newspaper. The group insisted that their suppliers lived not in a *basti* but a 'business centre' (said in English), named as such on account of the wealth accrued in the dilapidated shacks.[8] The rhythms of these routines of work, sleep, eating, washing and hanging out were punctuated by conflicts documented in the pages to come, including struggles to lead the group, manoeuvrings for power, fights over territory, strikes, bombings and arrests. At times, relatively more mundane events also provided distraction from simply watching the bazaar: the arrival of an extorting elephant (when elephants are used to create inconvenience and pressure locals into giving money to the *mahout* [elephant keeper]), a night-time visit by *hijra*s, the sight of a naked man in the midst of madness, a pedlar selling medicines for sexual health.

Like most people, the *jhupri* labourers have a multitude of identities. They can be categorised in many ways, each label carrying with it a set of assumptions about how they should be seen. Within bureaucratic discourse they would likely qualify as the 'floating population ... the mobile and vagrant category of rootless people' as a recent census put it.[9] Viewed this way, they are seen as being separated from their *bari* and hence 'rootless people' (*chinomul*), which indeed was once the name of a children's shelter here. None to my knowledge can vote at Kawran Bazaar and they thus do not relate within this context as voters. Many do not have basic identity documents. In principle and in aspiration they are citizens, even if they are rarely, if ever, treated in ways that accord with that ideal. Within development discourse, they are the 'urban poor' or perhaps the 'destitute'. They were once street children (*potho shishu*). They sometimes call themselves *kangali*, an evocative and often offensive term referring to those in need or destitute, perhaps remembering their youth. As the pages to come will reveal, many are criminal by the letter of the law, though that does little to distinguish people here. Perhaps most usefully they can be seen as *sramik*s (labourers).

Though united by the hardship of their youth, it is their labour that keeps them together today. It is how they identify collectively, and what keeps them fed. One of the oddities of contemporary research in Bangladesh is that there has been much focus on the 'poor', yet hardly anything on labour. The *jhupri* labourers, in this lane of a bazaar, are then the tiniest fraction of the tens of millions of people who labour to survive in Bangladesh.

A City Rises

> You can come from Comilla, Mymensingh, Barisal, Rangpur – you can come from anywhere and stay here.
>
> —Hassan, *jhupri* labourer

Kawran Bazaar feels like an intruder in a more modern metropolis, separated crudely from its surroundings. When people arrive here from villages to find occasional work or settle, they are confronted not only with the size of the bazaar but also the cultural markers that divide it from the city: to the south a five-star hotel, to the west the trendy urban wear of the youth at the Bashundara City shopping centre, to the east the grand military-built Hatirjheel (elephant lake) ring road which has carved through old *basti*s and rubbish dumps, and adjacent, the imposing skeleton of the new Metro Rail. In between are large billboards displaying cricket stars or strikingly fair-skinned models and bright sparkling shops selling consumer goods – be it a Walton television or Bata shoe – all of which are surrounded by Japanese cars that now fill the roads at extraordinary expense to the elite (who pay the import tax to own them) and city (whose streets they clog).

Yet it is not the bazaar but the offices and shops that are the encroachers. Some labourers and residents remember how the bazaar was once surrounded by fields, waterways and a green (rather than concrete) jungle. Liton, for example, described fearing witches or female ghosts (*petni*) when he would go to relieve himself in the nearby jungle in his youth. But building a sense of the past here is difficult. If you were to walk around Kawran Bazaar and speak to people at random by day, many will have recently migrated, or been there for a few months before returning to their villages. A degree of transience among many labourers, scavengers and beggars is the norm. In recent years I have found that when I meet new people, the majority have known the bazaar for fewer years than me. There are many exceptions to this. Some labourers recall the fall of President Ershad (in 1990) or even Liberation (in 1971), many wholesalers have established themselves over decades and a few people were born and raised around the bazaar. The *jhupri* labourers recall events back to the late 1990s but little before. Many do not want to remember. To remember is to re-live the family breakdowns, the vulnerability, poverty and sadness. To remember the bazaar is to recall a history of violence, a time when gangsters ruled and bombings and killings were common. 'We don't talk about the bad old days. Why would we talk about these bad things?' one from the group replied to a question I had poorly phrased, looking away from me and not expecting an answer.

The history of Kawran Bazaar – the biggest market in one of the world's most populous cities and countries – is largely unknown. Despite its prominence today, it rarely appears in either historical or contemporary accounts of the city, and what can be learned about its past has to be gleaned from sparse sources and the stories of elderly residents and workers, the few with memories sharp enough to recall past events and characters in detail. Even the bazaar's name is subject to confusion. An entry in Banglapedia[10] claims it stems from a 'Marwari merchant' Karwan Singh who established a market here in the late eighteenth century. Locals have other stories. One long-standing resident argued the name comes from a (now) dried river which used to flow nearby, while others had stories of a *pir* (saint, holy figure) called Karon who once lived here.

The academic neglect of this bazaar reflects a broader disregard of Bangladesh's urban history. This is not to say there are no insightful accounts of Dhaka's past,[11] but rather that the city has not been the subject of major theorisation or drawn significant attention from wider historians. The city is most often passed over in accounts of the East India Company and British Raj.[12] It is then no surprise that the social and political lives of the city's labourers and poor have seen even starker inattention. Bangladesh has little by way of labour histories and aside from references in nineteenth-century texts, there are to my knowledge no historical analyses of the lives of the urban poor and working classes here. This obviously has major implications for how urban and labour history are understood in the country. It also shapes how labour and politics are seen today. It means that contemporary analysis is easily left unanchored, disembedded from the city's and the country's past. We have little sense of the extent to which mobilisation, struggles and lived experiences today reflect the particular political and economic landscape of the early twenty-first century and how far they are rooted in earlier hierarchies and politics. Understandably most people care little for these questions. Although Dhakaites love their city, for many migrants it is just a means to an end; a pitstop to fight off rural poverty.

For them, the city's charms are hard to find, the luxuries of the rich unattainable. When asked, the *jhupri* labourers would often express the thoughts of many: Dhaka is 'filthy', 'a bad place', 'a mess'.

An alternative explanation for Kawran Bazaar's name lies not in a Marwari merchant, but towards the southwest of the bazaar, partly hidden behind walls plastered with posters promoting Awami League politicians and a thick layer of gaudy green paint. It is here that we find the earliest reference to the area, in the bazaar's sole mosque, built in 1680 under the instructions of Khwaja Ambar Shah, said to be a once powerful eunuch, from whom it derives its name. Very little is known about the figure of Khwaja Ambar. Some suggest he was not a eunuch at all but a wealthy local merchant, yet diaries from the time note a 'khajah ambar' as an officer of Shaista Khan, the Mughal governor (*subahdar*) of Bengal and uncle to the then emperor.[13] Eunuchs commonly served the Mughal elite, and 200 years earlier the throne of Bengal had been briefly claimed by former East African slave eunuchs (*habshi*s) in a little remembered episode. Ambar is commonly thought of as Shaista Khan's 'chief eunuch', a powerful and likely coveted position, able to dispense patronage and control access to royal opportunities.[14] Wider sources from the time document a eunuch 'Khwaja Ambar' as a figure close to emperor Aurangzeb. If these figures are the same, Ambar came from an illustrious line of eunuchs and later rose to even greater prominence in the Mughal court.[15]

Such mosques were often built as part of a caravanserai, also transliterated from Persian into English as 'Karwan sara',[16] offering an alternative explanation for the bazaar's name. As across the Muslim world, *serai* were small compounds containing an inn, a mosque and a bazaar, used by travellers for security, to rest and restock.[17] The bazaar sits to the east of what is today known as Kazi Nazrul Islam Avenue, which it has been speculated was once part of the Grand Trunk Road that for centuries linked South and Central Asia as a crucial trading route. The epigraph on the mosque indicates there was also a well here, a *serai*, garden and a brick bridge reaching over a nearby canal towards the city in the south. The canal is known by many names, one of which is 'Kairowan Nadi' (caravan river).[18] The tomb of Ambar himself, perhaps improbably, is said to lie below the mosque. For the *jhupri* labourers, the roots of the bazaar do lie in its mosque, however in a more evocative way, as Liton described it:

> This bazaar's name is 'Karon' Bazaar. You know Ambar Shah mosque? Ambar Shah was like a *pir* [saint]. Karon Shah was his younger brother.

Ambar Shah built this mosque. Karon Shah was mad, he used to smoke lots of *gaza*. He started the business here with a small *arot* [wholesale market], which eventually become a big *arot*, so Kawran Bazaar is named after him.

When the *serai* was built, the heart of Dhaka lay around 5 kilometres to the south, largely hugging the banks of the Burigunga River. Dhaka had emerged as the political capital of Bengal after the region was wrested from the sultanate to form part of the Mughal Empire in the early seventeenth century. By the mid-1600s, the Portuguese missionary Fray Sebastião Manrique estimated the city's population to be around 200,000, placing it on par with many major European capitals. The city was wealthy on the back of the world-famous muslin, which had long been exported around the world. There are hints then that Dhaka had a glorious past. Later accounts describe the city as having had large suburbs 'covered with gardens and houses', extending 13 miles north to 'Tunghy' (Tongi), which even today is to the north of the city.[19] An English merchant Thomas Bowrey from Wapping, who visited the city in the 1670s, described Dhaka as 'an admirable Citty for it's greatnesse, for it's magnificent buildings, and multiple of Inhabitants [*sic*]'.[20] Some sources note that at its height under Shaista Khan, the city was home to 25,000 weavers, and the large Mughal force of 40,000 soldiers and their assistants was housed in the area later known as 'Kawran' among other places.[21] Some even place the city's population at around 900,000–1 million in the seventeenth century,[22] a figure that would have made the city close to if not the largest city on earth, rivalling Constantinople and Beijing. In origin Kawran Bazaar was likely then a strategic resting point before arriving in a wealthy city,[23] and a journalist born in the area suggested there was once a gate here, where travellers would wait for permission to enter the city.[24]

Though the heights of the city's past are unknown, the depths to which Dhaka fell are clear. By the early eighteenth century, the capital of Bengal had moved to Murshidabad and the region's textile industry had declined terribly, as Karl Marx long ago described.[25] By the early nineteenth century, the eunuch's *katra*, like much of the city, was in a dilapidated state. Dhaka was a decaying backwater, and the population fell to 66,989 as recorded in the 1830 census.[26] With the decline, the city shrank, retreating south. The then north and northeast suburbs, where wealthy administrative, commercial and residential hubs stand today, were largely reclaimed by jungle. Any mosques or houses that remained there became dilapidated and travelling even to the Catholic community of Tejgaon just north of the bazaar was described as dangerous due to the encroaching jungle being infested with tigers. Grand mansions became small factories (as many are today), and Lalbagh Fort along with the *boro* and *choto katra*s in old Dhaka was overcome by nature, as evidenced by etchings from the period. As the city contracted in size and houses fell into disrepair, people moved from the suburbs to the centre, building 'make-shift houses on the sides of the main roads' as one historian describes.[27]

What the everyday life of the bazaar would have been like is difficult to gauge in detail. Accounts of the city's past document how urbanisation was fed by not only opportunity but also desperation. In living memory people can recall seeing death on the streets due to rural hardship, for example, during the 1943 famine. This has been a recurring phenomenon throughout the city's history. Mr Day, an East India Company collector, describing the famine of 1787, when rains had flooded much of the country including the city itself, wrote:

> The poor, homeless and penniless, crowded into Dacca, and though ten thousand of them were fed daily by subscription, these formed but a fraction of those who stood in need. Hundreds died of starvation in the streets of the city, until Dacca became a scene of horror unparalleled even among all its many vicissitudes.[28]

Another account describes how during these events, 3,000 Muslim families moved to the city, with women cleaning grain while 'the greater number are employed as masons, bricklayers and day labourers, in digging wells and erecting the mud walls of huts'.[29] Some were reportedly so desperate they were reduced to selling their children into slavery for a handful of rice.[30] Slavery was a common outcome. Sex work was another, and sex workers were 'to be found in every bazaar and in considerable numbers in Dacca city'.[31] Brothels were plentiful, and 'not unfrequently the scenes of assaults, thefts and homicides'.[32]

We can assume the *serai* fell into disuse at some point in the eighteenth century.[33] In 1832 Henry Walters' 'census of the city of Dacca' noted the remains of 'three Katrahs or Caravan-serais',[34] likely including that described here. It continued, however, to be known by some as a *katra*, more specifically, it seems, as a *bhagtiya katra* (*bhagtiya* meaning a 'dancing boy' in Hindustani).[35] James Wise, a civil surgeon in Dhaka in the late nineteenth century, wrote that many 'nars', who were boys or girls known for dancing or music, 'inhabit an old Sarae, or caravansary, called Bhagtiya Katra, built in the seventeenth century by an eunuch named Khwajah Ambar'[36]. *Serai*s more widely in the period were seen by Christopher Bayly as absorbing the near destitute and associated with 'groups of robbers'.[37]

The image of the area as home to outcasts, travellers and criminals is one that still resonates today. Yet the scale of change witnessed since this low point in the bazaar's and Dhaka's history is staggering. Some estimates suggest half a million people arrive or are born in the city every year.[38] From being a minor capital at Liberation in 1971 and home to a million or so, Dhaka has swollen to house roughly fifteen or twenty times that number today, depending on how you draw the boundaries of the city.[39] It is hard to find any place in the city out of earshot of construction work, and it is projected to continue climbing the rankings of the world's mega cities in the decades to come.[40] Kawran Bazaar has been central to feeding this growing city. By at least the 1970s, the area contained the city's largest wholesale vegetable and fish market, a hawkers' market, a significant *ghat* (boat launch), a large government godown across the railway tracks and a truck stand for transporting goods. It is well remembered by some locals how rural hardship led tens of thousands of people to pour into Dhaka in search of work following the Liberation War and then famine of 1974; and there are still labourers at the bazaar today who came during this period.

Today there are a number of large wholesale markets (*arot*s) across the city, and the edges of Dhaka hold huge garment factories sucking up surplus labour; then, however, Kawran Bazaar was one of the few major sites where people could look for employment. Most goods arrived via hundreds of heavily laden boats, and people found work as labourers (at the time mainly *coolie*s) transporting the goods in chains from the *ghat* to the market. Some labourers settled in the area, building more shelters overhanging the nearby canal, whilst others found a home in established *basti*s, and some simply slept where they could, often at the edge of roads under mosquito nets, on the *ghat* steps or next to the railway line. A long-standing resident described there being over 10,000 people living in the open or in makeshift shelters between Kawran Bazaar and Tejgaon alone in the late 1970s and early 1980s, with all the *coolie*s spoiling the area by 'shitting and pissing' everywhere.

As labourers would lie down to sleep, their surroundings by today's standards were still in some ways rural: paddy fields, jungle and waterways, with few buildings except the eunuch's mosque, and children playing cricket and football on an empty field where the Sonargaon hotel stands today. Yet Dhaka was to grow at an almost unimaginable scale. As Kawran Bazaar has grown with the city, so too has its notoriety, such that today the area is often considered a dangerous place by night, conjuring up images of criminality and violence. Locals portrayed it as the sort of place you would see a man walking along with a woman on each arm, where people would openly gamble, where there were prominent brothels, 'bashoman' (floating) prostitutes, a '*dwee* number market' (number two market, meaning a market for stolen goods) and a bazaar so lively by night that you could easily forget the normal rhythms of life. Meanwhile the *basti* adjacent to the bazaar, which grew as labourers moved in, became the largest open drug market in the city.

Kawran Bazaar is then symbolic of the strains the city faces. When it rains, the sewer water flows through the bazaar's lanes, in places up to your knees. When it is hot, the stench of putrid goods is potent. It seems to exemplify the list of ignominious titles the city has gained: most densely populated, least liveable, worst hit by extreme heat. It is easy to paint a picture of a city overwhelmed by such challenges, suffering under the chaos they bring. The visuals of the bazaar also suggest it belongs in a different city, as my description at the start of this section evokes. This would almost be to portray the bazaar as disorganised. Yet it is far from it. In fact, it is meticulously ordered, a place where even fallen vegetables are made use of, and it is also a window into how the city is run, how Bangladeshi politics is organised and how ordinary people seek a place within it.

Fifty Years of Politics

> Do you know what Bangladeshi politics is? It's capture, beat, cut, slash, rip, escape!
>
> —Salam, a *jhupri* labourer

Kawran Bazaar has witnessed fifty turbulent years of Bangladeshi politics. Throughout this history, it has been a constant moving cog in the life of the city, a place from which political leaders and gangsters have risen, from which people have mobilised protests and muscle and from which money has flowed in every direction. There are then many senses in which Kawran Bazaar has fed Dhaka city. To begin to understand politics at Kawran Bazaar and to understand the politics of Bangladesh through the bazaar, we need to first situate ourselves within the context of the nation's political life since its birth in 1971.

Bangladesh emerged from a bloody Liberation struggle and war against Pakistan under the leadership of Liberation icon Sheikh Mujibur Rahman – known as the 'father of the nation' and 'friend of Bengal' (Bangabandhu) – who led the country's first elected government under the Awami League.

Of the many challenges faced by Bangladesh's first administration, one of the greatest was developing a security apparatus that was sufficiently stable, loyal and well equipped to maintain a basic level of order. In many ways, this has been a perennial challenge for every government since. Indeed, most governments through the country's history have ended in assassination, coup, mass uprising and/or military intervention. This is not to say that political life through these decades has not been animated by major ideological currents and ideas, but to simply emphasise the importance of muscle to political competition and authority, a sentiment that Salam evokes in the quote that opens this section. Politics here has been shaped by questions regarding secularism and the place of Islam in society, by prominent left-wing movements, the charismatic personas of major leaders and the visions they represent and ultimately the idea of Bangladesh as a nation. Perhaps the largest ideological battleground has been that of democracy, and indeed the country's political timeline is typically seen as demarcated between periods of democratic and authoritarian military-backed rule, with a question mark placed on how precisely we can define the present government.[41]

Though the ideological cleavages are real and such labels are useful as broad heuristics, such a framing misses many points of continuity across such periods, along with differences beyond them. Some scholars, for example, point to the pervasiveness of patron–clientelism and factionalism across this history,[42] or the consistent enmeshment of party and state.[43] The concept of clientelism, focusing on the threads of unequal dependency that weave through society, has been a dominant paradigm for understanding the nation's politics. It was a core concept in the tradition of village ethnographies and underpins more macro attempts to visualise the nation's politics.[44] The sister concept to patron–clientelism is factionalism, referring to the horizontal intra-group competition occurring within the context of vertical patron–client ties. In the early 1980s, Peter Bertocci elaborated well on this view:

> [A]ll parties in Bangladesh are continually beset by factionalism. One is tempted to envision the party process as a plethora of groups organized along patron–client lines, or what one might call in the Bangladesh context *dada–dal* relationships, in which a leader (*dada*, a term for different types of senior male kinsmen) and his followers (his *dal*, 'party' in the sense of 'faction') compete for power in a constant shift of alliances, splitting off from one formalized party grouping to seek alliance with another, be it one actually in power or another in opposition. The result is the persistent party and subgroup

realignment so salient a feature in Bangladesh politics, the perennial emergence of innumerable splinter groups and their eventual withering away in most cases. The *dada–dal* character of national party politics is well documented for local level politics as well.[45]

A fundamental purpose such ties are envisaged as serving in Bangladeshi politics is establishing and sustaining sufficient strength to dominate rivals. Crudely, this has meant the ability to mobilise coercively in a manner that overwhelms the opposition. Political authority has thus been closely associated with this capacity. This is not to say that such characteristics are the sole, or even predominant 'quality' required of a politician and party, but simply that politics needs muscle to impress and compete. Managing this capacity has thus been a central political task, and the manner in which it has been achieved has been a defining feature of each government. Understanding how this has been managed differently by different governments is thus crucial to appreciating the nature of Bangladeshi politics, the place of syndicates in political life and how this shapes the lives of people like the *jhupri* labourers.

Bangladesh's liberation struggle was successful on the back of a guerrilla movement (and Indian military support) in which a myriad of different armed groups had operated under the banner 'Mukti Bahini' (Liberation Army). These ranged from large-scale militia–guerrilla groups (such as Kader Siddiqui's 'Kaderia Bahini') to brigades under senior renegade Bengali officers from the Pakistani Army and the predominantly student-led 'Mujib Bahini'. Many such groups subsequently had a detrimental effect on local law and order. As Zillur R. Khan writes 'many peasants, students, and worker groups who took up arms and received guerrilla training to fight the Pakistani army during the 1971 liberation struggle became marauders and ravaged the countryside after independence'.[46] Others had political ambitions and different visions of what Bangladesh as a nation should look like, and thus managing the competing interests of such armed actors was central to Bangladesh's early politics.

Political authority then was highly 'dispersed' in this period and order contingent on forming a coalition that could actively draw together coercive actors to dominate nationally. A key challenge in doing so was persuading existing *bahini*s to surrender and remobilise under groups closer to Mujib, as well as keeping in check elements of the military perceived as insufficiently loyal. Efforts to ensure arms were surrendered were only partially successful, and created dissatisfaction when Awami League leaders were appointed to positions of authority over the guerrilla leaders who so far had de facto control over large swathes of the country.[47] An early step taken by Mujib to solidify his control was to found the Jatio Rakkhi Bahini (JRB, National Security Force), a paramilitary group which swore an oath directly to him and incorporated members of the Mujib Bahini and Kaderia Bahini, growing in strength to around 25,000. The JRB has been described as 'the AL's [Awami League's] armed branch'.[48] The sizeable force was designed as a counterweight to the military, which albeit not equal to the military in sheer numbers, reportedly had access to superior resources such as AK-47s while the military was left with rifles dating from World War II,[49] in many cases lacked uniform[50] and for most of his term in office only had three aged tanks.[51] While the Rakkhi Bahini had some success in providing order and controlling black-market trading and smuggling, they also developed notoriety as the henchmen of the government, involved in corruption and extrajudicial killings, particularly of leftist groups.

Alongside a politicised paramilitary group stood auxiliary wings of the Awami League such as the Jubo League (the youth wing of the Awami League), which also served coercive functions. The 'Lal Bahini', for example, was an armed contingent of the Sramik League (the workers' wing of the Awami League), used to control industrial areas, and was complicit in acts of violent repression. Alongside them was the lesser known 'Nil Bahini' (Blue Force). Juggling such a coalition proved extremely difficult, however, with factional divisions, splinter groups and purges common. There are reports that between Liberation and 1974, around 3,000 members of the Awami League were killed either in factional conflict or as a result of attacks from underground leftists.[52] Factional fault lines lay within the coalition between the youth and senior leaders in the bureaucracy as a result of alignment during the Liberation War, and most importantly between the military and prime minister.[53] Mujib's ultimate step to counter such discord and a deteriorating economic and political situation was transforming Bangladesh from a parliamentary democracy into a one-party state under the Bangladesh Krishak Sramik Awami League (BAKSAL, Bangladesh Peasants and Workers People's League), incorporating the Communist Party as well as other minor parties into a party organised around the Awami League. Under BAKSAL all other parties were banned, and civil servants had to become members.[54]

The disorder that followed Mujib's assassination saw a series of coups and countercoups as elite factions within the military competed for control of the state. The military-backed and later civilianised regime of General Ziaur Rahman brought a radically different approach to the relationship between the military and political institutions, arguably 'welding the two inseparably'.[55] At the same time, it also established an alternative source of political authority through the formation of the BNP and an array of auxiliary groups, such as the student body, the Bangladesh Jatiobadi Chhatra Dal (JCD). Zia immediately increased military expenditure from 7 to 20 per cent of the national budget,[56] enhancing the benefits of soldiers, while also bringing the officer class into positions of bureaucratic authority such as chairmanships within public corporations and positions of police superintendents.[57] Under Zia the number of military personnel increased by around 50 per cent. A significant part of this was achieved through disbanding the Mujib-aligned Rakkhi Bahini and incorporating its personnel into the military.[58]

Zia also ensured coercive strength outside the military, hence founding the 'Combat Batallion',[59] which had parallels to the Rakkhi Bahini. The police, too, were strengthened and relied upon in the face of numerous attempted coups during his regime.[60] Zia's 'gram sarkar' (village government) introduced a new tier of government at the lowest level. Alongside these sat 'Village Defence Parties' (VDP), designed to consist of 150 people in each village, and intended to create an eventual 10-million-people-strong force to maintain order, operating under the administration of the home ministry.[61] These VDPs also formed 'Youth Complexes' which offered training to unemployed youth and gave them the ability to collect toll from ferry *ghat*s and markets.[62] One source indicates that by August 1979, 60,294 VDPs had been established, incorporating over 900,000 members.[63] These were arguably of direct political importance, serving to solidify Zia's regime on the ground. They were at times chosen with the guidance of government officials and MPs,[64] served as a mechanism for mobilising support behind the BNP and had similarities to the 'Basic Democracies' of Union Councils seen under the regime of Ayub Khan.[65]

The transition following Zia's assassination in 1981 eventually led to a military coup at the hands of the then chief of the army and later president Ershad. It has been argued that it was only due to factional divisions within the military that Ershad did not step in straight away,[66] the risk being they would be deeply unpopular given the public's dislike for Zia's assassination. After taking power, the character of the government again reverted to direct military rule, with the military taking on a significant role in state administration, a National Security Council formed of military chiefs and the armed forces receiving disproportionate increases in salaries and posts in the diplomatic corps and large corporations.⁶⁷ In 1985, the entire cabinet had a military background.⁶⁸ Rather than rely on the police or a specialised police unit for domestic security, Ershad's power base in the military served this purpose, with the vast majority of district superintendents being from a military background.⁶⁹ This was accompanied by wider institutional political changes, including the abolition of the *gram sarkar*, and attempts to incorporate the military more directly into district-level governance through the Zila Parishad Amendment Bill of 1987.⁷⁰ Opposition to Ershad's reign and Jatiya Party (the party established by him) rule, however, escalated in the late 1980s, when students, the Awami League and BNP together mobilised, particularly in Dhaka city, in mass protests to force Ershad from office.

The return to parliamentary democracy and national elections in 1991 saw the military take a step back from public life. The democracy that emerged saw the election of the BNP under the leadership of Zia's wife Khaleda Zia (1991–1995, 2001–2006) and the Awami League under Bangabandhu's daughter Sheikh Hasina (1995–2001, 2009 to the present). General elections between 1991 and 2009 were based on a system of 'caretaker government', whereby an ostensibly neutral administration directly oversaw national elections, thereby preventing the incumbent from utilising the apparatus of the state to their advantage. Though one step removed from domestic politics, military intervention remained a possibility through the 1990s and 2000s, as proven by the extended caretaker period of 2006–2008. A key challenge for both the Awami League and BNP has been to contain this threat which each attempted to achieve in part by politicising the officer class. It has been argued, for example, that during the 1990s the BNP's first term in office saw the promotion of officers aligned to the late president Zia, followed by the promotion of officers aligned to the JRB during the Awami League's term.⁷¹ Whoever has been in power has meanwhile politicised the bureaucracy, juggling appointments to promote favourable officers and relegate others.

General elections under a caretaker government meanwhile unleashed intense competition between and within parties, as candidates sought to build and defend authority under party banners following the constrained party mobilisation possible during the period of President Ershad.⁷² The period saw a rise in 'muscle politics', continued widespread national strikes (*hartal*s), the politicisation of everyday life and by the late 1990s a widespread sense that crime had deeply permeated the country's politics. Rather than seen as vehicles for ideological projects, parties became seen as tools for rewarding and organising the strongest members of the coalition.⁷³ Affiliate and associate bodies of both the Awami League and BNP proliferated at the grassroots, with students (*chhatra*), youth (*jubo*), workers (*sramik*) and volunteers (*swechasebak*) prominent among the many groups found locally. This system began to fall apart, however, when the military-backed caretaker government formed in 2006 overstepped its mandate and ruled for two years in a failed attempt to bring radical reform and rid the country of this political corruption. This period came to be symbolised by the term '1/11' on account of the military intervention in support of a new caretaker government on 11 January 2007.

The history of Bangladesh since the Awami League was re-elected in late 2008 has been shaped dramatically by its decision to repeal the caretaker government system, leading to three highly controversial and widely criticised general elections in which it won landslide victories (in 2014, 2018 and 2024). The grip that the Awami League has on key institutions of the state such as the judiciary and military, as well as on so-called civil society and society at large, appears to have intensified greatly. This period has also seen a new wave of scholarship from Bangladesh shedding light on the careers and strategies of politicians and activists, and the hold they have over political and economic life. Insightful accounts of muscular student politics have demonstrated how this profoundly shapes not only the lives of higher education institutions but also wider towns and cities, and indeed the nation as a whole.⁷⁴ Other work has focused on the criminal profiles and machinations of political bosses such as MPs and mayors, and the grip they have on economic sectors.⁷⁵ A further body of work has examined the micro political economies found in urban settings such as *basti*s, in which political leaders and state officials capture and extract services and resources.⁷⁶ Beyond such parties, some have explored Bangladesh's 'crowd politics' including the popular agitation against Phulbari coal mine,⁷⁷ student movements in Dhaka⁷⁸ and protests by trade unions.⁷⁹

This book builds on such emerging literature by focusing further down the political hierarchy to the everyday political life of the streets, to the labourers, vendors and muscle that look up to those with designations, but are profoundly embroiled in establishing, feeding and contesting the authority of those in office. It offers a detailed ethnographic account of the complex tapestry of de facto authorities found in everyday life and reveals how people navigate their place within this world. Rather than being the preserve only of local elites, the ethnography demonstrates the depths to which syndicates permeate everyday life. By tracing the connections between these street-level 'intermediaries' and the wider political landscape historically, the chapters to come substantiate the theoretical approach to the relationship between syndicates and political order outlined in the Introduction. By studying how the nexus of crime and politics has changed over these decades, a unique contemporary history of Dhaka and Bangladesh emerges, helping us better understand the Awami League's dominance today.

Notes

1. I had previously worked on a poverty reduction programme in Bangladesh between 2010 and 2012.
2. Labourers often referred to their *bari* or *gramer bari*, their village home.
3. Children grow up quickly here. On the one hand they watch cartoons and play fight under the eyes of the staff of NGO shelters (which as of 2022 have closed) or play cricket in the nearby Sher-E-Bangla Nagar Park. On the other, they learn to act like adults: smoking cigarettes, getting into fights, building and proving their capacity to operate in a grown-up world. A field worker with the boys at the bazaar once described their lives like this: 'There are no limits here ... everything is unlimited. If he wants to slap a girl, he can do it easily. He can "eve tease" easily. If he wants to steal, he can do it without end. That's why they don't want to leave this life.' In many ways the group of labourers and the support they find there become like family, regulating behaviour and providing advice.
4. A Sramik League leader described the major advantage of the bazaar as its accessibility from all sides, and it being a market where you can get everything.
5. Goods are sometimes also delivered to other holding spaces, known as *ghar*s or *foot*s.
6. E. Lewis (1868: 25).
7. The group used to have an arrangement whereby they would pay the police 100 taka a day to ignore their gambling. When they decided collectively to stop playing (because they were losing too much money and not being able to eat for the rest of the day), they stopped paying the money. The police subsequently came and found they were not playing but said, 'Well, you are all sitting here together so I will say you are playing, so give me 100 taka!' under the threat of arrest, as Liton described it.
8. A younger driver once told me:

   > You see the *basti*, it looks poor from the outside, but inside they sometimes keep 2 or 3 crore taka of goods in the room; they have a fridge and TV in their room, they purchase land in their villages. But one blow can make them lose everything. RAB could catch them.

From late evening until around 8 am, women (and less so men) huddle outside their homes on either side of the railway line over large baskets holding mounds of marijuana. Hidden from view they also sell harder and more expensive drugs such as *yaba*. Drugs are reportedly supplied primarily from Myanmar and India, and they pour into the market, being dealt and consumed there. According to the *jhupri* group, the vegetable trucks are used to conceal and deliver drugs around the country, and I have met rickshaw *wallah*s who come to buy drugs to sell around the elite neighbourhood Gulshan (often to foreigners, they claim).

9. Bangladesh Bureau of Statistics (2014: 6).
10. The online national encyclopaedia of Bangladesh. See 'Kawran Bazar', https://en.banglapedia.org/index.php/Kawran_Bazar (accessed 4 January 2024).
11. For example, S. Ahmed (1986).
12. This neglect of the city's past at least in part reflects its relatively minor role in the subcontinent during much of the East India Company and British Raj era. This can be qualified by noting important movements that emerged here, such as the Muslim League and revolutionary group Dacca Anushilan Samiti in the early twentieth century. Prior to and following the British, however, the city's importance is self-evident, yet undeservedly neglected.
13. As noted in the diaries of Sir William Hedges from the early 1680s, extracts from which were cited by J. T. Rankin (1918).
14. The position of chief eunuch was a trusted and powerful one, responsible for the inner lives of rulers (such as harems and wealth) as well as serving as military leaders, diplomats and brokers in the power struggles surrounding the court. Sending young native eunuchs as revenue payment was common until the early seventeenth century, particularly from Sylhet (Hambly 1974).
15. Khwaja Ambar was a protégé of Khwaja Talib, the trusted eunuch of emperor Aurangzeb himself. Ambar would go on to inherit his patron's title of Khidmatgar (personal attendant) Khan in 1704, suggesting a privileged position within the Mughal hierarchy (Faruqui 2012: 240).
16. Other sources indicate that Khwaja Ambar, described as a 'subordinate official of Shaista Khan', similarly built a mosque in Patna in 1688–1689 (Ahmed 1998: 388).
17. In Bengali a *serai* is termed a *katra*. It is then likely that at some point the mosque formed part of a *katra*, similar to but less grand than the famous *boro* and *choto katra*s that lie in ruins in old Dhaka, partially consumed by recent and poorly constructed housing. Bradley-Birt (1906: 268) notes that the 'Bara Katra' built by Shah Shuja, the son of the man who built the Taj Mahal in Agra, was never used for its intended purpose as his palace, but was rather used as a caravanserai, 'a public halting-place where travellers and the poor might find rest and shelter'. Some scholars have equated the term *katra* in the context of

Dhaka with a marketplace or 'royal market' (S. Sen 1998: 26), on account one assumes of the close association between royal patronage and markets.
18. This canal had many names – for some it was the Pandu River or Neri Khal; more recently it had been Iskaton Khal, but another name was 'Kairowan Nadi'. Karim (1964: 6) translates this as 'Caravan River', speculating that this may have been the name of the river in the 'Muslim period'.
19. Taylor (1840: 78). It is difficult to know the extent to which the city really extended and care should be taken not to romanticise this period of Dhaka's history.
20. Bowrey (1903: 150).
21. Rudduck cited in Khanum (1982).
22. See Bradley-Birt (1906); and S. Ahmed (1986). Others suggest it peaked at a population of around half a million in the late seventeenth century (Karim 1964: 92).
23. One historian notes that building the bridge and *serai* would have been 'a great service to the caravanians' as the 'Pandu river was of great strategic and commercial significance in the growth of the city of Dacca in the Mughal period' (Karim 1967: 302), with a branch weaving southwards past Narinda in the heart of the city.
24. Although no evidence of such a gate exists, it has been argued that this was an important check-post in Mughal times (Taifoor 1956: 213).
25. Marx (1953).
26. Walters (1832).
27. Ahmed (1986: 149). This decline was felt across the district and beyond. In the late eighteenth century, for example, Dacca district reportedly had around 650 markets, a figure which had decreased to 336 by the early twentieth century (S. Sen 1998: 162).
28. Cited in Bradley-Birt (1906: 238).
29. Taylor (1840: 310).
30. Ibid., 305.
31. Allen (1912: 60).
32. Taylor (1840: 282). It seems that by about the late eighteenth century 'Dacca and its neighbourhood furnished the greatest number of the children whom the low Portuguese of Dacca, Calcutta ... used to purchase and collect clandestinely, and export by sea' (ILC 1841: 18). Female slaves were often part of harems, and those sold into slavery in Dhaka were generally girls, having been 'decoyed away from their parents ... under pretext of marriage ... and disposed of either to public women, or to rich individuals as servants' (15). Wandering *fakirs* were identified as some of these tricksters. It is possible that some form of

slave market had existed previously in Dacca, though the most noted was in Hooghly, north of modern-day Kolkata in West Bengal.
33. In the mid-nineteenth century, Taylor wrote that 'there are no serais in the district, and the few persons that travel by land, therefore find board and lodging at ... Akharas, or at the shops of the Moodees or dealers in grain' (1840: 295).
34. Walters (1832: 536).
35. Shakespear (1834).
36. Wise (1883: 352).
37. Bayly (2012: 386).
38. Tayeb (2022).
39. Bangladesh Bureau of Statistics (2022).
40. Hoornweg and Pope (2017).
41. Democratic periods are seen as 1972–1974, 1991–2006 and 2008–2014, and authoritarian military-backed rule as being 1975–1990, arguably 2006–2008 and 2014 to the present.
42. M. Khan (2017); Basu, Devine and Wood (2018).
43. Suykens (2017).
44. M. Khan (2010); Suykens (2016).
45. Bertocci (1982: 993).
46. Z. Khan (1981: 552–553).
47. Mascarenhas (1986).
48. Codron (2007: 32).
49. Lindquist (1977).
50. Mascarenhas (1986: 34).
51. Ibid., 37.
52. Lifschultz (1979: 1331).
53. Obaidullah (2019).
54. Baxter (1998: 92).
55. Z. Khan (1981: 561).
56. S. Islam (1984: 558).
57. Ahamed (2004).
58. Z. Khan (1981).
59. Lifschultz (1979: 1339).
60. Z. Khan (1981: 561).
61. Maniruzzaman and Basu (1983: 132).
62. Ibid.
63. Z. Khan (1981: 560).
64. Franda (1981: 358).

65. The 'Basic Democracy' system had been an attempt to undermine political opposition by building a new support base at the grassroots, incentivised through access to government programmes (M. Khan 2010).
66. Maniruzzaman and Basu (1983).
67. Maniruzzaman (1992).
68. Codron (2007: 57).
69. Hakim (1998: 289) cited in Codron (2007: 57).
70. The Zila Parishad Amendment Bill of 1987 stipulated that military officers would be included in district-level government, as one of several appointed members chosen on the basis of administrative hierarchy and quotas. This was met with strong opposition amid claims that the military were playing a greater role in the country's political life which unified to pressure Ershad into not approving the bill (Huque and Akhter 1989).
71. Codron (2007).
72. The only election since 1990 not to have been administered by a caretaker government system was that of early 1996, which was boycotted by the Awami League and wider parties, leading to the institutionalisation of the caretaker government system and fresh elections.
73. Jahan (2018).
74. Ruud (2012, 2014); Andersen (2014); Suykens (2018); Kuttig (2019).
75. Ruud (2018, 2019, 2020); Kuttig (2020); Jackman and Maitrot (2021).
76. Hackenbroch and Hossain (2012); S. Hossain (2012); Suykens (2015); Lata, Walters and Roitman (2019).
77. N. Chowdhury (2019).
78. Jackman (2021).
79. Ashraf and Prentice (2019).

2
The Years of Terror

> In Dhaka people usually wake with the sound of crows. Here we woke with the sound of bomb blasts.
> —Former affiliate of 'Picchi' Hannan, living in the rail line *basti*

Before meeting the *jhupri* labourers, I had heard of Kawran Bazaar's reputation through old colleagues and friends. On the few occasions I had visited over the years, I had seen that by day it was a chaotic bazaar. By night, I was warned, it was one of the most dangerous places in Dhaka. I was unclear where this reputation came from and had heard only vague descriptions of *badmash* (criminals), *mastan* (gangster, thugs) or that 'there's lots of politics there'. I was thus surprised after getting to know the *jhupri* labourers to see little sign of violence other than the scuffles between labourers trying to reach trucks, and was told there were plain-clothes police stationed nearby, keeping a watchful eye over the market. I hence began to formulate questions about some of the terms my colleagues had used or that I had seen opaque references to in academic literature. *Are there* mastan *here? What do* mastan *do?* These questions largely fell flat. Some pointed my attention to the young thieves who stole mobile phones from passengers at the nearby Tejgaon railway station, some of whom I knew.

It was when I began to ask what the bazaar used to be like that replies became animated. Over subsequent years of research, labourers and political leaders here have conveyed consistent and evocative descriptions of the 1980s to 2000s: this 'was a time of chaos', an 'underworld' (*aparadh jagat*), an era 'of terror', a time when 'the whole bazaar was held hostage by gangsters' and 'guns were like toys'. A Jubo League activist well established in the area put it like this:

> The situation was terrible. It was even hard to enter Kawran Bazaar. Fear was everywhere, and everyone was scared. Theft and muggings were normal. It got worse after Ershad fell and the BNP came to power. People were murdered in broad daylight, traders were stopped by the gangsters [*santrashi*] and had all their money taken.

If caravanserais had a dark reputation under the British Raj, associated with crime and the off cuts of a city, then Kawran Bazaar's more recent past is true to form. The term most often used to personify this period is *santrashi*, which in its dictionary definition translates roughly to 'terrorist'. Though a source of terror, the figures referred to were not terrorists as imagined in English and other Latin-based languages. They did not espouse grand ideological goals but instead were far more akin to the image of gangsters or the mafia, the classic twentieth-century 'violent entrepreneur'. Indeed, another common term used is 'godfather', and in the media they were the 'top terror'.[1] These figures often had their name prefixed with a defining, colourful, if odd, characteristic: being *black, small, scavenger, destitute, chicken, Bihari, Sweden* or even BBC. In Naples, Roberto Saviano has noted how 'the anthology of nicknames is infinite' for the Camorra, and this equally applies here.[2] Such figures were far from unique to Kawran Bazaar, yet it was this area that was most intimately associated with their rise and reign. As they grew in strength from the late 1980s to early 2000s, the gravity of their activities increased. If in the early 1980s the *santrashi*s used machetes or knives, then by the late 1980s they used Molotov cocktails, by the early 1990s guns and by the 2000s petrol bombs, as a journalist here remembered it.

Many figures were born from the bazaar and nurtured by it into crime. The flows of people seeking a life in Dhaka provided the manpower to groups, with iconic figures and their men rising to power from the streets themselves. One-time labourers or scavengers were soon seen with guns, cars and the kind of wealth that was imagined, yet rarely seen among the poor. Long-standing NGO workers here recall the powerful figures who were once street children seeking shelter in their centres. The economy of the bazaar also provided the riches on which such groups could be built. It is hard to imagine that this bazaar with its fish and its fruit served as a basis for serious wealth, yet in a time before many of the major industries now seen in Bangladesh, this was a significant source of income. Alongside this, contracts from government departments and state enterprises headquartered here – such as the WASA, Titas Gas, Local Government and Rural Development (LGRD) and Petro-Bangla – became more lucrative. Tenders could be manipulated, controlled and profited from.

The sense of threat that infamous figures posed took on a life of its own. These groups appeared everywhere, yet also nowhere, simultaneously controlling the streets but becoming difficult to track down. Anyone could be affiliated. A trader in the area described how 'at that time we were even robbed by children. They used to come up to us, and pull up their *lunghi*, and they'd have a gun strapped to their leg.' Their threats appeared in a letter, a phone call or rumours of a name and reputation gained through murder and intimidation. The ambiguity of affiliation fed down to the streets, with opportunists freeriding on the fear. A former *santrashi* figure who served ten years in jail on murder charges, described this: 'Even sitting next to a police station people would mug you with an aubergine, pointing it at you under some cloth as if it was a gun.' Whilst today money is exchanged with relative security in the innumerable transactions that take place twenty-four hours a day, during this period, significant sums of cash would be hidden, kept concealed from outside eyes; 'even if you just took money out of your pocket, people would attack you, stab you and snatch it', as one wholesaler remembered it.

These figures and the groups at their command held such a grip on life at the bazaar that everyone was de facto aligned, complicit or subject to their interests. For people who grew up at the bazaar and nearby, there was a sense that 'to survive you had to be in a group', as one *jhupri* labourer put it. Many of the current *jhupri* labourers were themselves in these groups, and some have served prison sentences. This period is remembered for the pervasive sense of insecurity, where you could rarely sit in peace and where bombs would blast on one side, then the other. I was told repeatedly that though I could move freely now at the bazaar, back then I would have been robbed even before I lit a cigarette. Shakib, one of the *jhupri* group, recalled the period:

> During that time you couldn't sit here like you are doing now. *Santrashi*s were everywhere. Even when government people came, the *santrashi*s would ask them what they are doing here and invite them for tea.

These then were the years of terror.

Goonda Politics

> Kawran Bazaar was a beehive of gangsters [*santrashi*s].
> —Awami League leader, Tejgaon Thana

Of all the neighbourhoods in Dhaka, Kawran Bazaar is most closely associated with a long list of gangsters who once held sway in the city. Many emerged from the bazaar's alleys and nearby *basti*s to extort and rob and carve up the lucrative economy. It was often described to me as 'an area of terrorists [*santrashi*s] and godfathers'. Of all the figures to rise here, a man nicknamed 'Picchi' Hannan became feared above all. Hannan's role was so all encompassing that he has become mythologised, with his reputation aggrandised beyond plausibility. A Sramik League leader here described how 'he became so big, he controlled the whole of Bangladesh'. Picchi Hannan's story is a window into the entanglement of crime and politics between the 1980s and 2000s. It illuminates how the poor found opportunities within this and how political authority has changed since. To begin this story, however, we need to take a step back into the country's past, to the emergence of parties as serious political players in the region and how a nascent form of urban violent entrepreneur emerged.

When the East India Company wrested control of Bengal in the mid-eighteenth century, they took charge of a region in which wealth was largely rooted in land. Though central political authority was vested in urban centres, agricultural land was controlled by a tapestry of different local powerholders, ranging from *zamindar*s and their subordinates to local princes, supported by their militia. The daily threats to colonial control therefore emanated principally from the *mofussil*, such as the uprisings of *fakir*s or *sanyasi*s, bands of dacoits and their liaisons with *zamindar*s, unruly local leaders, and the general usurping of state authority such as when local *daroga*s were bent.[3] There were major threats to cities (for example, later in the Indian Uprising of 1857); however, these rarely stemmed from the character of the cities themselves. Eighteenth-century Calcutta, for example, was regularly prey by night to dacoits lurking in nearby jungles. These bands incorporated local Bengalis, men from others states and even Europeans, but were rarely embedded socially in the city and were therefore largely alienated from the ties and respect of the urban poor.[4]

By the end of the nineteenth and beginning of the twentieth centuries, however, we see a shift in the locus of elite anxieties around disorder and crime. One source of fear was the secret societies of the urban Indian middle classes, fostering the cause of independence. These *samiti*s (societies), as they were known, were branded terror organisations on account of their clandestine aim to achieve revolution through violent means. Many *samiti*s took the form of social clubs intended to foster nationalist ideologies, combined with the physical training required for direct action, often including the use of *lathi*s (sticks, rods).

Influenced in part by European anarchists and their bomb-making manuals, some *samiti*s obtained illegal arms and funded their activities through dacoity and the donations of radical wealthy benefactors. The most prominent among these was the Dacca Anushilan Samiti.[5]

Another fear stemmed from further down the social hierarchy. Indian cities had seen much change through the course of the nineteenth century. Port cities in particular had grown with the rise of export industries and manufacturing sectors, such as the extensive jute factories in Calcutta where by the turn of the twentieth century there were an estimated 1.7 million migrants.[6] This changed the fabric of cities, with new and predominantly male communities emerging in sprawling *basti*s.[7] It is in this context that new vernacular forms of urban authority began to emerge. Rajnarayan Chandavarkar's study of Bombay, for example, argues that this period witnessed the rise in 'street-corner bosses, dadas and their followers, [and] ... youth gangs'.[8] His study describes how the local 'dada' came to prominence, straddling different worlds. They might have connections to the police, perhaps be a 'jobber' in a factory (a labour leader, discussed in detail in Chapter 4), patronise local temples and be linked to party politics, whilst often also running a local gymnasium (*akhara*).[9] They could be found on the sides of political parties, of factory owners, of the police and of workers.

Calcutta meanwhile gave birth to a label that has currency across the subcontinent: *goonda*. The term is of unknown provenance but today refers to a thug, and is shorthand for a style of muscular, criminal politics that seems to characterise much of the region.[10] When it emerged in late nineteenth and early twentieth-century Bengal, it captured a sense that new forms of authority, crime and threat to the elite were being personified in the city. These were neither the ordinary petty criminal (*badmash*) nor the dacoits (*dakat*). They were a seemingly new brand of robbers, cocaine dealers, brothel owners, racketeers, agitators, extortionists and smugglers. Most often they were seen as up-country migrants, sometimes the 'homeless' of the city who worked as 'carters, hawkers and coolies'[11] and occasionally even the upper classes and castes. Concerns about *goonda*s stemmed in part from the insecurities seen in a growing city shaken by economic instability. Elites complained of increased robberies and theft.[12] More profoundly, however, elite anxiety came from the sense that there were new political agitators rooted in the city itself. *Goondas* were perceived as not only criminals but also mobilisers of street violence in labour struggles, the non-cooperation movement and later communal Hindu–Muslim clashes in Calcutta and wider Bengal. The threat was perceived as so grave that it led to the founding of a *goonda* department or division among the detectives of the Calcutta police in 1920, and the Goondas Act of 1923, which notably gave the government the right to remove those they defined as non-Bengali 'goondas' from the city without trial.[13]

Much of what we know about *goondas* from this period stems from confidential police and political records, which by design cast such figures as a criminal threat to local and colonial elites. Yet in practice the people labelled as *goondas* were heterogenous, with diverse interests and identities. Agitators in favour of labour might be labelled as such, but so likewise could the muscle deployed by factory bosses to discipline the workforce.[14] Agitators in favour of non-cooperation might be seen as *goondas*, but the government themselves also mobilised these figures to suppress such movements.[15] It was then the 'skill of producing violence ... [which] brought the "subaltern" of the city in close proximity of the "elite" political and industrial bosses'[16] and it was the emerging hierarchies of the city itself which such elites drew from. As in Bombay, many *goondas* in Calcutta were linked to *akharas* and the physical prowess they could hone here. Some were *sardars*, the key intermediaries linking the working classes to business elites, such as in the jute mills of Calcutta.[17] The terms *sardar* and *goonda* thus refer to different roles, but the individuals denoted may be the same, and the skills of each may reinforce the other.

What we then observe during this period is the convergence of institutional politics and urban grassroots violent entrepreneurship. This sets part of the political stage for the century to come in the subcontinent. Central to the communal Hindu–Muslim riots, for example, was the patronising of community-level *goondas* by the respective Hindu and Muslim political leaders.[18] In the 1930 Dhaka riot, a government report from the period described the Muslim crowd as consisting of 'criminals', referred to in the Hindu press as *goondas*, and largely comprised of lower occupational groups such as day labourers, butchers, *coolies* and stall owners, whilst the Hindu crowd was formed largely of *bhadralok* youth and artisan groups.[19] By the 1941 riot there are clear references to the role of so-called local *goondas* in Dhaka. Those arrested after the events included 'Habib, Arman, Majed Sardar, Abdullah Boro Badshah and Rahmatullah', figures who had explicit links to Muslim League leaders who visited them in prison, 'stood as securities for their release on bail' and reportedly celebrated their release with a visit to the Nawab.[20] Dhaka was not as blessed with state resources as Calcutta. In a letter from 1943, the Superintendent of Police, Bakarganj, laments the lack of a detective department in the city, the main drawback of which he describes as the lack of 'direct touch with the goonda type of criminal' whom he identifies as 'primarily responsible' for the 'communal clashes' seen in the city.[21]

This period of history prior to the birth of Bangladesh is very poorly documented, not least as a result of the executions of Bengali intellectuals at the hands of the Pakistani Army and related militia during the Liberation War. What little we do know hints that the nexus of crime and politics in Dhaka changed notably during this period as the city saw dramatic political and demographic change under East Pakistan. As will be examined further in Chapter 3, Dhaka, unlike Calcutta, had a very distinct indigenous social–political hierarchy stemming from its Mughal roots, and oriented around neighbourhoods (*mahalla*s), their leadership under *sardar*s (headman) and the Nawab. *Sardar*s were respected figures but also, it seems, could be associated with muscle and violence. The locally famous Kader Sardar (the owner of the first cinema in Dhaka, Lion Cinema) was, for example, said to have gained wealth and power through his association with a 'cocain [*sic*] addict of the Nawab family' and through these ties became associated with 'muscle power'.[22] *Mahalla*s were also said to have been able to mobilise their own 'musclemen' and use the communal fund they controlled to support 'communal riots'.[23] The reference to *goonda*s and the Nawab seems then to suggest that criminal muscle was produced by the formal political structure of the city itself.

Following Partition, Dhaka became the capital of East Pakistan and the city saw dramatic change. The estate of the Nawab was abolished in the early 1950s and a new class of bureaucrats came to dominate the city and region's politics. It appears this new political reality confronted the older neighbourhood-based forms of authority. It has been argued, for example, that the government of East Pakistan acquired land owned by *mahalla sardar*s without compensation in order to expand the city. This was the case in Kalabagan, for instance, just west of Kawran Bazaar, which was reportedly owned by Alauddin Sardar and controlled through his 'muscleman' (a translation of the term *lathial*, 'clubman') Bashiruddin, who was also a local milkman.[24] Other famous *sardar*s such as Moti Sardar of Siddique Bazaar were also 'oppressed and humiliated' by the government, signalling the rise of a new middle class at the expense of the old order.[25] By the mid-1950s, the district magistrate portrayed the *sardar*s as being

> old, ignorant, corrupt people ... who made a living by doubtful means. They were assumed to maintain relations with the underworld; they receive some

money from the police for acting as informers, and sometimes they extort money from people who have much to answer for.[26]

In Calcutta some heroic community figures who emerged from Partition went on to political and criminal prominence (for example, Gopal Mukherjee).[27] By contrast in Dhaka it appears that the birth of East Pakistan usurped the traditional forms of authority – the relationships between the Nawab, *sardar*s and *goonda*s. But this history is patchy and difficult to discern and must, if possible, be addressed by future historians. We hence continue our story as far back as the memory of locals stretched.

The Rise of 'Picchi' Hannan

> In the time of Picchi Hannan there were thousands of syndicates at Kawran Bazaar.
> —Awami League leader, Tejgaon

It was from the hordes of labourers who sought opportunities in Dhaka in the aftermath of independence and the subsequent famine that the ranks of the gangs that came to dominate Kawran Bazaar were formed. As in Calcutta, where *goonda*s emerged in part from the migrants and the streets, so too was the case in post-Liberation Bangladesh. An older generation of people who grew up in and around the bazaar recall gangs being formed from the nearby *basti*s and labour groups here, creating 'terror' and doing 'mastani'. One journalist described how in the early 1980s gangs of Bihari children and teenagers came from their camps to rob and steal. More serious figures, however, came from the adjacent *basti*s, long associated with drugs delivered through the railway network. One figure of note was Piyaru Mahajan (Piyaru moneylender) from Koshipotti (butchers' place), who 'united all the butchers', after which there were the truck drivers and their helpers, who similarly 'united to start doing *mastani*,' as the journalist put it.

From the late 1980s, groups began to emerge here that would rise to heights far beyond the alleys of the bazaar. Each corner of the market, nearby neighbourhoods and indeed the city has its own history of gangs and leaders who rose to power, the big names that people still remember today. Picchi Hannan is the man most remembered at the bazaar, a man who by the early 2000s had gained almost mythological status. Though he ran the bazaar, by the early millennium many have never seen him or have tales of spotting him in a fancy car or disguise. Businessmen feared a phone call or letter mentioning his name, a sum of money and a deadline, while local murders evidenced the lengths his gang would go to. It is said that five–ten businessmen were kidnapped at the bazaar a day, a figure which may or may not be an exaggeration but either way expresses the gravity of the times. With his whereabouts unknown, Hannan was ubiquitous yet unseen. Anyone could count among his informers and allies – street vendors, traders, labourers, beggars or police constables – all helping keep track of who was earning and who could pose a threat. Yet Picchi Hannan had only fifteen years ago been a labourer, a poor migrant living at the bazaar very much like the tens of thousands found here today.[28]

Hannan's career began with his arrival in Dhaka wearing a 'torn half pant and a torn vest', as a childhood friend and now journalist remembered it. He joined his older brother and father, who had left their home district of Chandpur for the city in the 1970s and managed to establish a rice retail business at the bazaar. He is said to have been forced to come after failing his class seven school exams, there being little hope left for his education. Not knowing Dhaka, this friend showed him the sights of the city. They used to play cricket and football in the empty fields around the bazaar, where tower blocks and shops stand today. As he got older and stronger Hannan eventually found work as a labourer at the nearby godown. A Jubo League leader and one-time rival recounted how Hannan grew up around the 'bhanga gate' (broken gate) area near the bazaar, how at the warehouse he formed a small group of around five people from his home district and how 'he used to steal rice and fight with the guards if they tried to stop him'. Others described him beginning petty street muggings and threatening people, but with work at the warehouse being unreliable, he moved to the bazaar proper after a couple of years, where his notoriety grew.

At first Hannan slept next to his father's business under a mosquito net. Some claim he worked as a guard in the rice wholesale market, some that he became the *sardar* of a group of *coolies* and others that he was a *coil*, the person responsible for collecting the commission from the *paiker* after unloading goods on behalf of the wholesalers. All, however, emphasise how his reputation for fighting grew and how he began to earn, extorting money from traders at the various wholesale markets in the area. Crucial to Hannan's journey and future reputation was his involvement with a then powerful gangster named 'Sweden Aslam' and the protection they received from the ruling Jatiya Party in the late 1980s. 'Everything began from there,' as one rival put it. Sweden Aslam is infamous as an extortionist, tender grabber, gold smuggler and murderer who rose to power from the area of Farmgate, just north of Kawran Bazaar. Legend has it he killed a local leader with a broken Fanta bottle and his moniker 'Sweden' came from his frequent holidays in the country to visit extended family and escape the heat of murder charges.

Why this period presented opportunities for gangsters to rise to power across the city is little understood. One explanation is that they were nurtured by political elites in their attempts to compete. President Ershad's legitimacy, for example, was challenged by the activism of the Awami League, BNP, students and other civil society actors. He had attempted to consolidate his military rule through quasi-civilianising the regime and forming a political party (the Jatiya Party), much like President Zia had done forming the BNP. Sweden Aslam and Picchi Hannan are portrayed locally as having been sheltered by the Jatiya Party, and it is plausible that this was at some level a political strategy to nurture new forms of muscle to control the streets. Others have argued that by the mid-1980s '[t]he competition [between parties] was so fierce that possessing a sophisticated gun would promote one to a higher rank within the party or its affiliated bodies'.[29] Across the city local clubs also appeared in tin shacks where ruling party bodies would be organised. Much like we saw in the descriptions of the Muslim League patronising local *goonda*s, here again we have a convergence of street-level violent entrepreneurs and political institutions in the form of the *santrashi*s.[30]

The return to parliamentary democracy energised rather than curbed the rise of gangsters. With elections now regulated under the emerging system of a caretaker government, political power was up for grabs, and politicians from each party nurtured such figures in their attempts to dominate. Odd references began to appear in academic literature to the role of the local 'mastan' in the lives of the urban poor and by the late 1990s scholars were referencing '*mastan* politics' as an attempt to understand the particularly violent competition between the Awami League and BNP. Gangsters were not only thriving in Dhaka, but across South Asia. In Mumbai the likes of Dawood Ibrahim had become a household name. In Calcutta, the nexus of crime and politics that emerged in the first half of the twentieth century arguably solidified with local 'dons' and 'mafia' involved in extortion, racketeering, property and drugs, under the patronage of political leaders.[31] The term *mastan* was also used in West Bengal to refer to the latest incarnation of urban toughs standing at the nexus of politics and community, offering their services to political leaders and dominating local life.[32]

Hannan's own career accelerated when Sweden Aslam was imprisoned in 1997, splitting his gang and allowing Hannan to emerge as the premier 'godfather' of Kawran Bazaar.[33] From the late 1990s, Hannan's role at the bazaar became all encompassing: he created monopolies on goods, built and invested in property, demanded cuts from developers, owned fleets of buses and his men were a regular sight at Titas Gas and WASA tender openings, as one local contractor recounted. What he is remembered most for, however, are drugs and extortion. His men controlled at least two major drug spots here. One was behind the upmarket Bashundara shopping centre, a phensedyl spot where 10,000–20,000 bottles were sold a day. The *jhupri* labourers remember the long queues that would form as if they were for a cinema. Another site was the 'Kawran Bazaar rail line *basti*', where drivers would slow or stop trains to quietly deliver goods in an arrangement which continued until very recently.[34] It was from this bazaar that Hannan created an 'empire of drugs', as a petty dealer described it to me once.

Hannan's second major source of income was from extortion and racketeering, coercively mediating access to work and business. His hold on the bazaar was so great that it is widely felt that there 'was not a single business here who didn't pay him', as a number of rivals and political leaders put it. Most infamously, Hannan's group were known for their kidnappings of wholesalers and larger more prominent businesspeople, whom they would take to a quiet spot and demand hundreds of thousands of taka for their release. A Jubo League activist and trader at the bazaar remembered this time:

> Picchi Hannan used to get money from the wholesalers who did business here. Say you have a space in the market as a wholesaler, and he has four workers – one each from Rajshahi, Rangpur, Dinajpur and Khulna. They sleep on the footpath, so the terrorist marks the wholesale market and calls one of them, takes him to a corner and says, 'You have to give *chanda* to us every month. If you want to do business you have to give the money.' Or if there is a big businessman with ten shops, he will call him and say, 'You have to pay this amount by the end of the month.' This is how they earned money by threatening people. By controlling this market they never lacked money. And if a minister gives them shelter, because they use terrorists, and the terrorists are their main weapon, this is how they earned huge huge amounts.

The threat, as one Sramik League leader put it, was simple: 'He would kill you in the middle of the day. If anyone didn't pay, they would be taken to the corner of WASA and shot dead. It happened regularly.' Hannan's ability to execute these threats was built from his group, which is portrayed today as having had a thousand or thousands of members, almost exclusively from his home district of Chandpur. As Hannan took greater control, Chandpuri people rose in number and prominence, constituting, locals estimate, over 50 per cent of the labourers, traders and others at the bazaar at the time. The tentacles of his group extended down to the labourers and street vendors, who through their affiliation and loyalty to a *boro bhai* (big brother) could be drawn into the conflict or used as informers to report on the goings on at the bazaar. Some in the *jhupri* group had specific roles as informers or drug dealers, and some went about their normal work but through affiliation could be drawn upon when needed.

More specifically, Hannan's syndicate (as locals describe it) relied closely on a small group of 'bodyguards' who themselves had hundreds of men at their command. Some of these figures had also risen under the shelter of Sweden Aslam, such as a man often considered Hannan's second in command, Sahib Ali. Hannan and Sahib Ali were 'a pair', as a rival put it, 'if one of them was in jail, then the other one would be out'. An affiliate described him as 'the man closest to Hannan', one of the few to know the full extent of his assets. Similar to Hannan, Sahib Ali came from humble roots, the son of a man who mended plastic shoes and was an occasional rickshaw *wallah*, and who disowned Ali after he became a prominent gangster. Some in his inner circle were known by their job description as 'killer', such as 'Killer Liton', once a scavenger from the bazaar, and 'Killer Masud', who reportedly held a post in the Chhatra League. Others close to him include Shahidullah (alias 'Lebu Shahid'), Nazimuddin Babu (his second wife's brother and president of the Dhanmondi Thana Chhatra League) and allegedly Mamun, the owner of a tower block to the north of the bazaar. Hannan's 'cashier' was 'Hazi Ismail', a man once so poor he used to walk around in a torn *lunghi* but was later tasked with keeping account of all the extortion money the gang collected.

As Hannan's profile rose, he became distant from the bazaar, rarely seen in public for fear of assassination and operating instead through his representatives. He moved from den to den, from nearby Kathalbagan to faraway in Savar, protected by his bodyguards. A businessman from his home district described how 'he used to come in disguises to the bazaar, sometimes dressed as a coolie, sometimes under a veil'. A rival recalled seeing Hannan arrive at the bazaar on a rare occasion in the early 2000s: the police stopped his car near Sonargaon hotel, 'he slid down the window and showed the policeman his gun. The amount of arms he had there could have blown up the whole check post. He told the policeman he was Picchi Hannan and gave him a bundle of 20,000 taka and carried on.' This was after all a period in which the police relied on 'obsolete outdated hardware' while criminals were 'equipped with modern automatic weapons like AK-47 assault rifles'.[35] Such sightings reflect the mythos of the figure. As well as a 'top terror', he was perceived as benevolent and admired. It is this image that helps explain the degree of legitimacy such figures arguably achieved during this period.[36] He is said to have built a mosque in his home village, as well as a madrasah and orphanage. Another businessman from Chandpur described him as generous and kind, 'like Robin Hood'.

Behind the heroic undercurrent of Picchi Hannan as a benevolent figure lies not only violence against his enemies, but exploitation of the poor. Hannan is not remembered for himself targeting the poor but his group incorporated people who did, and his activities left scars on the lives of those they touched. Even today Kawran Bazaar is a hub for boys and young men who have become disconnected from their homes, some abandoned and some forced out through violence or neglect. By necessity many become involved in crime and drift into drug abuse. These 'unemployed', 'spoiled', 'drug addicts', as they were variously described to me, became the expendable lowest levels of his organisation, the type of members whom rivals claim Hannan would sacrifice to the state, when the local officer-in-charge (OC) or others needed to show action against their activities. Hannan was interested in quarters where the profit was the greatest, yet the rank and file of his group imposed their authority over ordinary traders and hawkers, and many claim that everyone, however lowly, gave money to his group one way or another.

Syndicates and Rivals

> One day I contacted the DB [Detective Branch] to tell them that Picchi Hannan had come to the bazaar. The official asked me, 'Why are you telling me this? Do you not have children? Do you not love life?'
>
> —Siddiq, a rival

Hannan is remembered as having once been the premier 'godfather' of Kawran Bazaar. But, as a childhood friend of his emphasised to me, we must remember that 'the godfathers also have godfathers'. Understanding Hannan's links to party politics is crucial to appreciating the nexus of crime and politics during this period, as well as the nature of political change seen since. Whilst nurtured by senior party figures, Picchi Hannan and other gangsters of his generation are not seen locally as having had or been part of a party. Parvez, a *jhupri* labourer, put it like this: 'They had no politics, terrorism was their politics.' A long-standing

Jubo League activist described how 'he had a godfather, but he didn't have a party'. Top-down it is easy to imagine that the intense party politicisation of society seen following the return of parliamentary democracy held a firm grip on these powerful figures, but in practice, though nurtured politically, Hannan's authority came principally from the streets upwards. The various organisational wings of parties arguably had little presence locally compared to *santrashi*s such as Picchi Hannan. A now Jubo Dal leader in the area who was a long-standing rival of Hannan's group described how at Kawran Bazaar 'there was no Awami League, no BNP. They had no power. At that time Picchi Hannan alone was the most powerful, and he had no party.' Hannan hence rose in power irrespective of the party in office.[37] He emerged under the Jatiya Party and was sheltered and backed by both BNP and Awami League politicians for whom he would channel funds, mobilise men and rouse voters. A Sramik League leader put it like this: 'He was a terrorist, he didn't have a party … he was mainly involved with BNP, but took money from both parties, X and Y [names of local politicians]; he worked for whoever he thought would give most advantage.'

Hannan's rule then rested on the violence and intimidation he could exercise over rivals through his gang of Chandpur migrants. It was built on the opaque shelter he received from senior party figures. But it was also premised on the alliances and friendships he formed and maintained with different groups and individuals across the city. For some, Hannan's reach extended little beyond the Kawran Bazaar area. For others 'he had groups from Tejgaon to Tongi' and 'the whole city was under him', as one of the *jhupri* labourers remembers it, echoing the legendary status he had earned. A journalist and friend in his youth described him as having had a hundred key men in his group, all of whom would have their own boys, who

> would watch to see if the police were coming to the drug spots, and look out for rival gangs. They had separate groups for these jobs. Like this they had people in FDC Gate, Kathalbagan, Kazipara, Farmgate, Agargaon, not only Kawran Bazaar.

Picchi Hannan's gang was thus a patchwork of different groups scattered across the city. Some were firmly subordinate to him, some were allies and others indebted or friends. These relationships are often referred to today as also constituting a syndicate.

When the *santrashi*s emerged in public consciousness in the 1990s, journalists began noting the alliances between prominent figures. To conceptualise these, they coined the terms 'five-star group' and 'seven-star group', which were said to represent the city's underworld coalitions through the 1990s. Hannan, it was said, formed part of the five-star group, led by a former Jubo League leader known as Liakat. One of the most infamous figures Hannan was aligned to was 'Kala Jahangir' (Black Jahangir). Jahangir was involved with the Chhatra League in Mirpur, was from a middle-class background and yet became notorious for killing a rival on court premises.[38] This propelled his reputation as a feared 'killer' and gave weight to his demands when asking for *chanda*. Their rivals were said to be the 'seven-star' group led by Subrata Bain, a rare Christian in the *santrashi* world, whose base was in the nearby Magh Bazaar. In practice, however, the alliances in these groups appear highly fluid and are hence difficult to track, with many figures suspected of the murders of their one-time allies. Indeed, some say Picchi Hannan later killed Kala Jahangir.

These alliances were formed across the city. Just north of Kawran Bazaar in Tejgaon, for example, was an ally of Picchi Hannan, a figure known as Selim, who many locals recalled looked like a cinema villain. An Awami League leader in the area described how Hannan and Selim 'were friends and would work together', how they were a syndicate. Selim emerged after the fall of a more powerful group led by 'Picchi Khalek' who rose to power in the 1980s during the Ershad era, and is remembered as a local 'godfather', infamous for extortion rackets and drug trading in heroin and phensedyl.[39] Some claim that Hannan killed Khalek, thereby allowing his friend Selim to rise. When Selim was later imprisoned, his wife took temporary control and was known as 'lady commando' before Selim was reportedly killed in remand in the late 1990s.

Hannan had rivals as well as allies. His control was never stable or sure, but constantly contested and threatened as others attempted to take his mantle or wrest their share of the lucrative streams he profited from. Many hated him and his group and tried to undermine and challenge them. It was the conflict between such groups that in part led to the violence this period is notorious for. When starting out in the 1980s, for example, Hannan is said to have had a rivalry at Kawran Bazaar with a *coolie sardar*, and in the 1990s one of his greatest local enemies was a leader in the transport sector known as 'Dano Mizan' (named after 'Dano' the powdered milk popular in Bangladesh that comes in a small tin and which thus referenced Mizan's diminutive height). Dano Mizan had risen to power as a labourer in the transport sector and was similarly involved with the Jatiya Party. Mizan's group members were also renowned as local *santrashi*s and came into direct conflict with Hannan in the early 1990s when the latter attempted to extort money from Mizan's brother who was a businessman in the kitchen market at Kawran Bazaar. On one occasion Hannan was outnumbered and attacked by Dano Mizan who it is said beat and stabbed him repeatedly, then thinking him dead, he left Hannan in a drain at the side of the road. Yet somehow Hannan survived and was taken to hospital where he recovered.

This event is remembered by some as a turning point in Hannan's career. 'After this he became a terrorist in rage'; 'he was desperate for revenge and formed his group,' described a follower of Mizan and now local Jubo Dal leader named Siddiq. Through the 1990s Dano Mizan was a prominent leader of the 'Truck Labourers' Cooperative Association',[40] one of the many well organised and powerful bodies in the transport sector, which – as noted earlier – had a history of leveraging its organisation to extend control in the local economy. Enmity grew with Hannan's group, particularly over a spot for selling phensedyl on the train line that was at the time run by one of Mizan's followers named Malik. This spilled into a low-level yet continuous conflict, skirmishes, shootings and beatings. Despite being well protected by his group, the stabbing of Hannan finally caught up with Mizan around the late 1990s or early 2000s, when Hannan targeted many of those involved in the incident. Mizan was killed, along with Aktar, a former transport worker, fish wholesaler and Awami League figure, who had been there when Hannan was thrown into the ditch. The follower Malik was also killed, enabling Hannan to take over the phensedyl spot.

Countless people were killed by Hannan's group during this period, irrespective of their political affiliation. Rivals who had grown up with him under the Jatiya Party were killed, such as 'Rana' of Kazipara, who reportedly had the tendons in his legs cut and was stabbed twice, north of the bazaar in Begunbari in the early 1990s. Three members of the Sramik League were killed for opposing Hannan's interests, including the thana president. Hannan's men killed the Jubo League secretary on the road to the southeast of the bazaar near Kamarpatti (blacksmiths' quarter). Hannan shot, but did not kill, the then thana president of the Awami League, now a leader in the transport sector and known as 'Hatkata Kashem' (cut-hand Kashem). Many BNP leaders were also killed. A long-standing Jubo League activist recalled the period: 'We tried to fight them but we couldn't grow as an organisation. It was a time of terrorists.'

Reflecting on these events two decades later, some today cast themselves as small-scale heroes, resisting the might of Hannan and his group.[41] Some challenged the oppression in this period in smaller ways. Local shop owners, for example, rigged up a hidden bell system under their counters, so that when

Picchi Hannan's men came to try and extort money from them, they could alert all the shop owners in the area, who would bring out sticks to threaten them off. This worked for a while but then the system changed, and Hannan's group started sending letters to their houses.

The conflicts of this period have scarred many families. After Dano Mizan was killed, a rivalry between the remnants of his group and Hannan persisted. Siddiq was once a local leader of the Jubo Dal in the ward, and today is in the same position but at the smaller thana level. He grew up knowing Hannan. Once Hannan usurped Malik in the early 2000s by controlling the phensedyl spot on the railway line, his group took control of the whole area. Siddiq claimed that 'the whole group entered the *basti*. They began to rape women in different houses and demand money. We are born in this place, so how can we let this happen?' Hannan's group demanded *chanda* from him and his brother, both at the time businessmen at the bazaar.

> I was involved with the Jubo Dal. He killed my leader, the secretary of the Jubo Dal Tejgaon Ward BNP. Picchi Hannan didn't see any party. He killed whoever talked against him. He harassed me a lot. What could I do? Should I just sit and die? I thought he would kill me, so I had to survive. We all have to die, so it is better to fight before we die. I fought a long fight with him.

Picchi Hannan is seen as having had the clout and connections abroad to source weapons for his gang. Some of his less established rivals had to look closer to home. Siddiq, for example, looked to Dhaka University:

> Arms were available from the student halls. At the time, if you went to fifty rooms at Dhaka University, you'd find guns in twenty of them. When we were fighting with Picchi Hannan we went to a JCD [Bangladesh Jatiotabadi Chatra Dal] leader, Langra Masud [crippled Masud]. Langra Masud was later killed in Mahakhali area in 2000. But Masud bhai as a student leader was good and liked us. He also had [a] problem with Picchi Hannan. He was anti-Picchi Hannan. For example, when we were in trouble, we went to him [Masud] and said, 'Brother, we can't survive, save us.' He would say, 'Take as many [arms] as you need, but give money for [the] bullets' ... He also gave us some men.

To escape the conflict, Siddiq's family had relocated to Gazipur, bought land and built a house and enrolled his brothers in local schools. On one occasion, however, his youngest brother, aged only thirteen, came to the bazaar to sell fish in the early morning, and was shot and killed. The accused was 'Killer Liton'.

'How can I stand it if this innocent child is murdered, the youngest of our brothers, whom I had bathed with my own hands?' On a later occasion Hannan's group also abducted another of his brothers, whom he managed to find and save at the last minute.

In the aftermath, Siddiq was implicated in eighteen police cases, allegedly at the behest of Hannan ('the thana would do whatever he [Hannan] said'). Convicted for the murder of a scavenger, Siddiq was given a life term, with the sole witness being someone from Chandpur (and allegedly connected to Hannan's group). Siddiq then served ten years in jail, during which time his wife left him and re-married to raise their children with another man. Siddiq paints his story as one of fighting against injustice. Despite his own reputation as involved in crime and having killed people, he claims, 'I never did extortion, I never kidnapped anyone,' and that whatever he earned, he spent fighting Hannan's group. But whereas Hannan earned 10 lakh taka a day, he had only 50,000 a month. At the end of his term in prison, Siddiq was left without his family, had scars from bullet wounds, was so poor he could not afford the 10,000 taka fine to be released and had to serve an extra year in prison as a result. He reflected:

> I lost ten years of my life in jail. It's not only my family. There are hundreds of families here who were destroyed by Picchi Hannan ... I've lost my family, my wife, whatever I saved was ruined in the war with him. We were forced to fight with sticks. But how can you use sticks against arms?

The Fall

> There are no famous gangsters [*santrashi*s] anymore. There are no 'area-based' gangsters. Picchi Hannan, Sweden Islam, Morgi Milan, you won't find these kinds of people. If you find people, they will be with the Awami League. They have a legal identity, this is the change that has happened.
> —Crime journalist for a national newspaper, Dhaka

It took more than sticks to defeat Picchi Hannan. It took more than arms from Dhaka University fed by student leaders. It took more than those segments of the police that had not been corrupted or intimidated by his group. It even took more than the army. Hannan's reign ended in a dramatic fashion, when he was killed in 2004 by the then newly formed Rapid Action Battalion (RAB), an organisation which has an admired but now stained history in fighting crime and corruption in the country. Events are unclear, controversial and mired in folklore, and two broad (and compatible) narratives can be discerned of Hannan's end, one more national and the other more local.

By the late 1990s and early 2000s, Dhaka's gangsters were out of control. The violence, kidnappings and high-profile murders were flagrant acts of criminality that seemed to belie the notion that the ruling party and state were in charge. Gangsters once nurtured by political leaders and regimes had become too powerful in their own right. At Kawran Bazaar, local leaders portray Hannan as a challenge and threat even to political elites: 'What can be done when neither an MP nor minister has power during the reign of Picchi Hannan?' Siddiq asked me. The political 'godfathers' of the 1990s and 2000s such as the Awami League and BNP MPs had become 'hostages' to Hannan, he claimed. Sramik League leaders described the local MPs as having 'no power, they had to do what Hannan said'. One business leader and senior national BNP figure described having to pay Hannan's brother when constructing a building here. Even the Awami League ward president portrayed political leaders as having been afraid of the *santrashi*s.

The first narrative then is that the utility to political elites of having such figures on their side had eroded through the late 1990s and early 2000s as their power grew. The *santrashi*s' political connections came to tarnish the parties, and leaders saw the advantage of reining them in. When the BNP returned to power in 2001, they did so in part on a platform of ending the reign of the 'top terrors' who had come to symbolise the corruption of politics and insecurity of life. A crime journalist outlines this view:

> Killing and injuring people used to be very common in Dhaka City. There used to be fights over taking control, robberies, extortion. At that time the BNP government thought that it can't go on like this. The people of Bangladesh elected me. I have to keep law and order. Law and order has to be maintained so what could be done? The *santrashi*s have to be arrested. Who does *santrash*? *Santrashi*s are sheltered by politicians, they have to be captured together. So they formed RAB and then the killings started. David was killed, Picchi Hannan was killed, he was killed, then another, that's how it started. That's how they stopped it. The way they rose to power is the same way they were destroyed.

The government's plan was implemented under the banner 'Operation Clean Heart', which initially saw little success under the auspices of the police and military. Local police were often, we must remember, underequipped, readily corrupted and intimidated by the brute strength and daring of Hannan's gang.

During the early stages of the operation, Hannan and many other figures took shelter in Calcutta. It was not until the government formed the RAB in 2004 that it began to see success. Clad in black, often wearing bandanas and seen leaning out of trucks and 4x4s, the RAB had a professionalism and reputation rarely seen in the country's domestic security agencies. They echoed the paramilitary force of the Jatio Rakkhi Bahini formed in the country's early years, and indeed soon followed their example with involvement in widespread extrajudicial killings, referred to euphemistically as *crossfire* and *encounter*. Today a number of leading RAB figures are on the American sanctions list. The BNP government drew up (or some say inherited) a list of twenty-three persons dubbed as 'top terror'[42] and the RAB's first high-profile success was the capture of Picchi Hannan.

Why Hannan returned to Dhaka from Calcutta is unclear. Some link his eventual capture and death not only to the new mandate and change in the apparatus of the state and politics, but more specifically to the controversial Dhaka 10 by-election. This then is a more local explanation of his fall. Through the 1990s two figures had dominated the constituency that includes Tejgaon and hence Kawran Bazaar: Abdul Mannan of the BNP and H. B. M Iqbal of the Awami League. During Mannan's second term in office in the 2000s, he split from the BNP along notably with the former president of Bangladesh A. Q. M. Badruddoza Chowdhury to form a breakaway party, Bikalpa Dhara Bangladesh, intended to confront the country's two-party system. This led to a by-election in the constituency, with Mannan facing a well-established BNP candidate, Mossadak Ali Falu, the political secretary to the then prime minister Khaleda Zia. One narrative heard from BNP supporters locally is that Falu persuaded Picchi Hannan to help him win the election, supplying muscle to intimidate the well-established Mannan. When Falu arranged to pay Picchi Hannan, he was instead located by the RAB, despite being warned off by accomplices who sensed a trap. One Jubo Dal leader put it like this: 'Picchi Hannan was put on the *crossfire* list by Falu. Hannan was in India at the time, but Falu asked him to come back. He used him in the election, otherwise he wouldn't have returned. After he came back, he was killed.'

There are many other rumours locally about the treachery and events leading to his death. Some claim that he was finally found in revenge for Kala Jahangir's murder in India and that a friend of Jahangir knew of Hannan's whereabouts in Savar. A journalist known to Hannan claimed that a businessman-politician who was constructing a building at Kawran Bazaar was involved. After being threatened by Hannan, he used the journalist to track down Picchi Hannan's number, after which 'I saw that politician helping take Hannan's body out of Dhaka Medical College.' The basic events widely agreed upon are as follows: early drives at Kawran Bazaar attempted to unseat Hannan and his group from the area, leading to the arrest of important affiliates such as 'Tel Mamun', but not Hannan himself. Hannan was located by the RAB in an area of north Dhaka called Uttara. A gunfight ensued, yet he managed to escape. He was tracked down in Savar and taken into custody before mysteriously ending up dead. Local rivals of Hannan claim to have played their part in his downfall. Before being imprisoned, Siddiq described having pleaded with the local police and Detective Branch to arrest him; however, his attempts were in vain due to corruption ('there was even an OC arrested with Picchi Hannan's own weapons,' he claimed). Even elements of the media were reluctant to write against Hannan, either due to fear or profit. With the tide against Hannan's group, however, one of Siddiq's brothers helped the authorities by identifying key members of his group, which he did wearing a veil and moving around in a police vehicle pointing them out.

In the aftermath of his death, Hannan's group have had mixed fortunes. Some from his syndicate tried but failed to take control of the bazaar, whilst others reformed themselves and no longer lead a life of crime. Sahib Ali was reportedly arrested with Hannan in Savar and shot at some point, leading to a leg amputation and then imprisonment in Dhaka Central Jail. After being released, he attempted to start the group up again, only to be allegedly killed by the RAB. A rival described Hazi Ismail and Sahib Ali having a dispute over money, and Ismail paying 30 lakh taka to the RAB to have Ali killed. Ismail today is still at the bazaar, running a warehouse and seen as having 'tens of millions of taka' according to one rival. 'Tel' Mamun, although arrested, managed to be released and took ownership of a building built with Hannan's money, where he runs a hotel. He is regularly seen today in photographs on his Facebook page, posing with Awami League leaders. Other affiliates including Hannan's brother-in-law Nazimuddin were reportedly arrested by the RAB in 2007, and then again in 2014 with *yaba* tablets, Nazimuddin being described in the media as a 'crime boss' and former Chhatra League leader from Dhanmondi.[43] 'Killer Masud' was arrested by the RAB in 2007. The lower-level ranks of his group also saw different fates. Today at Kawran Bazaar people from Chandpur have far less importance ('they have no status now,' said one Jubo League activist). Some from his group managed to start petty businesses with the capital accumulated,

The Years of Terror

but junior members simply became labourers, such that many labourers and stall owners have dark pasts that they try to forget.

Others labelled 'top terror' from this period were imprisoned and are still in jail, including the infamous 'Sweden Aslam' under whose shelter Hannan rose. Some argue he wants to stay in prison, and that were he released he would be extrajudicially killed. A former *santrashi* figure who served a spell in jail with him claimed how in jail he's able to 'get any food he wants, he can stay outside his cell until 9 pm'.[44] Some say Sweden Aslam still receives a small share of illegal profits made in the Kawran Bazaar area, with men based in the nearby Raja Bazaar (to the west of the bazaar) and he still attempts to have his men elected as local councilors. More widely, the 'top terror' from this period constitute a portion of the Bangladeshis issued a 'red notice' on Interpol's most wanted list.[45]

Some names still circulate in Dhaka, no one sure if the person even exists or if their reputations are just being leveraged to strike fear and extract money. In Kawran Bazaar, businessmen get calls in the name of 'Bhai Ashik' or 'Raja Ashik'. Ashik is seen as a 'top terror', said to have once been a student leader at Tejgaon College. Some Awami League figures reportedly use his name to extract around 5 lakh a month from the bazaar, yet businessmen are unsure if he even exists. Aside from these shadows, the only figures seen as being in the mould of the *santrashi*s are at a much smaller scale, such as the 'chhyachra goonda' (petty *goonda*) from the rail line *basti*, as Sramik League leaders here put it, but 'no one really counts them as important.'[46] The odd newspaper report suggests the remnants of the 'five-star' and 'seven-star' groups are still in operation, however limited their status may be today. People speculate whether the phone calls really come from these figures themselves or impostors freeriding on the fear they evoke.[47] The crime reporter cited at the beginning of this section described this shift as having become 'digital'. He continued:

> Now there isn't this gang system. It has become digitalised. What I mean is that the people who used to be the big *santrashi*s, they now live outside of Bangladesh, some are in India, some in Dubai, and some of them manage this *chandabaji* from abroad.[48]

During the caretaker government period, *santrashi* figures along with corrupt political leaders were carefully tracked down, many imprisoned and some killed. Local leaders sidelined under Hannan attempted to take control, such as Dano Mizan's brother, although he too was killed. For a period then, extortions and other exactions calmed. This, however, changed once the Awami League returned to power in 2009 after their landslide electoral victory. Hannan's body meanwhile is reported to lie in an unmarked grave in his home village of Santoshpur in Faridganj Upazila of Chandpur District under the name Abdul Hannan.[49]

Notes

1. *Daily Star* (2004, 2005).
2. Saviano (2011: 54).
3. Chattopadhyay (2000).
4. Banerjee (2009: 54).
5. Heehs (1992).
6. de Haan (1997: 924).
7. Ibid.
8. Chandavarkar (2002: 194).
9. Gymnasiums had an important political function, serving as a platform for a 'dada' to build and sustain authority in his setting, as well as for political actors or capitalists to seek henchmen for local control among those who had proven themselves in the gym and *lathi* fighting.
10. Most straightforwardly, the term may derive from the English 'goon'. Locally, however, there is reference to the term 'goonda' in the English–Malayo dictionary produced by the English merchant Thomas Bowrey for the East India Company in 1701. *Goonda* here means 'wavering', 'doubtful' or 'suspicious'. Given the importance of Bengal to maritime trading routes and the historical prevalence of spoken Malay in the trade in the region, this offers one possible hint to the origin of the term.
11. Nandi (2016: 31).
12. For some British police officers and officials, *goonda*s had origins in the 'lathials' (stick-carrying guards) that Marwaris had brought with them as they settled in Calcutta (Nandi 2016: 21; Bhattacharya 2004: 4278). The historian Sugata Nandi outlines arguments made by a Calcutta High Court advocate in the 1920s who claimed that Marwari guards fell out of pocket when their masters' incomes were diminished after World War I, pushing them to petty crime, which developed into reciprocal relationships with lower-ranking policemen (Nandi 2016: 43–44). By 1914, it was the Marwaris themselves who requested the Calcutta police to control them, with their former guards having got out of hand and subjecting them to robberies and other crimes.
13. There was fear that such legislation would enable the government to clamp down unfairly on political protest, leading to a proposed amendment that political activity would not be covered under the purview of the act. This was,

however, rejected on the ground that it would provide a base for *goonda*s to commit crimes during political movements and events without recrimination (Nandi 2016).
14. Simeon (1995).
15. Bhattacharya (2004: 4279).
16. Ibid., 4281.
17. Chakrabarty (2000 [1989]); and Ghosh (2000). Some *goonda*s were identified as those involved in 'labour negotiations', where labour *sardar*s stamped their authority on their trades, demanding a 'commission' from those involved, and were able to use violence against both the police and the poor (Bhattacharya 2004: 4280).
18. S. Das (1991).
19. A. Roy (2018: 116). Despite the ostensibly communal character of these clashes, it has been argued that until 1941 these were primarily driven by class rather than religious conflict, with moneylenders and bazaars bearing the brunt, on the back of the economic downturn and crash of the jute industry in the late 1920s (S. Das 1990; A. Roy 2018).
20. A. Roy (2018: 156). These 'links with institutional politics' (S. Das 1994: 2878) enabled some *goonda*s to avoid prosecution, as also did their connection with the lower echelons of the city's police department, who were in their own right a somewhat threatening intermediary in the lives of the poor. Nandi (2010: 46) quotes a Bengali Hindu *bhadralok* councillor in 1920s Calcutta speaking in opposition to the Goondas Bill, describing the 'toll', 'share' and 'poojah' that cart drivers, hawkers and *coolie*s needed to give to the police constables.
21. Superintendent of Police, Bakarganj (1943).
22. Mamoon (1990: 18). It is possible that the 'Majed Sardar' listed in the previous paragraph as arrested in 1941 was a *mahalla sardar*.
23. Ibid., 19.
24. Ibid., 21.
25. Ibid., 22.
26. Den Hollander (1990: 62–63).
27. S. Das (1994).
28. The story of Picchi Hannan, like all the other gangsters in the history of Dhaka, has not until now been formally documented (see also Jackman 2018). There are only limited public sources to consult, such as odd newspaper reports. Other than these, we must rely on oral history, and must thus remember that this account is coloured by the legendary status he has earned over the years, by the benefit of hindsight and by the legacy of violence people still feel today.
29. Hussain cited in M. Chowdhury (2003: 269).

30. Similarly, Ershad started the 'national youth party' (National Torun Party), which had a 'labour function', as one journalist described it, giving income to teenagers and young men as a way of patronising the labouring classes.
31. Tumpa Mukherjee (2017).
32. S. Banerjee (2017).
33. Some old student leaders at Dhaka University suggested that in fact Hannan rose to power under the patronage of a particular student leader in the 1980s, a connection the locals here do not make. It is, however, likely that a formative step in Hannan's career was his relationship to Dhaka University. At the time, Dhaka University operated almost as a little fiefdom at the centre of the city, where the student wings of various parties gained huge power and prominence due to their role in unseating President Ershad. A then Chhatra League leader at Dhaka University described Hannan in his early days coming to meet him as a sign of respect. One particular connection highlighted is that between Picchi Hannan and a former MP and president of the Chhatra League, known as 'Auranga Dada'. Auranga was seen as a 'godfather' of a particular faction of the Bangladesh Chhatra League, renowned for orchestrating a protest against Ziaur Rahman when he was in power, and even implicated in the murders of two Directorate General of Forces Intelligence (DGFI) personnel. Such figures emerged as crucial during the movement (*andalon*) against Ershad's rule, and are said to have nurtured armed cadres, accommodating them in a house in nearby Kathalbagan. Hannan is said to have spent time sheltering or even working at Dhaka University, although the precise relationship here is unclear. While Auranga Dada is important, locals at Kawran Bazaar claim, as one rival to Hannan put it, that these groups 'emerged in parallel all around Dhaka'.
34. Most drugs reportedly came from Akhaura Upazila in the east of Bangladesh, adjacent to the Indian city of Agartala.
35. M. Chowdhury (2003: 267).
36. Ahmed (2004: 100).
37. This is not to deny, however, that some similar *santrashi* figures arose directly within parties and retained a close partisan identity.
38. This was reportedly the brother of an MP who had been elected to a position of local leadership within the Chhatra League that he coveted.
39. Although born and raised in the area in a middle-class home, Khalek became a fugitive. He hid somewhere in old Dhaka and would visit the area with six minibuses, each full of armed men to protect him: 'Like a minister', as a local remembered it. He was on the side of the poor, 'never took money from us', and used to command thousands of people in the area, many of whom are still here 'but have now changed their lives and pray five times a day'. He was so powerful

that he did not care about the local councillors, or about the MP, and – as was the case of other *santrashi*s – 'he didn't have a relationship with politicians, he was just a terrorist, he had the power of arms', a local Awami League leader framed it, describing how his family had had to negotiate on behalf of the poor with figures such as Selim and Khalek. The Awami League leader remembers how Khalek was powerful yet was eventually tortured by the local OC who 'shoved a rod up his penis'.

40. Truck Sramik Somobay Samiti.
41. One man Kashem, for example, was a longtime affiliate of Hannan's family, and was friends with his older cousins, Hannan being younger than him. Although not involved with his group, he felt he had influence over them, being well established in the area. He described one encounter:

> Sahib Ali once picked me up. A hawker who used to sit near my business told me that Sahib Ali took 50–100 taka every day from them. They had to work all day under the sun and give them whatever little money they earned. When I heard this, I told him, 'Don't give them the money anymore.' That night Sahib Ali came to me with a pistol at his waist and asked me if I had told the hawkers not pay them the money. I told him that I did and he hurled some abusive words at me. I told him, 'Your mother still lives by grinding spices at Kawran Bazaar, how dare you speak to me like this!' He left me but came back with 10–15 men and told me he would cut my tendons. I said, 'I know who your father is, you could never do this!' I managed to contact a councillor who knew him, and he came to speak to Sahib Ali; a few minutes later Picchi Hannan arrived. Sahib Ali told him that I was spoiling their collection spot. I said, 'You take hundreds of thousands of taka from people, can't you stop taking from these poor people?' The councillor agreed I had said the right thing, and Sahib Ali even apologised to me. But he said that 'today I am apologizing, but whenever I get the chance, I will hurt you.' But I never crossed him again.

42. These were: Subrata Bain, Molla Masud, Kala Jahangir, Khandaker Tanvirul Islam Joy, Sohel Rana Chowdhury alias Freedom Sohel, Khandakar Nayeem Ahmed alias Titon, Khorshed Alam Rashu alias Freedom Rashu, Imam Hossain, Prakash Kumar Biswas, Abdul Jabbar Munna, Abbas alias Killer Abbas, Arman, Helal alias Picchi Helal, Shamim Ahmed alias Aga Shamim, Jafar Ahmed Manik alias Manik, Sagar alias Tokai Sagar, Moshiur Rahman Kochi, Kamrul Hasan Hannan alias Chhoto Hannan, Sanjidul Islam Imon, Jisan alias Monti Kochi, Moshiur Rahman, Picchi Hannan and Alauddin.

43. Bdnews24 (2007).
44. Another prisoner in Kashimpur jail (the new Dhaka Central Jail in Gazipur) described how *santrashi*s have 'everything they need' – mobile phones, food ordered from outside the jail, cigarettes, *ganja*, *yaba*, TV, some 'even have children from jail. If you give the officer in charge at the court Tk 10,000, he can arrange a room for you to spend two hours with your wife. Done.'
45. For example, Rasul Aminur ('Tokai Sagar'), wanted for murder and firearms charges, suspected by some to be in the USA; Trimoti Subrata Bain ('Suvra'), wanted on murder and explosives charges and Khandakar Tanvir Islam Joy of the 'seven-star' group.
46. The degree to which such *santrashi* figures have been controlled locally is also seen as reflecting the authority of the home minister, who is the local MP. As the Awami League thana president in the south of the bazaar put it: 'The home minister told them he would see them twice but wouldn't forgive them in the third time.'
47. M. Hossain (2017).
48. Another crime journalist described it: 'Now this kind of extortion takes place through bKash. Now almost everyone has a bKash account, sometimes they receive money through the account of a bKash agent or some other people in the area to avoid being caught in investigations.'
49. *Chandpur Times* (2020).

3

Chanda(baji)

> In the time of Picchi Hannan they used to take money from the rich, the business people. Now the leaders take from everyone. That's the difference between now and then.
>
> —Parvez, *boro bhai* of the *jhupri* labourers

As the remnants of Picchi Hannan's gang failed to retake control at Kawran Bazaar, the more egregious aspects of his reign calmed. Kidnappings no longer plagued the business community and threatening demands for payment became less frequent. The severity of crossfire and widespread arrests made it clear that the ruling party and state would no longer patronise and tolerate the likes of Hannan. Those who wished to emulate him would face the same fate. The decline in such *santrashi*s brought about a power vacuum, which for local leaders and cadres of the then ruling BNP represented an opportunity. As long as Hannan had been dominant, the various official wings of the ruling party had been largely sidelined locally, weak by comparison. Yet the condition of the party at the bazaar was still too fragile and politics too uncertain to take advantage. The years of fights and killings had taken their toll on the likes of Siddiq, and the resources of local leaders were depleted from violence and competition.

This power vacuum was prolonged by national politics, with an extended caretaker government in the period 2006–2008. It was widely alleged that during their term in office the BNP were attempting to have a favourable caretaker official in place for the 2006 election, prompting widespread protest. It furthermore seemed obvious to some that the democracy this system held together was one of the most corrupt on earth.[1] In response, the military backed a new caretaker government in early 2007. Rather than calling a general election within ninety days as mandated, it extended its rule to almost two years in a failed attempt to bring radical reform and rid the country of political corruption. At Kawran Bazaar this was portrayed as a period of comparative calm, where businesses ran largely unimpeded and flagrant criminality and violence were minimised by the significant presence of security agencies in everyday life, which continued to arrest, imprison and allegedly 'crossfire' *santrashi* figures. Yet neither Hannan's death nor two years of a caretaker government cleaned Kawran Bazaar of crime and violence. Instead, the eventual landslide Awami League victory in the late 2008 general election led to a radical reshaping of the political economy of the bazaar and wider city, filling the vacuum left by the decline of these gangsters.

For the *jhupri* group, the difference between the era of Hannan and today is stark. Rubel, the leader and *boro bhai* of the *jhupri* labourers, described the 'godfathers and *mastans* of Tejgaon'[2] as having 'no importance now,' that most of them were in jail and there was today 'no one like that'. For another in the group, the likes of Hannan 'have changed their lives. They've left to do different work like garments now'; 'there aren't *boro bhais* like before.' Some of the *jhupri* labourers described getting out of prison to find the bazaar completely changed, their boss dead and gang disbanded. But what is also clear is that while the likes of Hannan are no longer in power, many of the roles once played by his group continue, but now under a different guise. What differs markedly is not that criminality has decreased so much as it is organised differently. As Hassan, one of the *jhupri* group, once put it to me: 'The people with power now are those in the ruling party, they are the *boro bhais* now.'

There has been a dramatic shift in the political fabric of Dhaka city over the past two decades, closely shaping everyday life on the streets and the political life of the nation. This has been little noted by scholars, in part because the political history of Bangladesh is rarely studied from below. It has been common to write, for example, of 'mastans' in politics as if the term has the same resonance on the streets today as it did thirty years ago.[3] But we cannot understand the nexus of crime and politics or the character of political muscle and syndicates, if we do not appreciate this radical change. In essence, many of the roles once played by Hannan are now filled not by *santrashis* existing in collusion with (but at arm's length from) politicians, but politicians and state actors themselves. One crime journalist put it to me like this: 'There are only political *santrashis* now.' Despite the collusion between Hannan and political leaders, locals are very clear that he and others like him were 'not political,' meaning that their strength did not arise from status within a party, they did not have an organisational designation and did not promote the ideology of any party, but instead operated on the basis of their own muscle and connections. Where Hannan once manipulated prices at the bazaar, controlled tenders at government offices and ran protection rackets, today these are controlled directly by leaders and affiliates of the ruling party, in collusion with security agencies and other state actors. These networks and the hold they have on the bazaar are often described by critics as syndicates.

One way in which this transition can be felt and studied is through the organisation of the informal payments that permeate many aspects of business and work here, often referred to as *chanda* or *chaada*. A crime reporter at a national newspaper described the following:

> The *chandabaji* system in Dhaka has changed a lot. It used to be controlled by area-based cadre, *santrashi*, *mastan* with big names. In the past, each area had one big *santrashi*. If you went in a different direction, there would be another big *santrashi*. There aren't these 'big name' *santrashi* anymore. They are not a big deal. Now it is the people who do politics – the Sramik League, Chhatra League, the ones who are with the Awami League – they do *chandabaji*. The *chanda* system is basically now controlled by the police and the party, but primarily the police, who have a balance of power between them. There's also the RAB, and the informers, the people who give them information.

This chapter details how such payments are organised in Kawran Bazaar. In so doing it illuminates perhaps the most common form of syndicate in the country, one that permeates all towns and cities: protection racketeering. Rather than a marginal activity confined to actors in the shadows, this is state business, controlled by party leaders, their associates and wider government actors. Rather than undermining political order, it sustains it. Rather than being new, in many ways it is deeply historical. Yet it remains illegal, morally suspect and on the ground, is hidden from view, organised on the frontlines by opaque, petty intermediaries.

The Party Syndicate

> I will tell you what I think. Now there is even more oppression. Before we were hostage to only one person, now we are under the hands of many … Kawran Bazaar is basically an illegal place. People kill each other to earn illegal money. If you want to earn money you have to kill whoever is above you. This is how it works. It is full of dirty politics.
>
> —Siddiq, BNP leader

To understand the ubiquity of *chanda*, imagine for a moment an overflowing truck arriving at the market in the late evening or early hours of the morning. The goods are met by labourers, delivered to a wholesaler and quickly sold on. During this time there will be at least four moments where the truck has to pay *chanda*. On arrival they typically pay 200 taka as a cost for the privilege, a further 200 to unload, 200 to re-load and 200 to leave. Separately, tips (*bakshish*) worth 20–50 taka are paid to the person clearing the inevitable jams which clog the bazaar's arteries. Around 800 taka per truck is then charged, and over 500 trucks arrive daily. This is far from being the only source of *chanda* here. While wholesalers within the covered market operate under a committee and formal leases on city corporation land, many other wholesalers work instead from the roads. Here, for a stretch between 5 and 8 feet, around 30,000 taka is paid monthly. Sitting alongside them are small businesses on public land, selling vegetables, chickens, tea, cigarettes and much more. All pay daily *chanda*, ranging from 30 to hundreds of taka, depending on their size and profits. Small vegetable sellers that dot the sides of the bazaar, some of whom have scavenged the goods at night, make similar payments, ranging from 30 to 50 taka.[4] It is not an exaggeration to say, as Shumon put it to me once, '*chanda* is everywhere at Kawran Bazaar, and *chanda* is everywhere in Bangladesh'.

Chanda is the preserve of those in power, and often closely associated with another term: syndicate. Colloquially, the notion of a 'syndicate' is commonplace in Bangladesh. It is pejorative, typically used when looking at figures of political authority to denote the unfair hold they have over local economic activity. It is used to imply illicit forms of collusion between leaders and the state to control access to particular goods, markets or opportunities. At Kawran Bazaar, Hannan's group was described as a syndicate, while the particular forms of control his group exercised (such as a protection racket or a monopoly on a product) were described similarly. A syndicate thus refers to both actors and action. Today the bazaar itself is characterised in this way. Labourers speak of the 'Awami League syndicate' being in power, referring to the constellation of different actors organised around the party who today are the *boro bhai*s looked up to where Hannan, his group and others once stood. A syndicate is inherently associated with muscle and connections, the ability to take control and defend one's interest through mobilising men, threats and violence, utilising wider connections to senior political leaders and state officials to ensure protection.[5]

To those out of power or subject to its authority, speaking of an 'Awami League syndicate' is a way of denoting the fact that it is largely figures within or closely associated with the ruling party that control such privileges. In practice, however, there is no one system or actor under which all of the *chanda* described earlier is controlled. Some street vendors make payments solely to the local police stationed nearby. In Chapter 6 we will see how some pay *chanda* to the political leader of a hawkers' association. Common to all of the examples given here, however, is that those who collect such *chanda* are from within or closely connected to the ruling Awami League. Shamim, a *jhupri* labourer who himself described having collected *chanda* in the past during the era of Picchi Hannan, depicted this system at Kawran Bazaar to me:

> Every day money is extorted in the bazaar. Crores of taka ...[6] people take money everywhere in the bazaar. If today you are with the Awami League, you have power, which you can use to earn free easy money. Tomorrow if BNP are in government, then their men are in power, they make money and you sit down. Every day 500 taka for a shop is being paid. It works like this: I'll send my men, maybe four of them, telling them 'go and pick up the *chanda*' and they'll move around the area taking money from all the shops. They then take that money and give it to higher ranking people who are stronger in the area, like the MP [member of parliament] ... Once it goes up the chain, each person keeps a cut and a part is given to the police. It's a vertical chain with links to politics.

In Kawran Bazaar it is the Jubo League, Swechasebak League (volunteer league) and then Sramik League who are seen as most powerful. Across different areas of Dhaka, different bodies have local strength. The collection and distribution of *chanda* then reflects the particularities of local political power. One crime journalist described to me how 'in every area there is a local balance. It depends on who has "muscle power".' Street hawkers often describe there being an 'agreement', a 'mutual arrangement', 'contract' or 'distribution' between local powerholders, centring on the Awami League and the police. One way of framing these interdependencies is as a 'nexus' between an array of local powerholders – notably the security agencies (particularly the OC of the local thana), powerful political leaders and other government officials (in this case, those of the Dhaka City Corporation).[7]

To speak of the ruling party in Bangladesh is to reference an often opaque and complex array of bodies organised around the ruling Awami League 'root party' (*mul dal*), formed into layers of committees at different administrative levels, where hierarchy is often usurped by informal reputations and relationships. Party hierarchy does not translate directly into power. Whilst senior political leaders (for example, the MP) are clearly dominant locally, below them the precise Awami League figure of importance will be determined by a wide range of factors. These include the proximity of the leader to senior politicians (the local MP and other party figures), as well as their reputation and their grassroots support. Viewed from above, the strength of particular Awami League bodies then differs between areas. In one area it may be the Chhatra League that dominates, elsewhere the Jubo League and so on.

Control at Kawran Bazaar is often thought of locally in terms of its nine key areas, some of which are mentioned in Chapter 1. These lanes, the trucks that arrive there and the wholesalers and businesses that operate from them are divided between two key figures. Both figures are described as powerful, and as men everyone looks up to and whom Kawran Bazaar operates under. Both are from the Jubo League. The first is Kazi, a businessman and general secretary of the thana Jubo League. Kazi is portrayed here as being close to the MP (and current home minister) and leveraging his contacts to gain a hold on the management of public space at the bazaar. Locals described how the land was previously managed through a public lease under the Dhaka City Corporation (DCC). Some described Kazi as the one holding the lease while others claim the system has fallen by the wayside, and instead he 'has to manage the OC and manage the minister [the local MP]' and gained his role not through open tender but 'through negotiations involving the police' and the DCC, as a Truck and Covered Van Association labour leader put it. While labelled *chanda* by those paying such money, much of this is collected in the name of 'parking fees'. Newspaper exposés suggest that leases paid for by private companies led to the emergence of 'DSCC [Dhaka South City Corporation] toll collector[s]' extracting illegal payments on vehicles.[8] Formally, Dhaka North City Corporation leases the right to charge 10 taka between 7 am and 7 pm, while parking is free at night.[9] Trucks are supposed to pay only 50 taka to arrive at Kawran Bazaar, but in practice the exactions made greatly exceed what is formally permitted.

The second figure is Saad, the Jubo League general secretary of ward number 26 at Kawran Bazaar, once seen as merely an ordinary businessman in the time of Picchi Hannan, but now extremely powerful, both respected and feared. Of the two, Saad is a more public figure locally, often seen holding court, surrounded by dozens of followers (young men, petty traders, labourers). Hierarchically, however, Saad looks up to Kazi, who outranks him in the party, although Saad is said to have close links to a more senior figure in Jubo League politics in the north of Dhaka.

If the 1990s and early 2000s were seen as representing the 'criminalization of politics',[10] the situation today represents something notably different. Instead of gangsters connected to but largely outside the formal party infrastructure playing an increasing role in politics and the economy, what we have today is the deepening involvement of political and state institutions in everyday life and crime. To turn the phrase above around, this can be seen as the politicisation of criminality and violence.[11] One impact this has had is to bring a far greater degree of stability to everyday urban life. Extortion, violent competition and struggles are still common – as will be explored in subsequent chapters – however far less severe. By comparison with the past, the *jhupri* labourers describe life as *peaceful* and with *no tension*, descriptions that will later seem odd given the levels of violence and instability still at play. A crime journalist who grew up at Kawran Bazaar described the situation today:

> In Kawran Bazaar there are still conflicts among the [Awami League] affiliates and subgroups, but they are not exposed publicly. The senior leaders have divided up the area, deciding who can collect money from where.

Instead of competition between gangs and their figureheads, today competition largely exists within and between parties, and therefore is more closely subject to institutional disciplining, wider norms that reduce the severity of violence and the national political scenario. Local intra-party competition is less violent, and the inter-party violence now is more broadly a function of national competition between parties. Incidents of violence stemming from local rivalries, and certain forms of criminality such as kidnappings, have hence reduced dramatically since the early 2000s here and across the wider city. The scope for actors such as Hannan to emerge from outside these networks is minimal. A Sramik League leader put it like this: 'They can only rise again if the government allows it.' Siddiq reflected: 'The time of the terrorists won't come again. No "top terror" can come again without political shelter. If you have an enemy now you don't need a *santrashi*, as either the police, or RAB or the detective branch can kill them.' Put simply, party political leaders and the apparatus of the state are now firmly in charge locally.

Lineman, Informers and Muscle

Both the police and political leaders appoint the *lineman* to take monthly or weekly payments. It's local politicians and activists, whoever has political power, that decide who will have a position on the footpath ... In every area where there are shops on the footpath, they have *lineman*. Throughout the whole city there are *lineman* ... Sometimes I saw that one of the hawkers has been appointed by the political leaders. Whoever seems like a leader, whoever has those qualities, they become the person who communicates and manages everything with the police and the political leaders. 'You all give me a fixed amount of money and I will control everything', they say. I've also seen that the people who work as a police source, informer, they sometimes work as *lineman*.

—A crime journalist at a Bengali daily newspaper

Local political leaders, police officers and government officials rarely muddy themselves directly with this type of *chanda*. Instead, their authority translates onto the streets through a range of petty intermediaries. *Chanda* is closely associated with the figure of a *lineman*. *Lineman* are opaque actors, operating as links between street vendors, labourers or traders, and local political and state authorities. Each *lineman* is responsible for a 'line', a specific sector or area. In any given location where there are street hawkers, for example, a *lineman* will have clearly but invisibly delineated responsibilities known to all in the area. Were the city colour coded by *lineman* territory and viewed from a bird's eye it would appear as a patchwork. Little is known publicly about *lineman*, and there is no clear sense of how many operate in Dhaka. Estimates given to me (by hawker leaders and long-standing crime journalists) range from 500 to 3,000.

The precise organisation of *lineman* differs markedly. At Kawran Bazaar, most *lineman* are seen as operating ultimately under the authority of Kazi or Saad (Chapter 6 provides a contrasting case from the fringes of the bazaar). All lanes operate under these two leaders, yet day to day they are controlled by their subordinates, who in turn manage *lineman*. The basis on which these lower-level figures control the lanes differs. Some are said to pay a fixed sum of 20,000 taka a day to control the lane in an informal subcontracting arrangement, as well as an advance of 10 lakh taka to Kazi or Saad. Other figures are more closely associated with the various wings of the ruling party – the Jubo League, Sramik League and so on – seen less as buying the right to control the lane, instead meriting it on the basis of the muscle at their command. Each of these figures in command of a lane in turn relies on their own men to control the area. From the perspective of truck drivers, labourers and street vendors, it is these frontline figures who are the intermediaries dealt with on a daily basis, behind whom stand the senior *boro bhai*s of the bazaar.

Elsewhere in Dhaka the story is more complex. Some *lineman* are seen as being 'the police's *lineman*', as it was put to me by vendors on a number of occasions, some are local hawkers themselves and some even live on the streets, but serve as a link to the local police thana. In rare instances, the *lineman* is a local politician with a designation in the ruling party. *Lineman* operate away from prying eyes. They work hard at avoiding wider attention that will expose their activities knowing that, although endorsed by local powerholders, they operate illegally. One crime journalist described someone he knew just north of Kawran Bazaar: 'There is a *lineman* in Farmgate, who is a bearded man. If you see him, he looks like an angel. He has a long beard, religious clothes. He has this as a disguise so no people would suspect him as an extortionist.' When I attempted to meet and interview this type of *lineman* I was often told 'they will not reveal themselves'. Even when senior local figures attempted to arrange interviews for me, I would turn up at a lonely street corner and find the individual had gone home or suddenly could not be found. *Lineman* are 'forbidden' from revealing themselves, as a hawker leader put it once, as it would expose the illegal activities of those who shelter them. While informally I spoke to a number of such figures at Kawran Bazaar, their work remained a closed off subject, and they pretended to be local businesspeople. Such secrecy is perceived as crucial to managing these arrangements because although these practices are important to the financial resources of lower-level party leaders, they are not outwardly permitted by the party. In public consciousness, *lineman* are seen as extortionists and are particularly well publicised by the media during Eid, when they ramp up demands and a flurry of articles lambast their activities.[12]

At Kawran Bazaar *lineman* are seen as being low-level cadres of the ruling party, also characterised negatively as a *chamcha* (sycophant, yes-men) and *dhandhabaaz* (opportunists), operating in the nine lanes of the bazaar, ultimately under the authority of Saad or Kazi. Estimates from labour leaders suggest there are around forty *lineman* at the bazaar. Nearby the *jhupri* labourers, for example, a tall *lineman* called Rajib regularly collected payments from the tea stands at the sides of the alley, including for a time from Shumon's *khichuri* stand. Labourers described him as a *rangbaj* (criminal, gang member) and as having climbed the political ranks by being very nice to senior people, becoming a low-level leader of the Swechasebak League (Volunteers League) before moving to the Jubo League. *Lineman* are perceived as earning significant amounts of money and therefore looked at with jealousy and resentment by those beneath them such as the labourers in the *jhupri* group. Some *lineman* are seen as simply getting a daily wage, but Rajib is thought by the *jhupri* labourers, perhaps improbably, to have personally saved up around 15–20 lakh taka.

Lineman not only collect money but are also often political mobilisers, using hawkers to swell the crowds at political events. The ability to mobilise men in political rallies, events and fights is a fundamental skill of the Bangladeshi politician, and one that has been well studied in other contexts, such as in student politics.[13] All such events have an important 'signalling function'[14] to demonstrate to others your strength and worthiness for political status. In the context of university students in Dhaka and Chittagong it has been argued:

> The violent performances of mid-level leaders are mostly directed towards their direct patron, usually another mid-level or senior leader on the campus. Their ability to directly engage in violence and take the necessary risks – be 'courageous' – makes them highly valuable to a leader who needs to be able to control violence to help buttress his own position on campus. However, for more senior leaders, and certainly those looking for a career in party politics, the ability to control violence, rather than use it directly, is central. Their publics are party political patrons looking for reliable conduits for patronage on campus.[15]

For *lineman* affiliated to particular Awami League bodies, the ability to mobilise has a significant bearing on their standing within the hierarchy, indicating their capacity to show support for a local politician. For *lineman* a step removed from the Awami League, this can be part of their arrangement with locally powerful actors, and a key skill required of them to maintain their role. Hawkers often portray these relationships cynically, describing how *lineman* need to get them to attend programmes to support bigger leaders so that their status in the party is secure. Attending such events is described by hawkers as an 'obligation'. A prominent crime journalist described the relationship as such:

> Some big leader in the area might ask the *lineman* to supply people to attend the political programmes to support him. He would tell the *lineman*, 'do your business, I don't need money, you just supply men to attend programmes with me,' which is important for his political career. The *lineman* then manages different people in different ways, and whoever can manage people well can be a *lineman*.

As is the case with labourers, hawkers can sometimes be paid for attending such events; however, more often than not, attendance is an obligation, premised on the threat of violence. Hence, hawkers themselves describe the fear of being beaten, having their shops destroyed, being prevented from working on a stretch of pavement or even being imprisoned in false cases, if they refuse the demands of a *lineman*. A vegetable seller at the side of the bazaar near the *jhupri* lane once described to me what would happen if she did not pay the local *lineman*: 'He will beat me and throw away all my vegetables on the street destroying them. No matter what, we need to pay him ... I heard he once broke someone's bones by beating him ... he has a lot of people backing him up.' These threats are very real. In one case from elsewhere in Dhaka that reached the news, a street vendor was beaten to death by Jubo League activists, apparently for the sin of failing to attend their local rally.[16]

Among these street-level intermediaries can also be found raw 'muscle power' drawn upon by political leaders to establish and sustain their authority. Although the likes of Picchi Hannan and other *santrashi*s are long gone, it is the aspiring gangsters, the 'chhyachra goondas' who still operate, far smaller but cast in a similar mould. One example is Ahsan, a man in his early thirties who grew up on the railway line and was once affiliated to the BNP's Sramik Dal, though is now with the Jubo League. Ahsan 'runs the city corporation line', as a follower of his put it, operating adjacent to the railway line under the authority of Saad and collecting *chanda* from the trucks that enter and unload at this end of Kawran Bazaar. In control of the lane, it is he who manages a number of local *lineman*. According to one of his 'choto bhais' (younger brothers):

> Ahsan is a powerful man, you can't do anything [around the railway line] without Ahsan's permission. And he can do anything. He is a kind of Picchi Hannan category, he is involved in things like mugging, drug dealing, addiction, there is nothing that he doesn't do. Whenever they call us to move with them, we first see what the purpose is, whether it is good or bad. If they ask us to attend the party's programme, say an Awami League rally, we go. But if they say somebody has hit them, now we have to go to fight with them, I try to say I have work to do, but sometimes he insists and so I have to go. When you move together in a circle, sometimes you have to follow, but I always think if I commit something and then the police arrest me, who will get me released?

Some in the *jhupri* group described Ahsan as a 'small Sweden Aslam' and as a 'goonda,' whose group has a reputation for consuming 20,000–30,000 taka worth of *yaba* a day, as Liton put it. It is figures such as Ahsan who strike fear into the truck drivers delivering goods to the bazaar. A senior leader of the Truck and Covered Van Association put it like this:

People come in the name of the city corporation and collect money from each truck every day. This is run by the people from the upper level so we can't stop it. Big officials at the city corporation, the OC of the thana. If you don't pay you will be beaten. I am 52 years old and have been driving a truck for 30 years, but if a young guy comes up to me, demands money and I refuse, he can beat me. I won't be able to do anything. We can't fight them every day ... This is my home, this is my area, but I have to pay. It is difficult to cope with. I can resist them with my drivers and helpers, but they [the authorities] will side with them [the *lineman*]. I would then have to deal with that situation. Who would risk their lives to stop this?

The prominent *lineman* at Kawran Bazaar thus sit in a chain of command feeding up to senior local Jubo League leaders. In parallel, however, sits another hierarchy at the head of which are the security agencies, primarily the local police thana, but also the Detective Branch and RAB.[17] The police and party are often described as creating a balance, where their respective interests are negotiated and cuts are distributed from the myriad sources of illicit income. Far from any ideals about justice and law enforcement, the police are perceived by the *jhupri* labourers and local hawkers as a continuous and day-to-day nuisance. As one *jhupri* labourer put it to me simply – 'police means bribes, with bribes there is no problem, without bribes there will be no love.' Hierarchically, the police presence on the streets extends beyond those in uniform. Day-to-day it is not so much the police constable who is a presence at the bazaar but the police informer.[18]

Police 'source', or 'former' as they are known, are a ubiquitous presence in Dhaka and beyond. Although some operate covertly, many are easily identified locally as being close to the police, such that labourers can list them, tapping their fingers as they count them off. One younger *jhupri* labourer Mamun told me, 'There are many. Imran *former*. Shamim *former*. Lengra [meaning crippled] *former*, Sajid, Kalu ... He's so black that's why he's called Kalu.' Such sources are the ears of the police on the ground, known to pass information to them secretly, yet powerful not simply because they feed the police information but because they are known to do so. Lengra, for example, was a common sight at the bazaar, often high on *yaba* which he was described as getting for free at the rail line *basti*. He was also eager to chat and insisted on taking my phone number when I met him for the first time. Lengra had an interesting background.[19] He was described as having been a *mastan* in Mirpur, although also as operating under Picchi Hannan's group – but '"third class", the lowest in his group,' as the *choto bhai* of Ahsan put it.[20]

I learned that while Shamim was an important police informer, Sajid was an RAB informer, a figure of similar repute, who grew up at the railway line. Mamun continued:

> There are informers not just for drugs, but if there are other crimes like group fighting, or people bringing knives or pistols, it's his job to inform the authorities. If he sees anything like this happening, then he will call the DB [detective branch] and then the police will come.

Everyone wants to keep in the *former*s' good books. As Liton described it: 'He knows what's going on. If a policeman comes from Barisal and is transferred to Dhaka then how will he know what is going on? He can't. But Shamim knows. He gets a huge amount of money, he's very rich.' Rickshaw van drivers kept a good relationship with him, often taking drugs together, but he also regularly extorted money from them. The *former*s benefit from receiving payment from the police in exchange for information, but also collect *chanda* from businesses in much the same way as the *lineman*. 'He earns from both sides,' as Mamun put it. He has a contract (*chukti*) with the rail line drug dealers, for example. The *former*s play on their position, Mamun continued, 'they never show the real criminals,' because they benefit from them. When the police come on patrol, 'he tells everyone to stay hidden,' instead showing them other people whom they put in the vans, beat, extort money from and then set free. A *choto bhai* of Ahsan put it like this:

> Previously people could exploit names, by saying that he is a man of him or someone else, now that doesn't work. Now he can't do that so he moves behind police, sometimes helps police arrest one or two men and threatens those who are involved in drug dealings by saying he would have them arrested if they don't give him money.

Locals all acknowledge that Lengra 'knows everything' about the area, and he is unanimously seen as a '100 per cent bad person'.

In the absence of Picchi Hannan and the era of the *santrashi*s, it is thus the political leaders and security agencies who are dominant, present at the grassroots through an array of local coercive intermediaries such as Ahsan, Lengra and the *lineman* of Kawran Bazaar's lanes. While bringing a degree of calm to the city, the influence that Awami League leaders and affiliates have at the bazaar is tremendous and can reach down into all crevices of life. Not everyone looks back with despair at the era of Picchi Hannan. As the quote at the opening of this chapter suggests, this present period arguably represents a deepening of the exactions made by those in power on the economy. The president of the nearby Truck and Covered Van Association, where the likes of Dano Mizan had their base, reflected:

> The situation was actually better for us then. There was not extortion like there is now. Then it was the wholesalers who used to pay, they didn't used to take money from the cars and trucks. They took from the businessmen who were earning lots. Now in every corner there is the Sramik League, Jubo League, Chhatra League, Awami League, there is no end to the leagues.

A contractor and restaurant owner at the bazaar recalls how 'many were saddened by his [Picchi Hannan's] death, as he was good to them. If he were alive today, Picchi Hannan would be an MP or minister.' He went on to describe how 'young people' now come into the offices at the bazaar, create problems using the names of high-profile local politicians and control tenders (*tenderbaji*). With many government offices at the bazaar regularly issuing tenders, those in power here are able to manipulate such processes:

> The *tenderbaji* that we've seen in the last ten years is like nothing I saw before. All of the ruling party people come to the tender [opening]. They don't understand them much but they come and impose themselves. There isn't the fighting like before, but they get what they want very quickly.

In microcosm then, the past decade is associated with a deepening of the demands made on everyday traders and labourers. One perhaps partial explanation for this is the incentives and pressures felt by those managing particular lanes, and how this translates into the activities of their subordinates. A Sramik Union and Sramik League leader at the bazaar reflected on this:

> Think about it. He [the person controlling a lane] has expenses of 28,000 to 29,000 taka a day. Plus he has an investment of 10 lakh. So he has to earn at least 40,000 taka a day. So he doesn't care who lives or who dies. Everyone has to pay. They don't care if the driver has money. A truck driver who has come a long way is tired when he reaches Kawran Bazaar, and if he then refuses to pay he might be hit, so he is helpless and he pays.

The subject is sensitive. The same Sramik Union leader portrayed it as being senior leaders who benefit, not those at the lower levels, adding that 'if we tell you much more about this it will be a problem for you and a problem for us, you won't be able to stay here. We can't say everything.'

A Society of Syndicates

> The state–antistate paradigm doesn't exist. All there is, is a territory where you do business ...
>
> —Roberto Saviano (2011: 190)

Charles Tilly famously argued that early European states were analogous to protection rackets.[21] When we reflect on this claim in the context of modern nation states, constitutions and national anthems, it feels a stretch. The apparatus of the state cannot be reduced to so crude a role, and the ideals and ideas of national life are rich and complex. States are often at pains to emphasise their legitimacy and authority, and notions of syndicates, extortion and rackets are portrayed as the domain of 'organized crime', not the state. And yet at Kawran Bazaar, as across Bangladesh and indeed many other contexts, syndicates are the domain of those in office. Unsurprisingly these dynamics are denied or downplayed. In 2019, the local MP and home minister spoke to a shop owners' association at Kawran Bazaar, reportedly claiming:

> If you go 11 years back, you would see how many types of extortion had been there. There was hardly any month when [a] killing did not take place in [the] Kawran Bazaar area ... But there's no extortion now. Where is [the] extortion? Provide us information if there's any.[22]

However much those in office attempt to distance themselves from crime, it is clear at Kawran Bazaar and far beyond that there is a pervasive relationship between political authority and control over syndicates. This is not to exaggerate and tarnish all officials or politicians with this brush. Motivations, ideologies and bases for political authority all differ at the level of the individual. Yet as noted in the Introduction, a host of recent literature from Bangladesh has argued that the unlawful control exerted over economic resources by party leaders is far from an aberration in the practice of politics. Media commentary routinely argues that syndicates appear to be institutionalised. Shortly after the Awami League returned to power, for example, one newspaper piece warned of the 'virtual legitimization of extortion'.[23] One way we can discern the importance of syndicates in political life is through the often intense intra-party rivalries witnessed during elections. Recent reporting on a by-election in Dhaka, for example, suggests that the

Awami League competition seen for the party's nomination stems from the fact that the constituency is home to two motorways, two rivers and a large market, some of the city's prime spots for rackets, and that many of the contenders were the previous *chanda* collectors for the deceased MP.[24]

An obvious interpretation of such dynamics would be to see them as deeply corrosive and indicative of disorder and corruption. Such opinions are not hard to find at Kawran Bazaar. The police are lambasted as terrorists, political leaders as dogs and their activities as unjust and exploitative. That syndicates are widely seen as immoral is indisputable. Yet it does not follow that they are inherently disruptive and eroding of order. A counterintuitive reading of syndicates is to view them as, in certain contexts, in fact productive and sustaining of political order in Bangladesh. Syndicates are crucial to politicians (and thus to parties) because they are an important means through which the former accrue resources. This enables politicians to sustain their own authority locally, incentivises them to be part of that coalition and thus helps sustain dominance over political rivals. It motivates followers, it can mobilise people to rallies and it can help pay party seniors when needed. In broader literature this is often referred to as rent-seeking.[25] Syndicates are a quintessential form of rent-seeking, manipulation of the economy and the roles of the state to the advantage of those in positions of political authority.

The distribution of resources in this manner serves to solidify the control of those in power, whilst also reining in potential conflicts, by sharing resources with those who have the capacity to disrupt the political order. A prominent crime journalist reflected on the arrangements through which *chanda* is collected and distributed:

> It's actually quite a good system. It reduces the risk of frequent killing and fighting. It means that everyone [who is powerful in that context] gets money. Some get more, some less, but everyone has to be given something from the money collected.

The array of intermediaries and arrangements for accruing *chanda* can be seen as a way in which a local balance of power is sustained to prevent overt and widespread conflict. Viewed bottom–up, the experiences of such syndicates in practice are not as exploitative and morally devoid as discourse and moral indignation would suggest. *Chanda*, for example, is a subtle arrangement. From the perspective of those paying *chanda* it may be seen as a requirement backed by muscle, but it also an arrangement that facilitates the ability to run a business while avoiding formal systems of rents and leases. In some cases, such as street vendors, no alternative system is available. It is hence a cost containing implicit or explicit threats but one that can bring with it a degree of protection and security. More straightforwardly, *chanda* literally means a fee, a contribution or a subscription, given, for example, in the context of organisational membership, as we will see further in Chapter 4. The concept and practices associated with *chanda* are hence analytically and morally complex to categorise. This has been noted elsewhere in the region as well. In Mumbai, for example, similar payments are referred to as *hafta*. While *hafta* is often portrayed as 'extortion' depending on whom one asks, it arguably 'lacks normative content', such that its use 'points to the blurring of this bribery–extortion distinction because it refers to a practice that is simultaneously an exchange, an arrangement, and a negotiation'.[26]

Historically, *chanda* was 'subscriptions collected by a landlord from all his tenants on some memorable occasion' such as a marriage, wrote J. C. Jack, once the settlement officer of Bakarganj (today in the south of Bangladesh), in the early twentieth century. In practice, however, it was often 'taken on the flimsiest pretexts and with a painful frequency'.[27] *Chanda* sat alongside a range of other arbitrary, discretionary and indeed illegal demands that landlords and other authorities could make of those beneath them. These levies were collectively termed *abwab*. In the context of early twentieth-century Bakarganj, the 'chanda system' was deemed by one Revenue Officer as the most important means by which landlords made money from tenants, reporting that 'it seemed to be the chief concern of the māliks to invent any means, however slight, to demand chanda from the tenants.'[28] In some contexts the *chanda* and *abwab* collected by landlords often amounted to a considerable percentage of and could even be equivalent to the official rent.

Tax and everyday payments of *chanda* then appear at one level to be diametrically opposed. One is formal and the other informal, one sustains state services and the other fills the pockets of local party activists, leaders and officials. Yet in crucial respects the distinction is opaque. In liberal conceptualisations of the state and state–society relations, taxation is foundational to political order, representing the means through which the apparatus of the state sustains itself, through which services are provided, and crucially, part of the basis and social contract on which protection is given to citizens. In Bangladesh, formal modes of taxation are clearly crucial to the state coffers, yet also have limited reach in everyday life. Bangladesh has the lowest tax revenue as a percentage of gross domestic product (GDP) in South Asia.[29] Here it is *chanda* and other forms of syndicates that often characterise state–society relations. It is through such arrangements that a degree of protection or security is provided and at the macro level, it is in part through syndicates that political order is sustained.

But as already indicated, this is nothing new. It would be easy to see syndicates as a modern phenomenon, a product of contemporary politics and capitalism. The vernacular discourse of *syndicate*s, the *mafia* and *godfather* is popular in part because of Hollywood and Bollywood films, and criminological theories often take the modern state as a foundational reference point. As argued already, flagrantly criminal figures such as Picchi Hannan can be traced back in form to at least the early twentieth-century *goonda*s. In many respects, however, the structural roles played by these figures go back even further. When viewed historically, and in relation to the understanding of political order outlined in the Introduction, syndicates can also be reframed as a modern incarnation of even deeper aspects of the regional and urban political economy. What the discourse of syndicates denotes then is not an idiosyncratic aberration from the modern nation state but reflective of how society has been organised through intermediaries for centuries. To understand this, we need to revisit the history of Kawran Bazaar, Dhaka and the wider region.

Tax Intermediaries and the *Mahalla*

> It was after all, an act of exchange – the exchange of coinage as tribute for protection.
>
> —Christopher Bayly (2012: 397)

When Kawran Bazaar was a *serai* and market on the outskirts of Dhaka, occupied for a time by *nar*s ('dancing boys'), home to labourers and nearby a community of potters, it was likely subject to a meticulous system of taxation and control. Part of the way in which control was exercised locally during the Mughal period, and indeed under the East India Company and British Raj, was through the recognition of local powerholders as key intermediaries between state and society, as conduits of taxation and sources of order. By studying these forms of authority and the ways in which they were enacted locally, we can scratch beneath the surface of the term 'syndicate' to suggest that the relationships and authority it denotes are deeply historical.

During the Mughal period the second largest tax after that on land was known as 'sayer' (also written as *sair* or *s'āir*), taxes levied on transactions and travel. James Taylor, the civil surgeon of Dacca in the early nineteenth century, noted that these were collected around key points of exchange such as 'gunges, ghauts and bazaars'[30] where 'duties or customs [were] levied upon almost every article of life, and of imposts on trades, professions and personal property.'[31] Few items and people appear to have been excluded from this, and the Mughal sources Taylor draws upon specify taxes on goods ranging from paper to gold, hookahs to looking glasses and combs, 'for a goat, 1 to 2 annas were charged in the rupee: elephants and horses at the rate of 5 per cent.' An annual tax on vegetable sellers was levied, weighted to their sales, as well as on other trades, from a washerwoman to a fisherman. Sources from the mid-eighteenth century outline that 'chandina sair' was a monthly tax on shops and other buildings in the city, 'chauk nekas' a tax on items sold at market, 'bajintri' a tax paid by dancers and musicians, 'mirbarri' a tax on boatmen and 'dhup mahal' a tax on grass sellers.[32] Later in '1793 the importers of ganjah paid a tax (Koot Mehal) of Rs. 2–4 per maund, and the venders of it in the city, a duty varying from two annas to one rupee per month'.[33] A more obscure form of tax was known as 'Chundeena Dumdaree. A tax on bear[s], monkey[s], and snake dancers, on bird catchers, singers, fakirs and conjurers.'[34]

Such taxes were collected in a number of ways. Some came through an array of toll houses (*chaukīs*) and toll collectors, organised principally from the 'Shah Bandar' (imperial customs office or officer) likely situated at Mirpur, where trading licenses were also issued. Others came through a range of local intermediaries. These intermediaries played multifaceted roles, and the system of taxation reflected the nature of political authority in the city. Cities across the Mughal empire held 'no rights, exemptions or charters and had no distinct legal personality'.[35] They were not even governed principally at the municipal level but in effect 'self-regulatory' at the level of the *mahallas* (city quarter or ward), with Mughal officials confined to a more limited set of roles such as security.[36] Political authority was thus in many respects 'dispersed' or 'decentralized'. Today on the streets of Dhaka it is common to find a cluster of migrants from particular districts of the country squatting on pavements, or groups of labourers or beggars living together. In a far more institutionalised way *mahallas* were typically associated with a particular identity or group, such as an occupation, caste or people originating in a particular region.[37]

The *mahallas* of Dhaka are said to have been governed under the authority of a *panchayat*, a council of five (male) members, led by a *sardar* or 'mir-i-mahalla', also known by Muslims as *matbar*.[38] One view is that these *panchayat* associations under the leadership of *sardars* can be considered the 'trade guilds of Dacca' for both Muslim and Hindu groups.[39] Others contest such a view[40] and the place of guilds in South Asian history more broadly is debated.[41] It can be noted that in one of the few first-hand accounts of such *panchayats* (coming from a superintendent of panchayats at the beginning of the twentieth century), a distinction was made between *mahalla panchayats* and trade *panchayats*, which were described as the 'trade guilds of the Mussalmans of Dacca'.[42] Little detail is known about the relationships between Mughal authorities and *mahalla sardars* in Dhaka.[43] Elsewhere it is clear that they were crucial tax intermediaries. In Patna, for example, 'the impost on occupations and transactions within the bazaars of the town ... could be adjusted through the headman of the respective market or occupational group.'[44] At times Mughal *kotwals* (city police officials) regulated taxation through the appointment of the 'mir-i-mahalla', and by 'nominating the heads of the local guilds'.[45] Below the Mughal administrators in Hyderabad sat 'virtually self-regulating groups of specialised merchants, artisans, and semi-skilled labourers', led by 'intermediaries'.[46] Each commodity had a 'headman', as did the money-changers, dyers, porters and labourers. The point then is that various forms of intermediaries have long been inherent to the nature of state–society relations here, and there are parallels in the nature of authority exercised, and the nature of dependencies people sustained on them.

By design these arrangements also left much to the discretion of the officials or tax intermediaries. At times even the level of taxation varied, in part because the income of the collector was contingent on the amount collected. In Hyderabad, intermediaries were 'officially recognized, for a price' and to gain such a position had to pay an 'appointment fee' or tribute (known as *peshkash*), often a considerable sum and for a fixed period.[47] Many tax intermediaries thus operated as entrepreneurs, paying a fee or tribute to Mughal authorities for the right to collect revenue for a fixed period and within a certain jurisdiction. This is known as tax-farming. One way it was referred to in this context was as *ijara*. The assignment of a domain or area of revenue was termed a *jāgīr*, held by *jagirdars*.[48] The extent to which such positions were 'farmed' in Dhaka is unclear. It has been noted that at least for a period the status of *sardars* was inherited.[49] Certainly elsewhere in Bengal there is evidence that bazaars were later farmed. In the early days of British Company rule, for example, markets in Calcutta were either run on private land, for which the owner paid the company an annual rent, or they were contracted on a yearly basis to an *ijaradar*, who were often characterised as making unjust exactions on market sellers.[50]

What is also clear is that other parts of Dhaka's economy were farmed out. In many cases monopolies were granted on commodities, giving the sellers the exclusive right to transport and sell such goods at market, such as for the lucrative *paan* (betel-leaf), where 'the farmer of this trade (*paan mahal*) purchased zones of exclusive trade from the state.'[51] Far from being rare, '[t]he Nizamat era seems to have seen the formation of such rights in practically all types of commercial activity, even at the lowest rung of the market.'[52] Perhaps less lucrative, the 'Myeferosh' ('sellers of fish'), are described as having held as a 'class' a 'monopoly' on the ability to sell fish in Dhaka.[53]

By the late eighteenth century all lands belonging to the Mughal government in the city of Dhaka were transferred to the East India Company and administered under the Board of Revenue in Calcutta.[54] With this came the rhetoric of free trade, law and civility, and later in the nineteenth century the creation of ostensibly civic institutions such as the municipal authority. Many such tolls, taxes and monopolies were portrayed by the East India Company as regressive and unjust and 'exaction[s] under the general rubric of s'air were summarily abolished.'[55] James Taylor later argued that 'the rate of assessment and mode of collection were not well defined, and being in most cases left to the uncontrolled management of renters and their subordinates, these taxes were generally very arbitrary and oppressive.'[56] To the extent that such a view is justified (and indeed it is contested), coercive taxation likely had many causes. In part it probably stemmed from the difficulties in extracting money from people who would prefer not to give it. In the case of tax farmers, it could also derive from the incentives to not only recoup (an often high) investment but profit well from the position.[57] It could also be a product of the distance between the central and local power, and the ability of local figures of authority to enforce their interests through the means available.[58]

But conversely it also stemmed from the fact that intermediaries often provided not only taxation but order. In the estimation of historian John McLane, the Nazims' direct authority in the region was largely confined to towns, and 'ran thin in rural areas'.[59] Perhaps most famously *zamindar*s – later termed by one English civil servant as the 'great middlemen'[60] – were crucial intermediaries on whom the Mughals, East India Company and later British state depended. The meaning of the term *zamindar*s in the Mughal period is contested and most simply refers to 'holders of land'.[61] Under the Mughals, it was not strictly land ownership, but a right to serve as a tax intermediary and profit either from the surplus or from a fixed rate. It was a 'title to the constant share of a product of society',[62] a right that could be inherited, divided, bought and sold.[63] Below *zamindar*s stood 'chains of tax farmers',[64] sometimes up to five or more levels.[65] *Zamindar*s were responsible not only for rents and taxes but, at certain historical periods, also enforcing justice and order within their domains. This was customarily ensured in part through coercion, associated with the force of *danda* (stick, rod) and *dandaniti* ('the rule of *danda*').[66] *Zamindar*s maintained 'armed retainers' and in so doing represented a potential ally against uprisings or a source of sedition.[67] The capacity for violence could even be a prerequisite for being a *zamindar* and at times *zamindar*s under the Mughals were also the formal 'military commanders' (*faujdar*s) within their territory.[68] In the case of the *mahalla*s of Dhaka, *sardar*s were responsible for community management, justice and regulation of trade,[69] with one later source noting that the 'panchayat takes cognizance of all breaches of caste custom in respect of trade, religion or morality.'[70]

In practice various monopolies persisted and were created under company rule[71] and the dependency on local powerholders was far from ended by British dominance. For a time, company officials continued to rely on the Mughal 'daroghas' in managing customs, such as 'Rajkishor Rai at Dacca'.[72] More substantially it has been argued that in Bengal the British relied greatly on 'the powerful men in the mohullas'.[73] In the mid-1950s, a descendant of the Nawab described how in the past the Nawab 'ran the town. The sardars were a tremendous political instrument for the power of the Nawab against the British.'[74] *Mahalla panchayat*s and *sardar*s thus continued to mediate and manage communities within the city, an arrangement which at least elsewhere the government arguably used to 'penetrate' urban society.[75] Attempts to change urban taxes were hence organised through *panchayat*s, such as the early nineteenth-century introduction of a '*chaukidari* tax' to fund guards and ensure security,[76] and the short-lived income tax in the 1860s. Attempts by the political centre to reform local governance were met by the realities of local power. In the face of local resistance to the *chaukidari* tax, the then acting magistrate John Bardoe Elliot reportedly appointed 'government supporters rather than true leaders' to Dhaka's *panchayat*s to try and sway opinion.[77] The resulting 759 guards appointed, *dafadar*s (supervisors) and from 1816 a 'Sadr-Bakhshi' (chief pay master), seem to have acted as extortionists, with the *panchayat*s seen as grossly corrupt.[78]

This seems to support the argument of Christopher Bayly that in practice the imposition of such taxes only worked relatively effectively when there was 'virtual self-regulation' at the level of the *mahallas*.[79] As his analysis also suggests, diverse coercive intermediaries were a persistent feature of local life: 'Descendants of the "ancestral" owners of bazaars continued to lease and even underlease their supposedly extinguished rights to local strongmen who managed to collect large sums from the bazaar people,' a practice Bayly calls 'bazaar caesarism'.[80] The right to fulfil traditional roles (such as *kotwals* and bazaar headman) was 'rented out or sold informally'.[81] In essence then despite the rhetoric of free trade, civility and law, a 'headman system' continued:

> What occurred was that the commercialisation of 'shares' in the perquisites of authority, which had been a marked feature of the eighteenth century, was progressing at a local level. Almost every right or perquisite (including most notoriously the right to engage for revenue) was now up for sale. But what made the sale worthwhile was that within the 'little dominion' which was being put on the market, competition and the free market were still excluded. Here, political muscle, the authority of the headman and the rights of caste rank continued to operate to produce cash, labour or commodities.[82]

The point here is not to draw a direct historical lineage between the coercive tax intermediaries of the past and the figures of local authority today. Though such analysis may be possible, the documented history of Dhaka is too patchy to attempt this. Instead, the purpose is to highlight how very many of the characteristics which appear to mark contemporary syndicates and criminal politics as distinct in fact closely resemble far older modes of governance. The suggestion then is that behind the modern discourse of godfathers and syndicates lie ways of producing order, ways of structuring state–society relations and forms of power that are consistent with centuries past. This is odd given the ostensibly dramatic changes in the institutions of state and politics, with parties, elections, votes, councils and tax offices. Yet when we focus on the roles of intermediaries, we are struck by the aspects of consistency in the ways in which authority is produced and manifests at the local level.

Three points of comparison seem to transcend hundreds of years: (*a*) the existence of widespread forms of coercive intermediation at the grassroots used both to collect tribute or tax and provide order; (*b*) the fact that these positions are an entrepreneurial domain where positions of status are bought, won and fought for; and (*c*) the fact that ultimately these arrangements are a manifestation of 'dispersed' or 'decentralized' power, but also support the political centre as a conduit for resources (be they finances, muscle or broader political support).

When coercive intermediaries are a defining feature of how protection is gained, how everyday business transactions are conducted and ultimately how the state sustains order in society, then the distinctions between tax intermediation on the one hand, and syndicates and *chandabaji* on the other, may be more discursive than material.

Notes

1. See Transparency International's Corruption Perceptions Index, www.transparency.org/en/cpi (accessed 24 November 2023).
2. Kawran Bazaar is in Tejgaon Thana.
3. For example, Atkinson-Sheppard (2020).
4. The organisation of this differs, but 20 taka to a *lineman*, 10 taka to a policeman and 10 taka to the sweepers is a common arrangement. In the nearby Fokinni Bazaar (Beggars Bazaar) below the Tejgaon flyover, women carry their scavenged goods and lay them out on the ground, similarly paying money to the local 'Awami League club'.
5. For Arild Engelsen Ruud (2019: 265), the term 'syndicate' can be understood as a mafia. As he writes: 'A South Asian mafia is a syndicate of mastans who work in collaboration with local politicians and police, and this syndicate controls certain local resources: milk, sand, shrimp farming, real estate, bus routes and a host of other business opportunities.'
6. This is perhaps an exaggeration, although there are many other forms of payments collected at the bazaar.
7. For the notion of a 'nexus', see Brass (2003); Ruud (2018); and Jackman and Maitrot (2022).
8. Alam (2021).
9. Mollah and Hosen (2015).
10. M. Chowdhury (2003: 274); Sobhan (2004).
11. Jackman (2018).
12. For example, see Mollah and Khan (2019).
13. Ruud (2012, 2014); Andersen (2014); Suykens (2018); Kuttig (2019); Jackman (2021).
14. Suykens (2018: 901).
15. Ibid., 909.
16. *Daily Star* (2023).
17. This resonates with Jauregui's (2016) ethnography of the police in Uttar Pradesh where she documents not only the collection of petty bribes by low-level constables but also the roles of 'dalals' operating below the local chief station officer (SO).

18. This is not to say that other police are not present at the bazaar. They very much are. Non-uniformed Detective Branch police, for example, are stationed around the bazaar at night, as I discovered when chatting with Parvez on one occasion, and found my latest question about Picchi Hannan met with an unusual 'we don't know anything about this,' as the Detective Branch officer wandered up curiously next to me.
19. Lengra means crippled and is his nickname on account of having one disabled arm. This is the subject of much rumour and speculation at the bazaar. Older labourers and locals describe it has having been the punishment for leaking information about one group of criminals to another during the Picchi Hannan period. Others described how he had continued to demand *chanda* from the railway line drug businesses, who eventually became incensed and beat him ('they were too disturbed paying him money all the time so they beat him,' one labourer put it). Still others claim it was due to a bomb exploding in his hands in a previous era.
20. This is a long-standing practice in the region. Banerjee (2009) takes note of the Calcutta police 'dacoit department' in the mid-nineteenth century employing arrested ex-dacoits as informers.
21. Tilly (1985).
22. *Daily Star* (2019). Elsewhere, a deputy inspector of the highway police claimed, 'There is no instance of extortion by [the] Highway Police' (*Daily Star* 2018).
23. *Daily Star* (2010).
24. Mollah and Islam (2021).
25. One definition of rents is as 'a form of economic surplus that is appropriated by political means and extra-economic force' (Warnecke-Berger 2021: 6). In 'pre-capitalist' contexts, these are appropriated 'to benefit the ruling group' through 'simple and pure violence to the influencing of political structures and the creation of market imperfections, such as the control of markets or the exclusive ownership of certain possibilities of production' (Elsenhans 2021: 136).
26. Anjaria (2011: 61–62).
27. Jack (1915: lxxxix).
28. Ibid., cii.
29. Mavis (2022).
30. The way in which such revenue was collected also reflected the broader symbolic significance bazaars held, as signifiers of status, and sites in which patronage was dispensed by local powerholders. Markets 'carried the visible imprimatur of ruling authorities' (S. Sen 1998: 8). The collection of tolls was then the domain and privilege of local elites, who held responsibility for maintaining order. Often, the significance of such sites, was not primarily material, but symbolic (15),

associated with wider sources of power and spirituality, such as mosques and temples.
31. Taylor (1840: 197–198).
32. Karim (1964: 63–64).
33. Taylor (1840: 209).
34. Ibid., 201.
35. Hambly (1987: 448).
36. Each form of *sayer* tax was known as a *mehal* or *mahal*, with 'each Mehal deriving its distinctive appellation from the local name of the profession, trade or article that was taxed' (Taylor 1840: 198).
37. Hambly (1987: 448). Such a structure was common across north Indian cities at the time and found in other major urban centres such as Patna and Delhi. Even today Dhaka's oldest quarters attest to this, with a close association between place names, the communities that live there and their occupations, the most prominent example being Shankhari Bazaar, where a hereditary Hindu community of shell jewellery makers live. *Mahalla*s are still recognised as sub-ward urban municipal units, and in the 2011 census, there were noted to be 855 such units in the Dhaka metropolitan area (Bangladesh Bureau of Statistics 2013: 15).
38. Census of India (1901: 439)
39. S. Ahmed (2018: 18).
40. Karim (1964: 94).
41. Guilds are rarely studied in the context of South Asia, and often assumed to have played a very marginal role in urban life. The assessment of one recent historian, for example, is that formal guilds in the model of those in Europe rarely existed. The collectives we do find had 'blurred' boundaries between their socio-cultural identity and professional role, and their political agency was 'weak, random and obscure' (T. Roy 2008b: 97). Roy goes on to classify the collectives of producers and traders in nineteenth- and twentieth-century India in four categories: 'the Ahmedabad guilds, artisan panchayats, master-artisan collectives and merchant communities' (103). Yet other comparative research on guilds acknowledges diverse associations as 'guild-like', qualifying not on strict formal grounds, but rather as having characteristics of independence, self-governance, the occupational similarity of members and that they work towards the common interest of the group in any one of a variety of ways (Lucassen, De Moor and van Zanden 2008).
42. Azam (1990: 33).
43. Writing of nearby Bihar, Chatterjee argues that long before the British came, systems of leadership within trades had emerged, often called 'chaudhuri, mistri, or dangriya', existing within 'every trading, artisan or carrier group' – from

butchers to barbers, porters and scavengers – most notably in urban centres. These headmen were elected to lead *panchayat*s, translated by this author as 'professional organisations' (Chatterjee 1996: 57). As leaders they would receive a 'certain commission on all goods sold, or services rendered' (58) but be responsible for the management of the group. They acted as intermediaries between the workers and the government – paying 'tributes' to the administration and informing them of the condition of the workers.

44. Bayly (2012: 398).
45. Hambly (1987: 450). See also Bayly (2012: 373–374). These may have drawn upon earlier urban hierarchies. In Andhra Pradesh, for example, there is some historical evidence that guilds were conduits of state taxation, representing one form of 'tax-farmers' in the mediaeval period (Reddy 2007: 298).
46. Richards (1975: 186).
47. Ibid., 186.
48. Habib (1963: 112).
49. S. Ahmed (2018).
50. Sengupta (2015).
51. Datta (2000: 201).
52. Ibid., 201.
53. Taylor (1840: 245). More broadly, many figures of authority in commerce or the state held their status on the basis of payments to the Mughal officials. In the context of the profitable textile industry long associated with Dhaka, various roles were only able to operate on the basis of fees paid. Where, for example, goods were purchased not from producers but through middlemen and brokers such as *bepari*s and *dalal*s, these figures were managed directly by the Mughal state. They were regulated or appointed by Mughal authorities, to whom they reportedly paid a considerable fee for the right (see Mortimer 1852). Taylor (1840: 202) also references how 'bepparies and brokers' of items such as tobacco and betel leaf in Dhaka were similarly taxed under the Mughal system.
54. Taylor (1840: 205).
55. S. Sen (1998: 106). Crucial to the colonial project was reforming the intricate system of taxes, customs duties and tolls. Sen's account of this period argues that bazaars, other markets and *ghāt*s became the 'epicenter[s] in the battle for colonial conquest' (7).
56. Taylor (1840: 197–198).
57. Shaista Khan's rule in the late seventeenth century is associated with Dhaka's rise and prosperity; however, the economy was also frequently subject to monopolies and exploitation. As one scholar puts it: 'The activities of the subadars Sha'ista Khan and Prince 'Azimushshan in Bengal – was virtual extortion organised as

commerce,' enforcing a monopoly on salt and other commodities, and forcing loans on merchants to be quickly repaid at high rates of interest, all of this enabling a personal fortune from thirteen years as governor of Bengal estimated at 380 million rupees (Raychaudhuri 1982 :183).
58. When the British Company later attempted to abolish tolls on merchants, for example, Sudipta Sen notes how 'means of coercion [against *zamindars*] were seen as particularly necessary in the dense web of waterways around trading centers like Dacca, where small and everyday assertions of tolls from boats was very difficult to police' (S. Sen 1998: 98).
59. McLane (1993: 74).
60. Baden-Powell (1899: 34).
61. Habib (1963: 138).
62. Ibid., 159.
63. Ibid., 154.
64. Martin (2008: 19).
65. Habib (1963: 153).
66. McLane (1993: 78).
67. Habib (1963: 203).
68. *Faujdars* were also used to discipline *zamindars* (McLane 1993: 32).
69. All Muslims except the elite (*ashrafs*) recognised the *panchayats*' authority and the *sardars* from each *mahalla* met together to resolve wider issues. This meant ensuring people maintained customs regarding food consumption and interaction (such as smoking the hookah) with people from other castes. They restricted members from doing work that is of a lower, and sometimes even higher, status. They regulated within-trade competition – 'no member of a caste may endeavour to oust another from any employment he has obtained, by offering to do the work for a lower wage or otherwise' – and also organised trade strikes (Census of India 1901: 440). The meaning of *chanda* in this context differs slightly from that described thus far. The superintendent of panchayats at the beginning of the twentieth century described how the term 'chhanda' is a 'share' and for him it 'is solely used by Fakirs' (Azam 1990: 25), it being 'a general custom among Fakirs that the headman gets a double share: the Sardar is also entitled to this privilege' (25). Instead, the term 'tola' was used to refer to the contributions made by residents to the communal fund held by each *mahalla*, and to which all households contributed 'a fist-full of rice or four paisa in a pot every day' (Mamoon 1990: 19).
70. Census of India (1901: 440).
71. T. Mukherjee (2011: 157). As Rajat Datta argues, the rise of the East India Company saw on the one hand, the reassertion of and centralised control over

monopolies on certain products (opium and salt, for example), and on the other, the discourse of 'fair trade' and attempts to abolish the intricate system of tolls and duties exacted by *zamindar*s and regional powerholders, with the exception of official toll houses in major cities such as Dhaka (Datta 2000).
72. S. Sen (1998: 112).
73. Bayly (2012: 379).
74. Den Hollander (1990: 59). This authority appears to have continued until Partition. Apparently when the Japanese were advancing on Bengal during the Second World War, 'the colonial authorities attempted to organize protection against air raids in Dacca. They failed completely because the *sardar*s, not having being consulted, did not cooperate' (62).
75. Yang (1999: 97).
76. An earlier attempt in the late eighteenth century had been made to introduce a 'police tax' based on levies collected from marketplaces, although as traders and shopkeepers resisted and in many cases simply migrated, the law failed (S. Sen 1998).
77. S. Ahmed (2018).
78. The secretary to the Municipal Committee, Alexander Forbes, wrote:

> The corruption of the Panchayats, the venality and extortion of the Duffadars [supervisors], the carelessness by which the tax has been allowed to fall into arrears and the rigour with which those arrears have been afterwards collected when almost forgotten by those who owed them, all these are deep causes of discontent. (cited in S. Ahmed [1986: 153])

79. Bayly (2012: 399).
80. Ibid., 246.
81. Ibid., 246.
82. Ibid., 247.

4
Labour Lords

> You need to keep a good relationship with the *boro bhai*s to keep safe or to get work. If you don't, then you can't sleep on the streets, you might be abused [tortured, beaten]. But then the *boro bhai*s themselves might also torture you or steal your money.
> —NGO field worker with boys at Kawran Bazaar

'If you want to know what it is really like here you must come at night,' I was often told when first getting to know the *jhupri* labourers. They spoke of the mess (*jhamela*) and the fighting (*ganjam*). The image they draw upon most to convey life here is the sight of labourers competing for work. By day the bazaar and adjacent avenue are clogged with imported Japanese cars, dilapidated buses, CNGs and rickshaws, all slowly inching forward in the shadows of the new metro rail, protesting each metre gained with a cacophony of horns. By late evening the traffic around Kawran Bazaar calms but is replaced with a different jostling for space. As labourers catch sight of arriving trucks, they speed their flat-backed rickshaw vans towards them. Rather than face forward, they often reverse, running while swivelling the handlebars so as to arrive ready to receive sacks. With neither brakes nor chains, the labourers are masters of weaving and dodging obstacles at high speed, forcing each other off course and lobbing insults at rivals. Those who arrive first wait the least, are likely to get more of the goods to deliver and hence higher payment at the end of the night. Fights and injuries are common. Liton described the scene as: 'The van drivers barricade the truck[s] like an army.' The image then suggests chaos, a ruthlessness and precarity for people relying on their health and needing to work here day to day to survive and support families. In reality, however, the majority of the trucks are not unloaded in this manner and the *jhupri* labourers rarely race for work. Instead, most labourers wait in a queue (*serial*) or follow instructions from a labour leader. Work, in other words, is highly ordered. Yet the claims of precarity that the *jhupri* labourers evoke with these images are still very real, only materialised in a different way. Risks stem not so much from the need to race and jostle for work, but rather from the dependencies which give order to work.

Like the *jhupri* labourers, many others in Dhaka also find work on the streets and in public spaces. Traders run businesses selling everything from clothes and electronics to drugs. Sweepers sweep, beggars beg, scavengers seek recyclable goods and sex workers clients. Though not without their differences, there is a commonality to how such people are organised, often operating as small groups and relying on some form of leader. These leaders are referred to differently. Sex workers often look to a *dalal*, scavengers sometimes to a *boro bhai* and many street vendors to the head of an association. But the most common term for such leaders is *sardar*. *Sardar* is a way of referring to a 'headman'[1] or foreman, a low-level labour leader who has responsibility for a small group of manual workers. The term is well established and common across the subcontinent and beyond. Nineteenth century sources define 'sar-dār' in Hindustani as a 'chief, a head man, commander'.[2] 'Sardār-ī' is then 'chiefship, supremacy, domination, lordship, rule'.[3] Historically, labour leaders were identified as ubiquitous 'intermediaries between employer and employee', found in tea plantations, mines and factories, but also in bazaars and transport terminals such as train stations and ports.[4] In the 1980s and 1990s, certain *sardars* had leveraged their authority among men to mobilise in the gang of Picchi Hannan, or even form rival groups to him. We have already heard of the various leaders (some termed *sardars*) that operated across communities in Dhaka historically.[5] At Kawran Bazaar, *sardars* are more colloquially termed *hordars*.

Today at Kawran Bazaar *sardars* are locally prominent intermediaries organising the movement of fresh goods, situated between the wholesalers and the trucks bringing and carrying away goods.[6] They typically organise a range of labour, including the *coolies* (those carrying goods in baskets on their heads), the helpers (those facilitating this, unloading or loading by hand) and the rickshaw *baan* (van) drivers (those carrying goods in flat-backed rickshaw vans). As with the *coolies*, some rickshaw van drivers operate at night under the control of a *sardar*, a senior and powerful figure who often rents people under him their rickshaw vans, coordinates with the wholesaler and truck drivers regarding the arrival of goods to be unloaded, determines who can and cannot work under him and subsequently pays his workers. These details are written in a ledger. Typically, the *sardars* have agreements with *arotdars* to unload certain goods at a certain price, requiring a *dadon* (advance) in part as security that the goods will be safe under their possession.⁷

Labour leaders are common not only in the bazaars of Dhaka, but across factories, construction sites and other industries. They play crucial, wide ranging and poorly understood roles in the lives of the working classes. Labour leaders were a figure of fascination in labour histories and early twentieth-century colonial discourse but are oddly neglected by academics today. The few studies that do examine their roles in Bangladesh indicate they are still a prevalent and important figure in the lives of the poor.⁸ The story told here from the lanes of Kawran Bazaar is of the various guises that labour leaders take and their crucial role in navigating the political landscape on the back and behalf of labourers. Labour leaders are intermediaries and political entrepreneurs, as well as friends, advisors, sources of security, comfort, love, and also risk and exploitation. They provide a daily anchor in the lives of labourers as figures of respect and often operate through a variety of *samiti*s (societies, associations) in the form of cooperatives, unions or mutual-aid associations.

As intermediaries, they derive power from their ability to navigate, building unity and strength from below, whilst carving opportunities above them and fending off risks. On the one hand, labourers are subject to the interests of political leaders, routinely rounded up to swell the crowds at rallies and events. They form the muscle base of local politicians and parties. As we saw in Chapter 3, the chains they work within are also looked to as a source of capital to enrich petty party leaders and cadres. On the other hand, leaders with a group of labourers under them are entrepreneurs. They utilise their capacity to mobilise politically, orchestrate acts of political violence or intimidation, seek opportunities for more work or gain status within the party hierarchies above them. Labour leaders thus profit from their ability to navigate this landscape, holding together groups of labourers, surveying the terrain for opportunities and always wary of those who could usurp their position. This chapter examines the *boro bhai*s, *sardar*s and *samiti*s of Kawran Bazaar as crucial forms of intermediation in the lives of urban labourers, and that for many, often function in effect, as syndicates.

Boro Bhais

> If you want to work at Kawran Bazaar you need a *boro bhai*. If you don't have one, you can't get work. If you don't have one, you won't be safe.
>
> —Shakib, *jhupri* labourer

*Sardar*s often have their name appended with the term, hence the most proximate and powerful *sardar* to the *jhupri* group, Dulal, is known as 'Dulal *sardar*'. Dulal is now elderly. He described to me having worked at Kawran Bazaar for over forty years and having once had forty rickshaw van drivers under him. He arrived in the bazaar in 1975 and became a *sardar* with the support of his cousin who was an *arotdar*. *Sardar*s typically receive daily rents from the vans they own and rent to drivers (approximately 80–100 taka per van), along with a significant cut of the fee charged for the group to unload or reload the goods. For managing this Dulal relies upon a trusted worker, Kashem, who has worked for him for twenty years, initially as a van driver for sixteen years, and then as the supervisor of the vans and workers, keeping vans secure, collecting money and dealing with problems as they arise. The rough division of payments is often understood by the *jhupri* labourers as follows: from a fee of 20,000 taka for unloading and distributing goods in one night, the *sardar* would allocate 10,000 taka to the *coolie*s, 5,000 taka to the rickshaw van drivers and take 5,000 for himself. Some estimate that Dulal *sardar* earns about 1.5 lakh taka a month, others far more. What is clear is that he has achieved things few below him have. He has three children all of whom have studied to the masters level and he also owns a local pharmacy in the nearby area Farmgate which his son manages.

The *jhupri* group have a complicated relationship with Dulal *sardar*. As teenagers many laboured under him, learning the job and ways of the bazaar under his direction. Over time, however, the relationship has soured, as the story in Chapter 5 will tell. When asked if the group had such a leader, the *jhupri* labourers were adamant: 'We are all brothers, we have no *sardar*.' This would also be expressed bluntly as 'we don't have a *sardar*, we have a *serial*'.[9] Of the eighty rickshaw van drivers in the *jhupri* lane, only ten operate under Dulal *sardar*. The remaining seventy organise work through a 'serial'. A *serial* refers to a nightly lottery, used as a system for organising the way in which a group of labourers unload goods from the trucks.[10] This *serial* most often takes the form of pieces of scrunched up paper being drawn from a hat, and people being allocated their turn in the queue accordingly. The *serial*s are associated with certain areas (*bhag*), and hence the *jhupri* labourers have the *serial* associated with their lane for trucks that are not under the *sardar*.[11] Some trucks then are a free-for-all, others are controlled by a *sardar* and some operate under a *serial*.

Despite the rhetoric of not having a *sardar*, the *jhupri* labourers are much more intimately connected to the logic of a *sardari* system than they present it. Alongside the feeling that 'we are all brothers', the group have clear hierarchies, at the head of which are the 'big brothers' (*boro bhai*s). There are three *boro bhai*s in the *jhupri* group, who operate at times together and in sync, and at times in competition. A younger van driver in the group described these figures: 'Parvez bhai is top. Then Rubel. Then "mission Azad".' These *boro bhai*s play comprehensive and dense roles in the lives of the labourers. These roles are shaped both by the personal histories of these individuals and the group, as well as the wider political economy in which they find themselves. A younger labourer in the group described their role:

> Rubel and Parvez are in control. They don't work. They don't stay here, but if there is any work it is under their control. Parvez and Rubel are our brothers. It is their responsibility. Everyone is with them. They are in charge otherwise there will be disorder, there will be arguments, do you understand?

Like brothers, they are looked to for advice and support on a daily basis. The relationships are spoken of in terms of *love*, and whether they 'adore' each other. Like family, they are seen in moral terms, judged to be good, to be fair, to be ethical or otherwise. Part of the solidarity and bond between the labourers and these *boro bhai*s is that they are all rooted in the streets of the bazaar. The three figures of authority are from the same 'batch' of children, as Rubel put it, growing up together in an old Aparajeyo Bangladesh (a local NGO) centre for boys, having moved there from the Chinomul Centre. Rubel and Parvez both grew up without parents at the bazaar, they were *tokai*, thieves and labourers and yet they have moved beyond that level, have done well, moved out of the bazaar and established a family life. The dependencies on the *boro bhai*s are all the more acute because most of the labourers have grown up disconnected from their own families.

The complexities of these relationships are then in part a product of the histories and childhoods of the group, who have been driven together by vulnerabilities, and their lives intertwined and interdependent to a degree that is difficult to appreciate. But the roles of these *boro bhai*s are also a product of the wider political economy in which labourers are situated, and which was outlined in Chapter 3 in terms of the patchwork of different party leaders, the syndicates they run and their close relationships to the security agencies. Managing work at Kawran Bazaar is partly about ensuring fresh goods are unloaded as required, taken to the right wholesaler and moved on at the correct moment. But the act of work and managing labourers is also inherently political. From the perspective of local party and state authorities, economic opportunities and the accrual of capital are treated as resources that they can control at the local level. As was argued in Chapter 3, the local economy is a source of funds for those in power to both sustain themselves and to prosper from. Who works and how much they gain, therefore, must contend with such authorities.

From the perspective of the *jhupri* labourers, relationships with figures and groups of political authority are not only something to withstand, but opportunities to be taken advantage of. Political leaders need manpower. They need muscle to fight with local and party rivals to establish dominance. They need men to bring to political events, demonstrating to their party seniors that they are strong and important locally. Although labourers have low social standing, they are politically valuable, looked at by senior leaders as a resource to be drawn upon. They are also a threat to be controlled, potentially able to mobilise behind rival leaders. The role of the *jhupri boro bhai*s is thus to navigate this world for the *jhupri* labourers, positioning the group in relation to the political infrastructure in a manner they judge will be advantageous to them. Put in other terms, they mediate this relationship. Each of the three *boro bhai*s in the group plays a different role and has a different strength, enabling the *jhupri* group to maintain the work they have and seek opportunities.

Rubel was often described to me as dressing and acting like a *mullah*, with his white *panjabi* and constant use of overtly religious language. Some termed him 'Rubel *mullah*', and for those critical of him, his appearance is one way he has cultivated authority among the group. He owns six rickshaw vans, which he rents out on a daily basis to others in the group,[12] but more importantly he holds some of the contracts for unloading trucks and delivering goods to the wholesalers. He is thought by some to be earning 3,000–4,000 taka a night.[13] Rubel emerged as a leadership figure among the *jhupri* labourers in childhood, when he was a 'team leader' as others put it in English, organising the scavenging and stealing of fruit and vegetables at night, and their sale in the early morning. While Rubel primarily manages work and owns a number of rickshaw vans, Parvez is more closely linked to politics. At the time of my fieldwork, he ran a small *samiti* (society, mutual-aid association), collecting deposits from each of the labourers (discussed further in Chapter 6). Crucially, he positions the group in relation to the broader political landscape, sketched in the sections to come. He actively engages the group in political events and violence for a price. One of the labourers described these *boro bhai*s:

Rubel *bhai* never wants to create violence [*ganjam*]. That's why everyone goes to Parvez, because Rubel doesn't like problems and doesn't want to get involved. Rubel *bhai* says 'I eat my own food, I don't want to get involved in bad things, but if you need any suggestions, I will give you some good advice.' That's why everyone goes to Parvez *bhai* because he goes everywhere for fighting. I have observed Rubel, he [is] always doing good things.[14]

The third of these big brothers is Azad, known as the 'fireman' (as Rubel described whilst indicating a pistol), the kind of man who is dangerous (now indicating stabbing motions), and infamous locally for having served twelve years in prison for crimes committed during the era of Picchi Hannan. His particular skill, others in the group explained, was that he had the knowledge and courage to build bombs. Although seen as a *boro bhai* of the group, Azad is not a labourer, but a guard for papayas and collects 100 taka per truck that arrives in the bazaar and protects it from theft.

The *jhupri* labourers then look to each of these *boro bhai*s for advice and support on a daily basis. They ask for small loans and require their leadership if there are tensions or fights. The names of these leaders carry respect locally. 'If there is a problem, just give my name,' I heard both Rubel and Parvez say on occasion when instructing a labourer on an errand. The obligations that followers have to these *boro bhai*s range from being asked to run errands (such as fetching tea and cigarettes, as is customary in any hierarchy in Bangladesh) to the willingness to fight. These dependencies are also a source of jealousy, resentment and discontent among the group. The labourers in the group have to trust in the strategies and direction given by their *boro bhai*s, the work they secure for them and the wider political relationships they develop to seek opportunities. Unlike most of the labourers, these *boro bhai*s have homes in *basti*s which they return to during the day, and which mark their status as different from most in the group. They also earn far more than the labourers as a result of their status, and thus are brothers who have grown up at the bazaar, lived the same life as the others but now stand above them.

From Jobbers to Unions

> [U]nion fees replaced *dasturi*.
> —Dick Kooiman (1977: 324)

The image of labour leaders as morally complex, exploitative yet crucial figures in the lives of the poor is a familiar one within labour history from the

Indian subcontinent. In colonial discourse, labour leaders were referred to as 'jobbers', the now-antiquated English term for brokers or middlemen. They were the quintessential intermediary, found in factories,[15] coal mines,[16] tea plantations,[17] bazaars, transport terminals and boats.[18] At times jobbers were themselves ordinary workers seen as having more authority and standing among men and thus sent out to recruit labour from within their networks of kinship, caste and their home villages. Like Rubel and Parvez, however, the role of the jobber went far beyond the strict domain of work and was portrayed as encroaching on almost all aspects of life. Jobbers were not

> merely responsible for the worker once he has obtained work; the worker has generally to approach him to secure a job, and is nearly always dependent on him for the security of that job as well as for a transfer to a better one ... they may finance him [the worker] when he is in debt and he may even be dependent on them for his housing.[19]

Jobbers sat in command of small 'jobber units' often consisting of dozens of men.[20] The structural role played by jobbers brought scope for a degree of personal wealth and status, and with it, exploitation of those subject to their authority. By the early twentieth century, labour leaders were increasingly associated with corruption and the mistreatment of the working classes. They were seen as an 'evil' force,[21] detrimental to the dignity and lives of labour, and equally to the efficiency of the economy. 'The clutches' of the jobbers were portrayed as keeping workers 'in permanent bondage'.[22]

The list of accusations levelled against *sardar*s was long. They were seen as unfairly indebting labourers,[23] exercising control through physical violence,[24] unnecessarily dismissing workers and taking the salaries of fictitious labourers.[25] But perhaps the most common claim which led them to garner a poor reputation was that they took *dasturi*. Similar to *chanda*, *dasturi* is a term for a fee or 'customary commission'[26] on a transaction and dates to at least the seventeenth century.[27] In the context of labour, *dasturi* is most often seen as a regular cut of wages given by the worker to the jobber. The 1929 Royal Commission on Labour in India (RCLI), for example, described how 'in many cases a small regular payment has also to be made out of each month's wages'.[28] In other cases, *dasturi* was the cost of recruitment into work. Jim Masselos, for instance, argues that the sweepers of Bombay made three payments: *dasturi* of a month or two's pay to acquire work from a jobber, a monthly cut of their earnings and a fee when returning from leave.[29] The payment of *dasturi* was not merely a financial transaction, but 'a sign, a representation, of the sardar's authority',[30] and the authority of jobbers such that we can characterise them as 'labour lords'.[31]

In Dhaka today the term *dasturi* has largely fallen out of use, except among the sweepers in the city, who make hushed yet routine payments to petty officials as a condition of work. In his ethnography of a *basti* in Dhaka, Khan references the continued role that *sardar*s play in mediating access to work and also in bringing labour groups from rural areas to the city. Similar to the account from colonial India, he writes that 'many wage labourers have to pay the sardars ... an amount of their earning and accept any sort of work the sardar offers.'[32] With the authority of *sardar*s extending beyond the gates of the workplace and into the *basti*s of cities across the subcontinent, their role at times overlapped with that of a *goonda*. Dipesh Chakrabarty described how in his own fieldwork in jute mills around Calcutta *sardar*s were 'often described ... as well-known goondas'.[33] At times the descriptions we encounter of *sardar*s closely resemble those we saw of *goonda*s in Chapter 2; they were known locally as 'dadas', respected and feared in their communities, at times running gymnasiums and extortion rackets and utilised by factory owners to control the workers.[34]

In contrast to the discourse of *goonda*s as antithetical to the authority of the colonial regime (albeit one qualified by references to the colonial state deploying *goonda*s), here we find the opposite to be often true. Jobbers were foundational to the functioning of capitalism and the authority of capital, operating as a crucial cog in the day-to-day management of the workforce.[35] *Sardar*s were hence in many contexts a 'mode of labour control'[36] and 'agent of discipline'.[37] This at times meant that *sardar*s could be seen as indirect agents of the colonial state. In the context of Bengal, for example, large industrial workplaces arguably functioned as 'nexuses' with the government and police. Jute mill managers 'dominated municipal boards, controlled the local police force and acted as judicial magistrates of mill towns.'[38] This has been described as a 'manager raj', where British (often Scottish in this case) managers of private industry were in effect local representatives of the colonial state. For workers then the colonial state was often perceived as a 'protector of the interests of capital'.[39] At times, the role of *sardar*s within this equation was even more explicit, for example, when they formed part of civil guards for maintaining order in industrial areas.[40] To the extent that *dasturi* was crucial to the exercise of the authority and interests of *sardar*s, this form of 'corruption' can be seen – as Dipesh Chakrabarty has argued – as constitutive of rather than antithetical to the operations of capital and colonial authority.[41]

Yet this image of the jobber needs to be qualified in a number of important regards. For some, such a characterisation of jobbers as coercive and all-powerful borders on caricature.[42] Rather than being 'monolithic and homogenous', labour leaders were arguably 'a rather motley, indeed heterogeneous, group'.[43] Hierarchically, we can, for example, think of 'head jobbers' as well as 'lower jobbers'[44] (historic sources in Dhaka similarly cite 'head-sardar', 'sardar' and 'sub-sardar', with reference to municipal waste workers).[45] The conditions under which such leaders operated were also radically different, from factories and mines to ports and bazaars. Some operated within the bounds of a clear organisational structure, and others under an array of local, traditional and municipal authorities. At times then the character of the relationships cultivated with workers could resemble less oppressive dictates, and more 'patronage and vertical loyalty, strengthened by kinship ties or common origin'.[46] *Sardar*s can hence be seen as socially embedded,[47] needing to situate themselves within the 'moral economy of the neighbourhood'[48] and potentially undermined by other forms of authority and patronage. There were 'competing locations of power and alternative sources of patronage to which workers could turn',[49] and *sardar*s thus needed to 'remain responsive to the needs and expectations of the workers',[50] as if balanced on 'a tightrope'.[51] Where the interests and loyalty of *sardar*s in practice lay was highly contextual, at times configuring squarely on the side of the management, and at other times more aligned to workers.[52]

Through the course of the twentieth and thus far in the twenty-first century, academia has lost sight of labour leaders in the mould of jobbers. This, in part, is due to the fact that jobbers became perceived as less crucial to the management of labour, thus featuring less centrally in our understanding of working-class politics. It is also due to fact that new forms of intermediation have emerged claiming to represent the interests of labour, shaping their relationship to the workplace and wider state. The most important of these are of course trade unions. On the face of it, unions and jobbers could not be more different: the jobber stands as a hierarchical mechanism of control for management, whereas the union in ideal form is based on principles of 'voluntary' and 'contractual' relationships, with union leaders elected by workers, and in an important sense therefore their 'equal'.[53]

The history of trade unions in South Asia suggests that the difference is often far less pronounced. As trade unions began to emerge in the early twentieth century, they ostensibly posed a dramatic threat to the authority of jobbers. Jobbers juggle their own interests with those of their workers and their workplace, and enforce these through patronage and coercion, whereas the promises of unions were that they would promote the class interests of the worker. In some contexts workers clearly saw hope in unions as a counterweight to the factory 'henchmen' (*sardar*s),[54] and an alternative route for grievance redressal and representation.[55] In practice, many of the unions that emerged around the large industries in Indian cities were distant from workers, led by well-meaning urban intelligentsia but with little ground support.[56] In the case of the jute mills of Calcutta, for example, although union numbers rose dramatically in the early twentieth century, they had very few subscription paying members, little democratic or constitutional coherence as organisations and were only as strong as the 'personal loyalty' leaders could elicit from workers.[57]

Where unions gained traction, this was often due not to the ousting of jobbers, but their integration. The threat posed by unions did not of course go unnoticed by jobbers, who had to either join the union or side with the workplace, in either case potentially undermining their own authority.[58] In practice, *sardar*s could be found on all sides of protests. In the case of the 1919 textile workers strike in Bombay, for example, jobbers appeared 'as strike leaders and strikebreakers as well as mediators'.[59] Among the mill workers of Bombay, most unions emerged in collaboration with jobbers who often in fact acted as 'union president'[60] and where 'head' jobbers were particularly important.[61] Similarly in Bengal, many early unions in the 1920s such as the 'Bengal Central Labour Federation' were founded with the cooperation and leadership of *sardar*s, who represented workers at union events.[62] Such unions were in effect 'controlled by intermediaries like the sardars'.[63] As the influence of *sardar*s weakened among workers, so too did the role of the unions which depended upon them.[64] Even when not at the helm, the strength of unions drew from the authority that jobbers held over the workers. For example, jobbers 'were entrusted with the task of collecting subscriptions in their departments, money which they were supposed to hand over to the trade-union officials' and the payment of *dasturi* was replaced with the payment of union fees.[65]

Jobbers could hence be seen as 'entrepreneurs',[66] for whom balancing the interests of unions could represent new opportunities for social mobility. Jobbers themselves formed unions, at times to promote their own interests, with some forming unions to hinder the working classes. Rajat Ray, for example, takes note of the colourful Sheikh Samir, 'a cocaine and opium smuggler' who formed a rival union to the Indian Seamen's Union to shore up his position as a shipping broker.[67] Although the urban working classes had been politically active through strikes, protests against employers and wider political movements,[68] the emergence of unions in this period indicated the involvement of labour in 'institutional politics'.[69] As political parties sought to form and patronise trade unions, 'Jobbers, no less than dadas or neighbourhood power brokers of diverse sorts' became crucial to how this was achieved.[70] The extent to which this promoted the interests of the working classes differed. At times, unions were founded and grew on the back of arrangements between union leaders and employers, as was the case with Muslim-League-aligned unions in the jute mills of Bengal in the 1930s.[71] H. S. Suhrawardy arguably intended to use *sardars* and other intermediaries to 'reinforce the authority of the mill managers',[72] and provide a base for the Muslim League in Calcutta.

More recent work from South Asia on the grassroots politics of trade unions paints in many respects a similar picture. After independence a shared feature of trade unions across much of South Asia has been their proximity to party politics. Major parties in India and Bangladesh have trade unions closely aligned to them, which typically dominate when the party is in office, and serve as a party base, source of support and at times, muscle. There are clearly significant differences – particularly at the sub-regional level in India – but it is these dependencies on parties which are often identified as a key source of union weakness.[73] In reality, political leaders often straddle parties and unions, such that the interests of parties and local leaders often become the de facto practice of unions.[74]

Andrew Sanchez's work on Tata Motors in Jamshedpur, Jharkhand, for example, reveals the widespread sense of complicity between the prominent Tata Workers' Union and the company management, to the detriment of casual workers. With an effective monopoly on union mobilisation, there is then much substance to the belief that 'the union is in the grip of an organised criminal subversion, in which violent entrepreneurs enter trade union politics to extract bribes from industrial capitalism.'[75] In the coal mines of Dhanbad (also in Jharkhand) this political economy is clear and stark. Here, many labour *sardars* historically operating in the mines became union leaders, in so doing solidifying patron–client relationships and assuming 'the color of a mafia-type organization, with a monopoly on vulnerable labor'.[76] As union leaders, many such figures operated within the Indian National Trade Union Congress (INTUC), with some becoming criminal politicians and controlling territories as 'gangsters'.[77]

Analysis of strikes in the tea plantations of Kerala suggests that a major driver of these is the perceived corruption of union officials colluding with plantation owners to the detriment of workers.[78] Party and trade union leaders are often the same people, union coordinators within the plantations are also security guards and supervisors and unions leaders are perceived as enriching themselves and offering their children opportunities at the expense of workers.[79]

The point then is that ostensibly dramatic shifts in the character of intermediation can conceal profound consistency in the nature of relationships between labourers and those above them. In principle, the role of a jobber is diametrically opposed to that of a union; however, their history within the South Asian context suggests they in fact play similar political roles, with familiar end results from the perspective of labour. Like jobbers, unions are today often portrayed as instrumental principally to the careers of their leaders, at times sustaining hierarchical and exploitative relationships with workers and ultimately serving the wider political interests of parties and those they are closely linked with. The differences between payments made in the name of *dasturi* or union dues can be difficult to discern if they both uphold relationships that play similar structural roles. Unions often, it seems, operate as coercive intermediaries.

The Strength of *Samitis*

> There is no end to the societies [*samitis*] at Kawran Bazaar.
> —A leader of the Jamalpur labour cooperative association

For labourers less established at the bazaar, *sardar*s are a common source of work. Teenagers moving between the streets and children's centres or men freshly arrived or staying a short period, all find opportunities through them. For them, the *sardar*s provide a rhythm, a degree of security and regular employment which, even if the income is lower, is much valued. In their eyes *sardar*s are prominent and powerful, but surveying the bazaar as a whole, *sardar*s are not what they once were. We saw at the beginning of this chapter how wider forms of labour leadership have life among labourers. Parvez and Rubel manage work and provide the comprehensive roles long associated with *sardar*s, yet by contrast are framed as being 'brothers' not headmen or leaders. They too are only small players in the context of the bazaar. More powerful labour leaders here are positioned not as *sardar*s, but as leaders within labour organisations, colloquially referred to most often at the bazaar as *samiti*s (associations, societies).

The term *samiti*, like 'association' in English, has very wide usage. Early twentieth-century unions in the context of Bengal were referred to as *samiti*s,[80] as they sometimes still are today. Literature has understandably focused on the roles of trade unions in the working-class politics of South Asia; however, we need to cast our eyes more widely to appreciate the complex associational life we find here. The term *samiti* can also denote cooperatives, savings groups or other workers' associations, all of which are extremely common in the bazaar, in Dhaka and across Bangladesh. This heterogeneity is not new. We saw in Chapter 3 that 'guild'-like organisations were common in Mughal cities, operating as a crucial mode of intermediation and governance, linking the working classes to the wider city and state authorities. Sparse references since suggest that by the late-nineteenth and early twentieth century, the notion of a guild was no longer applicable. In 1883 James Wise, for example, refers to workers' 'unions,' which he clarified was his translation of the Bengali term *dal* (group, faction).[81] The term *dal* today often has explicitly factional connotations, and the brief descriptions that can be found of these *dal*s in historic Dhaka also indicate that people of the same caste and trade were divided. Taylor for example writes:

> The Hindoos in their social intercourse are divided into societies or clubs called 'Dulls.' There is often more than one of these societies in the same caste, and even the several members of a family not unfrequently belong to different dulls.[82]

These associations were portrayed as providing entertainment, managing the caste and fining members for breaching custom. 'Societies of a somewhat similar description' also existed among certain groups of Muslims, Taylor notes, for example the 'Myeferosh', the outcast 'sellers of fish' mentioned earlier as having once held a monopoly on the right to sell fish. These were led by a hereditary president who 'levies a contribution daily from each member of the society, and in return gives them a feast at the end of the year'.[83] Here then we find what seems to amount to a form of *dasturi* or *chanda*, in relation to a leader organizing labour into some form of association. A later source notes Myeferosh were organised into a 'union or dal, presided over by a Paramanik [headman]'.[84] Similarly the Hindu spice or medicine dealers had 'six powerful dals, or unions, in Dhaka city, the Dalpatis, or head-men being persons of great respectability'.[85] The Hindu pottery and brick makers (*kumhar*s) had two 'dals, or trade unions, one known as Islampur, the other as Bhagalpur ... the headman is styled Paramanik',[86] and the Hindu garland makers (*malakara*s) also had two 'unions' in Dhaka. The Hindu washers (*dhobi*) had no 'permanent union (Dal); but whenever disputes arise, or their interests are endangered, they quickly form one, reserving for such occasions a headman, or Para-manik'.[87] Leading one of these *dal*s, or *panchayat*s, was a powerful position, and as such was, according to some, 'much coveted'.[88]

The point then is that it did not take unions to organise the urban working classes collectively.[89] Understanding labour hierarchies today hence necessitates being attentive to not only the diverse characteristics of and political roles played by unions, but also the broader array of *samiti*s and hierarchies that exist. To visualise this, imagine once again heavily laden trucks arriving at Kawran Bazaar. The drivers and helpers who bring the goods into the bazaar may well be members of the 'Truck and Covered Van Association'. The owners of the trucks meanwhile are likely members of the 'Bangladesh Truck and Covered Van Owners Association'. As goods are unloaded onto the flat-backed rickshaw vans, some labourers are members of small *samiti*s run by *boro bhai*s such as Parvez or by *sardar*s who also often run *samiti*s, yet a far larger group are members of the 'Kawran Bazaar Van Drivers' Union'. If *coolie*s are also unloading goods, they too will likely look up to a *sardar*, though many from the district of Jamalpur are organised as the 'Labour Cooperative Society'. The baskets on the top of the coolies' heads are, however, owned privately, and the owners organised under the 'Basket Owners' Society'. As the goods arrive in the bazaar they will come under the authority of the wholesalers, who themselves operate under various business associations including the 'Wholesale Owners' Society'. If any of the above stop for a break to buy a cigarette or tea, it is possible the shop will also be organised under a *samiti*, such as that of the shop keepers to the south of the bazaar whom we will discuss in Chapter 6.

In other words, a range of workers' and business collectives are dispersed across Kawran Bazaar. Larger organisations often have formal registration with a government department, either as unions or cooperatives (under the social welfare department or cooperatives department).[90] Below these, however, exist a myriad of different *samiti*s, which often take the form of a savings group or mutual-aid association, yet play diverse and complex roles in the local political economy. Similar observations have been made in other sectors, such as transport, where a wide range of often politicised associations operate.[91] Although rarely studied, small mutual-aid associations are extremely common across Bangladesh.[92] One study of 14 administrative unions in the country found a total of 323 informal *samiti*s, organised around occupation, interest group, area or family.[93] Similarly, a 1990s ethnography of a *basti* in Dhaka describes how 'it was almost impossible to find anyone who was not involved' with a *samiti*.[94] From roughly the same period, Stuart Rutherford found variations of informal *samiti*s operating between neighbours in slums or lower-class neighbourhoods, and among occupational groups such as garment workers and rickshaw drivers.[95] Outside of Kawran Bazaar I have observed *samiti*s in almost every context I have researched with the urban poor, such as the beggars outside the Supreme Court organised under an almost quadriplegic *samiti* 'cashier' who denied the presence of the savings group he was widely known to run;[96] sweepers living in Osmani Udyan Park paying into a *samiti* run by their *sardar* and street traders under an array of informal *samiti*s that seem to come and go, not to mention the (largely unsuccessful) attempts by local NGOs to organise the urban poor into small groups and facilitate savings.

A central practice of smaller *samiti*s is grouping together people to collect regular savings, safeguarded by a leader.[97] Wider analyses of such savings groups or mutual-aid associations recognise them as being a common form of organisation among poor people, one that is neither modern nor particular to any society or context.[98] Systematic and comparative research on such groups emerged most clearly within anthropology in the 1960s,[99] although studies of particular forms of savings groups, such as the 'friendly societies' of the United Kingdom and beyond, go back further. A key analytical distinction made in such studies has been between rotating savings and credit associations (ROSCA) and accumulating savings and credit associations (ASCA), the former relying on a rotating system of savings and credit distribution and the latter accumulating capital, which often serves as a pool from which members can take loans.[100] A *samiti* can in practice refer to a ROSCA or ASCA, and group structures associated with NGOs or microfinance institutions (MFIs) are often also identified by this term.[101]

Taken as a whole, the *samiti*s at Kawran Bazaar have significant coverage among the workers. The Truck and Covered Van Association claims 7,000 members here alone, while the Van Drivers Union has 580 members (from a total of around 800 van drivers at the bazaar). All such *samiti*s require regular payments to their fund. As with the tolls exacted by Picchi Hannan's group or those by the *lineman* of political leaders and the police, the dues of membership to a *samiti* are termed *chanda*. Members of the Truck and Covered Van Association pay 20 taka a day as *chanda* when leaving the bazaar, and members of the Labour Cooperative Society pay a similar amount to their leaders. In the case of the Tejgaon Van Workers' Union, the van drivers give 10 taka *chanda* a day, receiving a receipt for their contribution. In larger *samiti*s, these dues are also collected by a *lineman*. The Van Workers' Union for example has three *lineman*, each collecting around 120–150 taka contributions a day from van drivers at key points in the bazaar, and receiving a salary on this basis. Above *lineman* sit the leaders of such *samiti*s. In some cases – such as the Van Workers' Union – government registration necessitates a formal committee elected every three years, in which there are eleven members, most importantly including the president, secretary and cashier. Smaller *samiti*s are more one-man bands, created through the strength and character of their leader.

The benefits conferred by membership of a *samiti* are typically framed by the leaders of workers' societies in terms of health and welfare.[102] The welfare fund of the Truck and Covered Van Association, for example, has an emergency loan of up to 20,000 taka accessible in the event of illness or injury. If a worker is permanently injured and left unable to work, or dies at work, then it is claimed members raise a far larger sum to gift their family, around 100,000–200,000 taka, based on contributions. The association's president described them asking 'your brother is suffering, won't you stand beside him?' For the Van Workers' Union, if you are sick you have access to funds, and if you die, your family will reportedly be given 20,000 taka.[103] Contributions are also made for the wedding of a daughter.

Critically, *samiti* leaders also often have the responsibility to manage the everyday work of labourers, usurping the traditional role of the *sardar*. By contrast with the *sardar* who manages the contracts for his *coolie*s and van drivers, in the case of the Van Workers' Union, the daily work of labourers is managed under a *serial* by the union. To gain access to work as a van driver in much of the bazaar, membership of this *samiti* is a requirement. The man on the ground for managing work day to day is the *lineman*. A leader of the union described it as:

> say a labourer comes to work today, and has an argument or fight with a truck driver, *minti*, *arotdar*, or other labourer. To solve this types of incident we have three designated men who move around the market and see if any problems occur. We pay their salary from the fees paid by the members. Say one labourer gets injured in a fight, then the treatment costs have to be arranged with the fund raised through the fees … When a case is filed following a fight, then he will be helped with this fund to get him released.

Ostensibly then such organisations exist to represent worker, and therefore class, interests. Leaders frequently spoke of their *samiti*s in terms of bringing unity, strength and support to the workers, countering the precarity of everyday life. Yet the extent to which worker interests and welfare lie at the heart of such *samiti*s is readily questioned by outsiders. Rubel, for example, often lambasted the Van Workers' Union, claiming on one occasion that it was 'just a "show". Really it is politics'. Organisationally it is very clear that locally important *samiti*s exist synergistically with the ruling party. Leaders of *samiti*s are also leaders of the various affiliate and constitutive bodies of the Awami League. Liton put it to me once like this: 'It's the rule that whoever runs these [*samiti*s] will be part of the Awami League.' Most leaders of the Van Workers' Union, for example, are also leaders in the local branch of the Sramik League, and this overlap has similarly been observed in other sectors including transport.[104]

The suggestion that such *samiti*s are really about politics, is a way of questioning the intentions, worth and activities of these organisations. For many, the fee for membership in an association can often be a thin veil for local leaders taxing workers to enrich themselves and those around them. A crime journalist who grew up in the bazaar similarly reflected this more critical view:

> Many of those who were once involved in terrorism have now come under the shelter of politics. Because they are politically involved, the police and RAB don't want to control them, and they know they can get away with extortion, like in the transport sector, where every vehicle, bus, truck has to pay 50 to 500 taka per day. They collect it for so-called labour welfare or social welfare to avoid legal consequences. They might give a token or a receipt for the money you pay, saying that if a worker falls sick or gets injured, they will arrange treatment or arrange [a] funeral and burial if any worker dies. This is just an excuse. Actually the expenses aren't much. If they take 2 crore taka, they are spending at most 10 lakh, which is not much, but they do it in this way so that it looks legal. Welfare of the workers is just an excuse.

The claim then is that such societies are far closer to being syndicates than they appear from the outside. Indeed, it is common to hear such *samiti*s lambasted by those outside them as exactly that. This more critical view of trade union politicisation and the self-serving behaviour of union leaders finds resonance within the limited wider literature on unions in Bangladesh.[105] In the early post-liberation years, for example, trade unions in industry had a reputation for 'large-scale corruption and jobbery'.[106] More recent work highlights how the desire of parties to solidify a base has led to widespread politicisation and divisions among unions, such that union leaders often switch political allegiance to align themselves with the ruling party. In the garments sector this has meant that labour is only weakly unionised, with the dominant unions and federations interlinked closely with the ruling party; meanwhile smaller organisations are highly marginalised.

From the perspective of the labourers at Kawran Bazaar, the political involvement of their leaders can be crucial to sustaining their access to and stability of work, but also comes with responsibilities and risks. This often implies that labourers are embroiled in the political strategies and loyalties of their leaders. At times, this can simply mean attending rallies and other events, enabling the union leaders to demonstrate their own strength in mobilising manpower for more senior local leaders. The President of the Truck and Covered Van Association, for example, is also the joint secretary of the Tejgaon Thana Sramik League: 'I am in both so there is a good relation. Whenever they [Sramik League] have programmes we move with them to make them a success.' This political connection enables such organisations to protect the workers. One *lineman* of the Van Workers' Union put it like this:

> If we have a problem on the road, we have leaders, and they look after the workers. Our leaders are involved in political parties, some of them in the Sramik League, some Swechchasebak League, so they have power.

Yet in other ways and times the political involvement and authority of *samiti* leaders can be a hindrance and threat to the workers themselves. Where a condition of accessing work is effectively membership of a *samiti*, the act of work means entering into a relationship of dependency on politically aligned labour leaders, and being subject to their interests. The risks of this are numerous, and explain the *jhupri* group's contentious relationship with the Van Workers' Union, as well as the complexities within their own group. Parvez and Rubel have a long-standing suspicion of these other *samitis*. Early on in my research I observed the Van Union *lineman* collect 10 taka *chanda* from the rickshaw drivers, and asked Parvez why it was not demanded of them also. He replied: 'They can't, if they try we will fight them.' When they were growing up and starting out as van drivers at the bazaar, there similarly existed a *samiti* purporting to represent them, called the 'Rickshaw Van Workers Union' (Rickshaw Van Sramik Union). Unlike today, however, the union was not aligned to the then ruling party (the BNP) but instead to Picchi Hannan. Parvez recounted their experience:

> We used to have an organisation of van drivers in the time of Picchi Hannan. His men helped us, and we cooperated with them. He had a brother, a cousin, not a sibling, who is still here and involved in [the] Awami League, his name is X. He's not strong like he was before. Now he's just a normal person. But then he was involved with us as the leader of the organization. But he stole so much of our money, and from then on, I don't trust anyone.[107]

Their distrust in the *samiti*s of others did not, however, prevent them from running their own. Part of Parvez's income, at least during the 2014–2015 period of this research, came through organising the seventy labourers under him as a *samiti*, which functioned, at least ostensibly, as a savings group where each labourer deposited 10 taka per day. Rubel had previously run a *samiti* within the group, each member having given him 500 taka, from which he is said to have only returned 150. More fundamental to the suspicion felt by Parvez and Rubel towards the Van Workers' Union was the political strength of the union. Parvez once reflected:

> There are two sides [to work at the bazaar]. Our side is stronger. We have put our names in that organization, but we are not taking this slip [paying *chanda*]. Because they have some rules. People of the organisation are involved in politics. Their control over us would grow and that could become a problem. So, we have some conditions to being involved. If they want us to be members, they have to sit with us. They can't interfere with our work or our internal issues. The risk is that they try to control our work for their own benefit.

The argument of the *jhupri* labourers then is that this union is an explicitly political organisation, and their involvement with the union would put them under the authority of the political leaders heading it, making them vulnerable to the demands such leaders may make. Despite the claim that 'our side is stronger', of the approximately 800 van labourers there are at the bazaar, 580 are union members, while the remaining either operate under *sardar*s, *boro bhai*s such as Parvez and Rubel or independently. Parvez and Rubel know that they cannot compete with the union directly for work and that if they do, it will put them up against a far larger group of labourers, politically aligned to the ruling party. Younger drivers in the *jhupri* group under Rubel and Parvez are hence suspicious of the union. Tohin, one such labourer associated with the *jhupri* group, described it in these terms:

There's a *samiti* but I'm not a member of it. If I join with the *samiti*, they will start calling me. The whole country is becoming political, so different parties will keep calling me 'hey, why don't you come ... hey, come here ... you drive a van but you don't come with us!' I know all of them, but I pretend I don't know them. There's no advantage bringing enemies into your life.

The argument here then is that alongside the array of intermediaries described in Chapter 3 as operating under the local Jubo League and security agencies, we find that labourers themselves operate under an equally varied set of intermediaries, organised around *sardar*s, *boro bhai*s and various *samiti*s. These are integrated into the political hierarchy in complex ways, most notably through the political affiliations of the labour leaders. Such leaders frequently sit within various societies or unions, which in practice often arguably operate as a form of coercive intermediation linked to the ruling party. The hold that such leaders have over labourers and the manner in which they extract *chanda* or union dues, is often perceived locally as a syndicate, and referred to in these terms.

The *jhupri* labourers are not members of the local union and exist in a precarious position. For much of my research their anxiety seemed to stem from the threat that their access to work would be diminished. As the research continued, however, it became clearer that other games were at play. Liton, for example, described membership as meaning they would be seen as 'legal', claiming people 'can call us *santrashi*s, but they can't call them *santrashi*s because they have an ID card'. The assertion that this relatively small group of labourers living at the side of the bazaar could be called terrorists or gangsters could easily feel like an exaggeration. In early 2015, I realised it was not.

Notes

1. Wise (1883: 83).
2. Shakespear (1834: 1065).
3. Ibid., 1065. Across the subcontinent, a range of terms are used to describe figures playing broadly the same role. Discussing the labour at the docks, for example, a report noted 'shipping companies ... employ foremen, known variously as *tindal*s, *mukkadam*s, gang *maistrie*s, *jemadar*s, *joliwala*s, or *sardar*s' (RCLI 1931: 185).
4. RCLI (1931: 23)

5. Of labourers in particular we hear only the odd reference in Dhaka. James Taylor, for example, writes of the 300 street *coolie*s in Dhaka in the 1840s

   > who belong to the districts of Purneah and Bhagulpore [both today in Bihar]. This class of people have been settled here for about 150 years; they live in sets, each consisting [of] twenty persons under the orders of a sirdar, who regulates their work, and divides their earnings among them at the end of the month. (Taylor 1840: 311)

6. *Sardar*s also existed, at least in the past, among thieves. A journalist who grew up near the bazaar described to me the *churi sardar* (leader of thieves) of a previous generation called Anda, meaning egg, because he and those under him particularly stole eggs. He was described as a strong man and no one could beat him in a fight, but he also had 'a big heart. If he heard you hadn't eaten, he would go down the road and steal a chicken for you. Then he would sell it and feed you rice … He couldn't stand seeing people's misery.'
7. The cost of the labour is generally borne by the *bepari*, and either paid by the *bepari* directly, or more likely the *arotdar*. These goods are then bought up by *paiker*s, who pay a commission to the *arotdar*, sometimes paid through a 'coil' (a job some say Picchi Hannan once had).
8. Bertocci (1970); Wood (1994); I. Khan (2000).
9. *Sardar*s are a source of security and jealousy. Among the *jhupri* group there is a common sense that labourers are not paid the real rate and that the *sardar* takes an unfair cut, being able to do so due to a labour surplus. A teenager Parvez, affiliated with the group, yet not old enough to work as a van driver and working as a helper unloading pumpkin trucks, said to me once, 'We know that we are being paid less but if we don't agree then he will be approached by anyone else. There is no shortage of people who will do any job.'
10. More broadly, a *serial* can refer to a group savings system.
11. In other areas there is a mixture of *serial*s and *sardar*s. In practice, the system is cheated. As Shakib said, 'there's a serial, but whoever runs the fastest, they get the money. The serial doesn't work.' Liton complained that 'every night there's fighting. Not everyone is honest. Even though there is the *serial* people lie, they pretend they are in the *serial* when they aren't really. So then people fight.' Some exist at the edges of these systems, picking up bits of work as they can, in between the *sardar* and the *serial*. Liton put it: 'Sometimes there aren't *serial*s for the work. We have built relationships with the *bepari*s and the *coolie*s, and I know the *arot*s well, so I can take these goods. There are so many *ghar*s, if you know them, you can find work.'

12. Particularly where there are no *sardar*s, it is people who own vans who are looked to. You need to have a good relationship with a *boro bhai* (in this case, simply someone who owns a van) in order to be able to rent one and thereby get work.
13. Though they do not self-identify as having a *sardar*, it is worth reflecting on how in fact the group could operate without someone taking on this structural role. The logic behind having a *sardar* is to reduce the transaction costs of moving goods for the wholesaler. The *sardar* manages the contract, organises the labourers and ensures the efficiency of the process. Without a leader of some sort, the wholesaler would have to deal with tens of van drivers, which could easily become inefficient. It is Rubel then who controls some of the contracts on which the *jhupri* labourers work. A primary difference seems to be that he is identified as one of them; though senior, he shares the same roots, has grown up in the same way and therefore retains a common identity.
14. Rubel was, however, far more involved in organising violence than this quote suggests, as will become clear in Chapter 5.
15. Chandavarkar (2008: 123); Chakrabarty (2000).
16. Simeon (1995).
17. Sumita Sen (2010); Evans (1997).
18. Balachandran (1996).
19. RCLI (1931: 23)
20. Kooiman (1977).
21. RCLI (1931: 24)
22. Burnett-Hurst (1925: 48) cited in Chandavarkar (2008: 126–127)
23. In certain contexts, such as in the coalfields of Jharkhand, labourers were indebted to their jobber on recruitment and these debts persisted for extremely long periods (Goyal 2018: 556–557).
24. de Haan (1997); Chakrabarty (2000 [1989]); A. Sen (2002); Bhattacharya (2004).
25. A. Sen (2002: 3957). Also see Chakrabarty (2000 [1989]: 110).
26. Chakrabarty (2000 [1989]: 108).
27. Naqvi notes that in the mid-seventeenth century *dasturi* was a 'well known local custom … [that] was allowed on all occasions of sale of goods' (Naqvi 1964: 335). Early dictionary definitions see it as 'perquisites paid to servants by one who sells to their master' (Shakespear 1834: 859).
28. RCLI (1931: 24).
29. Masselos (1982: 113–114).
30. Chakrabarty (2000 [1989]: 108).
31. Chakravarty (1978: 283).
32. I. Khan (2000: 42)

33. Chakrabarty (2000 [1989]: 10).
34. See, for example, A. Sen (2002).
35. For some, *sardar*s 'modelled themselves on the traditional village landlord' (Evans 1997: 92) embodying 'pre-capitalist' modes of coercive control (Chakrabarty 2000 [1989]). Others (for example, Chandarvarkar [2002]) have critiqued this as an orientalist rendering of the forms of control exercised.
36. A. Sen (2002).
37. Chandavarkar (2008: 123).
38. Basu (2008).
39. Basu (2004: 15). As Basu argues, however, this was not a static relationship. On the one hand, we can see jute mill owners operating for a long period as a 'cartel' in the form of the Indian Jute Manufacturers' Association and their patronage by the colonial state, before Indian themselves became influential in the association. On the other hand, we can see expatriate capitalists as at times constituting a threat to colonial authority (18–20).
40. Ibid., 175.
41. Chakrabarty (2000 [1989]).
42. Sumita Sen (2010); Chandavarkar (2008); Bates and Carter (2017).
43. Chandavarkar (2008: 136, 141).
44. Ibid., 142.
45. Municipal Office, Dacca (1969).
46. Kooiman (1977: 314).
47. Chakrabarty (2000 [1989]: 108–110).
48. Chandavarkar (2008: 144).
49. Ibid., 144.
50. Ibid., 141.
51. Sumita Sen (2010: 4).
52. In the judgement of some, the jobber of the mill was more aligned to the workers – more a 'kind of proto-union representative' than a node in the management hierarchy – but for others (for example, the sweepers of Bombay) far more a top-down exercise of authority from the state. See Masselos (1982: 116).
53. Noted from Chakrabarty's (2000 [1989]: 132) characterisation of Gramsci's formulation of trade unions.
54. A. Das (1985: 28).
55. The government – driven by the threat of labour unrest, the founding of the International Labour Organization (ILO) and the need for improved economic efficiency – introduced new legislation to improve welfare and regulate labour, providing a framework for the operation of unions, although implementation and practice fell far short of the formal stipulations

(Chakrabarty 2000 [1989]: 71–72). This legislation necessitated registration, the auditing of finances, stipulated the membership of executive committees and forbade certain forms of protest, such as lighting strikes and pickets (Basu 2004: 197). Note that in his discussion of the unions in Bengal's jute sector, Chakrabarty oddly neglects the complex relationship between *sardar*s and such unions, despite the centrality of *sardar*s to his understanding of authority in the everyday lives of the working classes.
56. Basu (2004: 135).
57. Chakrabarty (2000 [1989]: 138).
58. A. Das (1985); Kooiman (1977).
59. Chandavarkar (2008: 161).
60. Kooiman (1977: 327); Chandavarkar (2008: 162).
61. Chandavarkar (2008: 141).
62. Basu (2004: 168–169).
63. Ibid., 169.
64. Ibid., 171.
65. Kooiman (1977: 324). For budding unions and strikes, the payment of a regular subscription by workers was of course a signal of commitment to their cause (A. Das 1985: 30), and we can only imagine the symbolic importance of jobbers facilitating this relationship. It is also important to note that prior to the legalisation of unions, there were instances of jobbers themselves establishing welfare associations.
66. T. Roy (2008a: 998); Basu (2004: 10).
67. R. Ray (1979: 84).
68. Gooptu (2001).
69. R. Ray (1979: 84).
70. Chandavarkar (2008: 196).
71. Chakrabarty (2000 [1989]: 201).
72. Basu (2004: 258).
73. Candland and Sil (1991).
74. Chibber (2005).
75. Sanchez (2016: 51).
76. Goyal (2018: 546).
77. Heuzé (2009: 161).
78. Raj (2019).
79. Leaders here receive 'chantha' (translated as 'dues') from workers and union costs are taken directly from their salaries by management.
80. Basu (2004: 136).
81. Wise (1883: 262).
82. Taylor (1840: 258)

83. Ibid., 258–259.
84. Wise (1883: 90).
85. Ibid., 272.
86. Ibid., 334.
87. Ibid., 262. E. Lewis (1868: 10) notes that among the Hindus the president is designated differently according to caste – he is 'styled "Dálpati" among the Brahmins, "Paramanick" among the weavers, goldsmiths, barbers and so on and "Mukia" among the Tepális [dealers in 'oil, grain, salt' (Lewis 1868: 6)]'.
88. Census of India (1901: 440).
89. It is interesting to note that when unionisation took off in Calcutta, it did so first not with the labourers of the mills, but the 'amorphous body of labourers' who fell outside the purview of industrialists (R. Ray 1979: 89). As Das Gupta also notes of the city, unions sat here alongside wider workers' associations such as the 'Mohammedan Association' among mill workers, the 'Sakti Samiti' (Barbers' Association), Lohars' (Blacksmiths') Association and Masons' Association. See Das Gupta (1994).
90. The choice between forming a union or a cooperative is in part logistical (registering with the labour federation, or with the cooperative department or bureau under the social welfare ministry), but also a long-term strategy. The president of one labour *samiti* here explained:

> The benefit of having a *samiti* registered as a cooperative is that if Kawran Bazaar is moved anywhere else we will have a claim for benefits to the government. But in case of a union, they can't have such a claim. Wherever the market goes, we will do movements with our demands. But if we don't have a registration, we can't claim anything.

91. Kuttig (2020).
92. Devine (2006); I. Khan (2000); Maloney and Ahmed (1988); McGregor (1989); Rutherford (1997).
93. Maloney and Ahmed (2008).
94. I. Khan (2000: 80).
95. Rutherford (1997).
96. Jackman (2022).
97. *Samiti* leaders are known by different names. In terms of their role within the *samiti* they are often referred to as the *cashier* (cashier), though other labels are also common in more sophisticated organisations including *shobhapoti* (chairman) or secretary.
98. Geertz (1962); Ardener (1964); Bouman (1995); Rutherford (2009).
99. Geertz (1962); Ardener (1964).

100. Early interest focused on ROSCAs while attention moved also to ASCAs from the 1990s (Bouman 1995). The difference then between ROSCAs and ASCAs is fundamental to the academic categorisation of these groups, and the basic distinction lies in how savings and loans are distributed (Bouman 1995; Rutherford 2009). In the case of rotating groups, members of the group are each in turn distributed the money deposited. For all members except the last this represents a loan against future savings. The existence of a ROSCA is time bound according to the size of the group and regularity of deposits. By contrast, in the case of ASCAs this capital accumulates, often serving as a pool from which members can take loans if needed. ASCAs most often also have clear time horizons, perhaps one year, after which deposits are returned (Rutherford 2009). ASCAs tend to have far more variables than ROSCAs and require more sophisticated forms of management (Rutherford 2009).
101. In the case of ROSCAs, a range of terms may be heard, including *loteri samiti* (a lottery association), *khela samiti* (a game association) or *serial* (meaning a line or queue, as we have already seen). See Rutherford (1997).
102. Similar fees are also taken in the transport sector (Kuttig 2020).
103. A leader of the Labour Cooperative Society described his motivation for forming the *samiti*: 'If he has an accident, who helps him? Now, if you have an accident, we bear the cost of treatment. If you can pay back the fees later, we will take it, but if not, we will pay.'
104. Kuttig (2020).
105. Ashraf and Prentice (2019); Islam (1983); Taher (1999).
106. Islam (1983: 169).
107. The mobilisation of labour groups in previous decades is difficult to discern. Many *jhupri* labourers themselves have personal histories in such groups, *sardar*s were known to mobilise in this manner and as this account suggests, Hannan's group had control over the labourers. Research from the late 1990s argued that 'the labour gangs are directly controlled by violent gangs either through their members or through their trustworthy nominees' (I. Khan 2000: 188).

5
Fighting for Carrots

> Will we really allow people to block our work? We're the ones who work for our rice. We can't sit silently. Shouldn't we fight for our own money?
> —Rakib, *jhupri* labourer

As months passed at the bazaar my claims of conducting research without seeming to do much were for many of the *jhupri* labourers really a distraction from a more obvious reality: I was unemployed. The group were then impressed by my swift change in status in subsequent years evidenced by a business card, jumping from a hanger on who drank too much tea to a 'professor', as they generously framed various post-doctoral positions. This admiration was accompanied by requests to detail my income and expenditure in minutia, starting of course with salary, tax and housing costs and later, at my own insistence, the much-dreaded nursery fees. Jobs are hard to come by in Dhaka and anything vaguely formal a distant dream for the *jhupri* labourers. Government positions in particular are rare and much coveted, often requiring extortionate bribes to acquire, similar to how jobbers once mediated work in industry. Many municipal sweepers in Dhaka, for example, are known to have paid up to 10 lakh taka to gain a job, bringing debts but conferring stability of income and other opportunities. A younger labourer in the *jhupri* group, clearly exaggerating, once claimed to me while looking at the road being cleaned that 'even the sweepers on this lane are government people, but only us labourers don't have papers.'

The *jhupri* group have few avenues for getting salaried jobs. Being the sons of labourers, fishermen, small-scale farmers or faded one-time *santrashi*s and having spent years apart from them, means family is rarely a source of strength. Few here can rely on family capital, security, contacts or opportunities. Whatever the *jhupri* labourers have, they have it despite this background. As children they learned to fend for themselves. The friendships formed here were not only their fictive *bhai*s and schoolmates to play and joke with, but something even closer, brothers to survive with. Viewed from the side of the *jhupri* lane, their world then is much smaller, framed by the corners of the bazaar. It is here that they can earn, and here that they seek opportunities. Even for Eid, some do not return to a village *bari* or family elsewhere but spend it with others in the lane during one of the rare times the bazaar is eerily quiet.

Some in the group have basic literacy from a few years in school before life at the bazaar, or the smattering of education they received in a non-governmental organisation (NGO) shelter. Many, however, are functionally illiterate, unable to read the newspapers that are written from nearby offices, sold on the streets of the bazaar and eventually return to their authors, forming the wrappers for the small bundles of marijuana the labourers sell on to journalists. Unfamiliar with schools and exams, they are educated instead in the ways of the bazaar. Politics is not something they read about, but that they live. The landscape painted in the previous chapters is one known through years of opportunities gained and lost by the *jhupri* labourers. Each has a story of being caught stealing and beaten in childhood, of paying the informer after being caught out in some way, of being a victim of extortion by a policeman, of the previous patronage of a *boro bhai* at the bazaar, of making their way through their youth into the *jhupri* group and the stories and reputations of the characters that surround them.

This world requires close and careful navigation: Little is stable, most up for grabs. Territory is taken and lost as some *boro bhai*s rise in status while others fade or fall dramatically, all shaped by the wider fortunes of political coalitions and leaders in which they are embedded. Seeking and maintaining opportunities within the bazaar is the everyday lifeblood of the *jhupri* group, the fodder of endless conversations, speculations and rumours. As the group look out at the bazaar, they do not simply see labourers at work, but are eyeing up the goods others are taking, aware that even the benches they sit on could be wrested away by others sizing up the stretch of dirty public land they use to rest on.

When the labourers see the *lineman* of a *samiti*, a union or under the auspices of Kazi or Saad, they see a threat and a future, a source of jealousy and hope. When they see political leaders holding court or their images on the posters plastering the bazaar, such as outside the eunuch's mosque, they see a potential *boro bhai*, or fantasise about themselves being the ones looking onto the lane against a bright backdrop, with digitally whitened skin. The avenues for opportunity are, however, limited. Being a wholesaler sitting in a chair giving orders, is attractive, yet unrealistic: How would you get the capital? And even if you did, who would respect you, knowing you grew up on the streets here? In the time of Picchi Hannan falling in with his or other gangs was a potential route to opportunity, although at least in his case, one in which those from Chandpur had status and the lower ranks ended with little, as some in the *jhupri* group found.

Yet the riches available to those above them are plain to see in every motorbike, every fancy Japanese car that parks at the bazaar, every expensive Marlboro or Benson cigarette smoked, every tender given out by the nearby government offices and every story of the wealth accumulated by those of status locally. Strategies to earn more are an everyday affair, someone selling something on the side, someone stealing a bag of carrots here and there, another thinking about a small business such as Shumon's *khichuri* stand or the small bundles of marijuana they once sold. Speculation on how to earn at times feels like clutching at straws. With me, it was questions about the logistics of visas to the United Kingdom. On one of the rare occasions I came to the bazaar with a friend, he was interrogated about his job and salary, and asked – only half-jokingly – if he could give them a contract for the health programme he was working on in a remote district.

What is also clear to the *jhupri* group is that even as labourers there are opportunities to earn. In good periods, daily income can reach 2,000 taka a day, more than respectable middle-class jobs in offices. For the *boro bhai*s of the group, there are routes to not only more work, but other opportunities and pockets of income. Money can be earned through mobilising the group with a politician. More could be gained if that politician is in or comes to power and allows the group's leaders to appropriate other local resources, such as the wide-ranging opportunities for *chandabaji*. Pursuing these in essence requires leveraging one of the few assets the group has: muscle. Indeed, the group's view of Bangladeshi politics often comes down to the need to fight, to intimidate, to cut, beat and attack. The task of the group's leaders then is to mobilise the group violently to gain more work, but crucially, to do so in a way that positions themselves advantageously within the political hierarchies laid out in the previous chapters.

Writing this in 2024 it might seem logical to observers of Bangladesh that any such political calculation would rest with Awami League politicians, who have now been in power for over a decade, representing the longest period of party continuity in the country's history. During the 2014–2015 period, however, this was not the case. Other opportunities presented themselves. The prospect of the

Bangladesh Nationalist Party (BNP) returning to office was very real, and for many – including the *jhupri* group – this was how they saw their route to power.

Jhupri Muscle

> You're one of us, so you will also have to fight!
>
> —Choton, *jhupri* labourer

To be one of the *jhupri* labourers you need to be a good fighter. Some of the older members of the group (those now in their mid-thirties upwards) came through the ranks of earlier gangsters such as Picchi Hannan. When they were out of earshot, others in the group would explain how notorious certain labourers I knew were, how they had been a powerful and dangerous *rangbaj* (criminal, gangster), known for carrying a pistol and shooting rivals. Being able to fight is a significant determiner of respect, and one measure I was judged by when becoming involved with the group. I constantly affirmed how I could never fight on account of my glasses as labourers compared their biceps favourably to mine, tested whether I could get out of grips or whether I could pick them up. Collectively, the labourers brag about fighting, about beating people up, about how scared they made someone and about how strong they are as individuals. These bragging rights are an essential part of the group's identity. They are renowned as the best fighters at the bazaar I was often told. I was safe because I was with them, no one would dare say anything. If they fight, then their enemies will run away to the remote hilly district of Bandarban. When looking on at an Awami League meeting at Kawran Bazaar with Liton once, he told me: 'We're not the ones scared of them. Those leaders are scared of us. If anyone's going to be throwing bombs it's us!' Though I never saw evidence of it, members of the group occasionally mentioned they had guns if needed.

Teenagers and young men growing up at Kawran Bazaar and wishing to work in the group have to demonstrate their loyalty, physical strength and *daring* (the English word is sometimes used) to older group members. A familiarity and willingness to fight is useful for the jostling of everyday life, for when another labourer gets in your way or someone inconveniences or disrespects you. On one occasion I witnessed it was simply the men who manage the bazaar's toilets and showers who were the problem, attempting to charge the group too much for their use. In response, they took me along to the toilets as they handed out some slaps to the attendants and kicked down some wooden panels, leaving me looking bemused by the side as an accessory to a broken bathroom. More seriously, this muscle is foundational to how the group seek opportunities, but it is only part of the equation. The other part of the story is whose orders they take, who they align themselves to and bet will bring the group up with them. Here we find the link to the array of political leaders and party wings highlighted in Chapter 3.

The *jhupri* group can be useful to political leaders for a number of reasons. Political leaders can command dozens of men directly but rely on dozens more by extension. Each leader or prominent activist in turn seeks to build relationships with men hierarchically, to be able to call upon them as needed to ultimately serve the interests of the leader above them. These networks are often opaque and fragile, with alliances contingent on shifting calculations for advantage. The *jhupri* group are then low down in this chain, not the lowest, but low. They are the expendable muscle that politicians call upon to fight on their behalf in territorial conflicts or fill up the crowd in rallies to demonstrate popularity. They are also the type of people looked to for more extreme forms of violence, if someone needs to be killed or a bus needs to be bombed in an act of overt violence typically seen in the run up to general elections or surrounding particularly contentious moments.

Rubel made it clear to me when we first met that morning behind a row of parked buses that the *jhupri* group were aligned to the BNP. It was common during this period for all sorts of groups, activists and leaders to align themselves with the BNP, even if they had been part of the Awami League during the previous term. In line with Bangladesh's habit of switching between the Awami League and BNP every five years it was for many people a reasonable calculation that the Awami League would not be re-elected. Prominent Chhatra Dal leaders in Dhaka would later reflect on this period showing me photos of the current Chhatra League leaders who had renounced the party and marched with them prior to the election. In the *jhupri* group's case, the relationship to the BNP came principally from Parvez, who during the 2014 election period had become close to a local Swechasebek Dal leader by the name of Muzaffar. Muzaffar was framed to me by others in the group as being Parvez's *boro bhai*. He is known to be wealthy, and that his father owns a five-storeyed building nearby. He was the BNP's candidate for the local ward councillor and became joint general secretary of Dhaka city north unit of the Swechasebak Dal. He would later be elevated to the central committee of the Swechasebak Dal. Though BNP public events were minimal during the 2014–2015 period, Parvez could be seen in pictures on Facebook standing among groups around the leader, eating at a local kebab restaurant or at closed door events, looking smaller and more sheepish than he did at the bazaar among the labourers. Muzaffar in turn was regularly seen on the campaign trail locally with the BNP's candidate for Dhaka North City Corporation Mayor and later saw a spell in Dhaka Central Jail.

Rubel was thereby affiliated indirectly to Muzaffar but did not himself directly have a *boro bhai*. Instead, he had what others in the group referred to as a 'political small brother' (political *choto bhai*), someone younger than him, but an important and useful relationship to maintain. This figure was the locally infamous 'chhyachra goonda' Ahsan who was described in Chapter 3, and at the time was affiliated not with the Awami League, but with the Sramik Dal. Unlike Parvez's connection, this was not cultivated with the idea that Ahsan would be in a position of political authority later, but instead that he was a source of muscle to draw upon, as we shall see. The third of the group's *boro bhai*s 'mission' Azad was similarly identified at the time as 'doing' BNP politics (*BNP kore*), and himself explicitly seen as a source of muscle (being known as the 'fireman').

Party affiliation then is not about the capacity of Parvez, Rubel and the group to vote. In fact, none of them are registered electorally at or near Kawran Bazaar. Underlying these connections was the calculation that the BNP would eventually get into power and that by demonstrating their support now they would be able to reap the rewards later. In the period of BNP–Awami League conflict immediately preceding and during my fieldwork, members of the group described how Parvez was paid around 30,000 taka per occasion to lead the *jhupri* labourers into fights and skirmishes ('He collects the whole 30,000 taka and keeps it all for himself,' as one put it). But the *jhupri* group's political affiliations are also more complex than this description suggests. I once asked Liton about the significance of the group's BNP affiliation.

Me: Which party do you support?

Liton: I support all the *dal*s! Why? I will tell you. The party has a five-year duration, and then the opposition party will protest and push you out of your 'position' and then I will follow another man. All men are good.

Me: I've heard that most of the *jhupri* labourers do BNP.

Liton: No, we do whichever party. Whoever gives us 100 taka, we go to their meeting. If someone gives me 100 taka, I will follow them. If the Jatiya Party gives me, I will go there. But some men, like Rubel, Parvez, they only do BNP politics. They only send men to support BNP. If they went to another party, then those leaders will say, 'You do BNP, so why have you come to Awami League?' and then they will be beaten.

During the time I spent with the *jhupri* group, it was relatively common for the group's labourers – though not Rubel, Parvez and Azad – to participate in political meetings. This happened most significantly during attempts by the BNP or Jamaat-e-Islami to call *hartal*s (strikes) and meetings in protest against the government. But rather than attending BNP meetings, members of the *jhupri* group would participate with wings of the Awami League. The group described how they would sometimes go with the Jubo League, sometimes with the Chhatra League and sometimes the Krishak League, but that they had not registered as members with any of them. The instances I witnessed involved senior members of the local 'Leagues' passing through Kawran Bazaar rounding up the troops. On one occasion I saw the Krishak League secretary from nearby Tejgaon pass by the east side of the Water Supply and Sewerage Authority (WASA) building, where a group of *jhupri* labourers were sitting. Walking along in his oversized suit with a clipboard, he was greeted by cheers from the group. He immediately gave 100 taka to the group for tea, and then said he needed twenty people for a meeting at Farmgate. Each person would receive 100 taka. I resisted calls from the group to come along, and the group left (after having tea) cheering the name of a local politician.

Questions of why the *jhupri* group attended such events given their professed allegiance to the BNP often came down to money: 'We can fill our stomachs'; 'they give us 200 taka'; 'we aren't working now'. It was true. Most of these events were during the day when they were not in any case working and they could earn a little extra to send to family or eat better. But alongside this economic incentive, sit more complicated reasons, resonant with Rubel's description (quoted in the Introduction) of their relationship with Awami League groups as a 'tangle'. Parvez explained:

> After the Awami League came to power, they forcefully controlled the country. Now in this situation we are under pressure. We have to take part in the political programmes. When they call, you have to attend, sometimes in Suhrawardy Udyan [a national memorial in the centre of Dhaka], sometimes in the Party Office.

The consequences of refusing to attend could be that Awami League leaders report them to the police, or even liaise with the police to have them arrested. Giving the appearance of supporting the ruling party is then crucial.[1]

By extension these affiliations touched the whole group. I once asked Rubel about the significance of the BNP links for the group and he responded rhetorically: 'Will the small brothers support the Awami League when their big brothers do BNP? No, if they do, the big brothers will get angry and pressure them to do the same.' The younger members in the group often, however, knew relatively little or were coy about these higher connections. On one occasion I asked Sayeed (a younger rickshaw van driver) who was above Parvez and he said: 'I don't know brother because we can't ask him who's above him. If I ask him, he will beat me.' From the perspective of the labourers, working in the *jhupri* group offers a structure within which they can earn a living, find support, protection, guidance and a system for saving money in the form of a *samiti*. Working under the *boro bhai*s provides a political status and opportunities; however, these come with high risks attached. You may be able to earn, but you risk being beaten, arrested or perhaps even killed; you may risk the livelihood and respect of your family and community.[2] To work in the *jhupri* group you must fight. I overheard Rubel telling a *choto bhai* once, 'either you will beat him or you will leave Kawran Bazaar, now you choose.'

A Carrot Syndicate

> Bengalis are bad. If you give them a chance, they will take everything, that's what we're like.
>
> —Dulal *sardar*

Figures of authority at Kawran Bazaar are routinely the object of the *jhupri* group's insults. The Awami League are called *santrashi*s, wholesalers are *cheater*s, the police and the Rapid Action Battalion (RAB) informers are seen as dirty characters and the cadres of prominent leaders, *chamcha*s. A personal level of hatred is, however, reserved for one particular individual: Dulal, the long-standing *sardar* of the *jhupri* lane. As already noted, the *jhupri* labourers' relationship with Dulal goes back to their youth, when as teenagers they many spent years labouring under his authority, learning their trade, the names of the *arotdar*s and the techniques for pushing the rickshaw vans. 'He taught us everything,' one described. Even newer members of the group such as Liton first worked under him 'I didn't understand the system here and so went with a *sardar* [Dulal].

But as soon as I understood [the system], that's when I left!' Through immersing myself in the world of the *jhupri* group I had heard all sorts of grievances against Dulal *sardar*: He was blocking their work, he was trying to take *chanda*, he was taking a cut of their earnings, 'he grabs the rights of the poor.' He was really a 'fake policeman' was one of the more unusual descriptions.

At its most basic, their dispute with Dulal concerned control over work. Within the *jhupri* group they felt they had too many men for too few trucks and looked enviously at Dulal's supply the other side of the *jhupri* lane. Not only did he have a greater supply for his men, but he was also making advances into their territory. He was trying to take *chanda*, as one driver put it, trying to take rent for the space they used to unload, thereby taking a cut of their earnings. During one of my first encounters with Parvez he had told me, 'the *sardar*s are thieves … if they try and stop us we will beat them.' The group felt that Dulal did not deserve his status, that what he had, should be theirs: 'He has houses, he has bank accounts, but are they really his? He has just taken these things from us' one labourer described. When the group discussed the Dulal problem, violence was at the forefront of their solutions. Liton would often explain how the group 'had to fight' to resolve the problem. For over twenty years Dulal *sardar* had controlled the contract to unload the carrot trucks coming to Kawran Bazaar, but towards the end of 2014 the *jhupri* group's disaffection with him was mobilised into action.

The intensity of these private remonstrations against Dulal *sardar* had alerted me to tension in the lane, but I was nonetheless surprised when I arrived at Kawran Bazaar one morning in mid-December 2014 and was immediately told of events the previous night. The anti-*sardar* sentiments that had been building for months had manifested into what was portrayed as an anti-*sardar* strike. By 9 pm the previous night, around seventy of the *jhupri* group had blockaded the main entrance to the vegetable wholesale market, demanding that Dulal *sardar* be got rid of. Feelings such as 'if we don't get the work, no one will!' and 'it is either us or the *sardar*!' were expressed to me. Blockading the bazaar was an assertion of the *jhupri* group's identity, that they too have a claim on work here and can leverage their size and strength to take territory. Not allowing the flow of goods for even a couple of hours could have had serious financial consequences at the market. The group knew, they later explained, that the market authorities and the wholesalers would either have had to give in or fight them off, a potentially dangerous move with a group so large, and difficult at such short notice.

Challenging a *sardar* who has been established for over twenty years disrupts the balance of power at Kawran Bazaar and directly affects more senior figures, changing their power base. Leaders such as Saad got involved, and there was reportedly even a *salish* (community dispute resolution) and intervention from the area's MP. Even though the group were known to have BNP connections, the strike was ostensibly successful. Negotiations with the Awami League leaders led to Dulal leaving the bazaar, fearing being beaten up and it allowed the *jhupri* group – led by Parvez and Rubel – to take over his contracts.[3] Rather than having access to only a few of the trucks in their lane, they took over all of them. One of the labourers Nazir explained:

> The carrots used to be controlled by Dulal *sardar*, it was under their system. But now we have brought them into our system. They unloaded them for twenty years! We didn't say anything, they didn't allow us to work them. Now we have become united ... and have pressurised them. We have taken control. Now we work by sharing them.

Word went at the time that Rubel and Parvez would not take the cut that Dulal was taking, and therefore the van drivers would benefit more greatly and equally. Over the days that followed a series of further meetings took place involving 'old people'[4] from the group who had moved on, and also local politicians including the then Tejgaon Awami League president. Though invited to attend, I stayed back, suspecting my presence might overly complicate events, as well as jeopardise future research. From this emerged what seemed to be an agreement that Dulal could keep the ownership of his twelve vans, thereby still earning his 1,200 taka rent a day, but would lose control over the contracts and with it his cut and status. Dulal *sardar* became simply Dulal. At that moment, the *jhupri* group included many (but not all) of his men, uniting the *jhupri* lane, recognising that 'they also have families and need to earn,' as one put it. This was the first year that the group had dared such a move, as Choton reflected:

> This doesn't normally happen. We didn't think about it before. We had a system here and we did not think about it. We were small before. We grew up here taking the abuse of the *sardar*. When we were young they used to give us 50 taka in the morning for breakfast. Money had little value for us then, we could live off 20 or 30 taka, but now we have families, and even 500 taka isn't enough.

In the days to come, however, it became clear that the class-based rhetoric which had motivated the struggle was a veneer. The goods came to be controlled not across the *jhupri* group through a *serial*, but instead through what was described as a syndicate.

Small syndicates controlling the labour for bringing goods to and from the wholesalers are portrayed as a more recent arrangement at the bazaar. These represent a fourth structure through which goods are conveyed, sitting alongside the mess of unruly competition, *sardar*s and *serial*s (mostly under the Van Sramik Union, but also *boro bhai*s such as Rubel and Parvez) as seen in Chapter 4. A syndicate in this context is where a politically connected group of labourers use their muscle and contacts to control goods that come into the bazaar. These are formed for particular goods during a season and the syndicate hence has a fixed duration, though can continue over years. Syndicates are particularly associated with winter when the supply of goods to the bazaar is dampened, incomes are lower and competition for work greater.

For the *jhupri* labourers, this was the first year that they had formed such a syndicate. In later years when I returned, I found that this had become a routine and yearly struggle, and extended from carrots to other goods such as Bangladeshi tomatoes. Liton later described it:

> Now you see that people form syndicates. The *sardar* system is now coming under syndicate[s]. Syndicates come from [a] 'political source'. This means that we have strength through relationships with [political] leaders. It's not the system of a *sardar* taking half our money. We have a relationship with the Awami League or BNP, which means that if others talk about us, then we can stop them. There are many people trying to take away the work from us.

The basic principle of a syndicate in this context is that a small number of labourers form a group and negotiate or take control of the supply of goods into the bazaar in liaison with more senior political figures. Other labourers outside of the *jhupri* group form their own syndicates elsewhere at the bazaar. Any attempt to take these goods means you will be shouted at, beaten and the labourers would 'bring their people,' as it was put. In later years their connection would be to the Jubo League, whom they paid 2,000 taka a day to, but in this instance, they simply took control.

This meant that work typically spread across seventy men was instead being controlled by around ten, led by Parvez and Rubel. Whereas incomes might normally at this time of year be as low as 300–500 taka, being in the syndicate brought an income of around 1,500–2,500 taka. Though he was not identified by most as having become a *sardar*, Rubel played a similar structural role.

His men monitored and recorded the arrival of the goods, and he took responsibility for paying not only the van drivers but also the *coolie*s. As a young labourer later described it, 'Rubel took the *sardari*.' Some in the wider *jhupri* group but not in the syndicate accepted this, reconciling themselves to the fact and saying that in any case they did not want to work more ('We have *boro bhai*s in our group, those who have been here longer. If we don't obey them, it will be chaos'). Others were adamant that this was unjust (Liton described how 'Parvez has ten bad people around him. If we say anything to him about this I could get shot or stabbed').

Despite the strike and formation of the syndicate, the victory was short-lived. The mood of triumph gave way to tension, and in the days that followed the group became subdued and reluctant to talk. When asking about events to later type up in my diary, I found the group clearly on edge: 'There might be a big fight. Someone might even get killed ... It's not safe to talk about these things ... Let's talk about something else.' Less than a week later it became apparent that Dulal, the elderly and experienced *sardar* of decades, was not to be stopped so easily. In the early evening of 21 December 2014, I received an innocuous seeming call from Liton, asking whether I was coming to the bazaar that day. Something about the tone of his voice struck me as odd. I arrived the next morning, a week after the strike, to find only a few of the *jhupri* group. Shumon approached me with his usual smile but winced as I shook his hand: It was swollen and cut. It transpired that the night before Dulal *sardar* had hired young men from the Chhatra League to come and fight off the *jhupri* group, enabling him to retake control.

Dulal's connection to the Chhatra League came through the wholesaler he supplied goods to and who was also described as eager to maintain the relationship with Dulal, rather than having to deal with the likes of Rubel and Parvez who had recently barricaded the entrance to the market. The wholesaler's son was a leader of the local Tejgaon College Chhatra League branch, and therefore able to mobilise a good number of his own men, while also reportedly drawing on those of the president of the city Chhatra League. The *jhupri* group meanwhile only had a few of their men, at the core the ten or so in the syndicate. Outnumbered, they called in an 'outsider' as it was put: Ahsan, the 'chhyachra goonda' from the railway line and his *yaba*-fuelled group, who were at the time affiliated to the BNP's Sramik Dal, and known for giving muscle backing to syndicates.

The group later portrayed how they were attacked outside a bank near the *jhupri* lane, yet were able to fight off the Chhatra League boys. When one of them attacked Parvez, the group retaliated furiously. One of Ahsan's men reportedly smashed a hook into one of the Chhatra League boys' heads, the victim having to be taken immediately to Dhaka Medical College Hospital. The group had committed what Rubel later described as the 'half-murder' of this *chamcha*, while their man Ahsan was also injured in the fight, after the Chhatra League targeted him and 'struck at his head.' The fight was so intense that in the middle of it they described not knowing who was on which side. One of the *jhupri* labourers later described their anger:

> We are poor people, we don't have money, they have the money, they hired boys from the university and college. What do they think about us? We drive vans and so don't have any power? We are van drivers but we have a good relationship with the *boro bhai*s and leaders. Our *boro bhai* doesn't get angry, but when he does get angry then he could do anything.

Importantly, however, not all of the *jhupri* labourers were in the fight. Some had distanced themselves from the group in response to the syndicate, and others creatively avoided the conflict. During the fight Parvez had called younger labourers associated with them to join on their side against the Chhatra League, but some resisted, as one young labourer Sayeed described it:

> I saw them fighting, and they started calling us to join. I was going to but I saw the fighting was so 'heavy'. I realised something terrible might happen and it could be bad luck for us to go there. If I had joined them and something happened like the police caught me, it would have been a tough time for my family. We aren't rich. We spend what we earn, so it would have been very difficult for us. It would take time for the news to come to the [Aparajeyo Bangladesh] centre, and during this time I would be in detention and the police would ask me many things ... I have no one to support me ... so that's why I didn't join the fighting. The leaders have money, so they can arrange this sort of fighting, and they can hire [a] 'killer,'[5] but we are children from poor families.

'But what did Parvez say when you didn't go? I asked after the event:

> At the moment I don't see him, I don't take care about him. If I see him he'll say 'hey, don't you know me? Did you forget me? After this fight you don't come to me. I called you to come to the programme and you didn't come. Go away!' I don't want to listen to that and don't need to go to him. I will be blamed, maybe he will say that he should beat me, so why do I need that? When I see him sitting there, I take my van the other way around.

Despite winning the fight, the *jhupri* group were defeated when the Chhatra League called in the police, forcing them to flee. The group scattered and the Chhatra League subsequently took control of the *jhupri* lane, posting men in the area to make sure they could not return. When I saw a few other members of the *jhupri* group at the bazaar the day after, they spoke to me in whispers, looking over my shoulder at the Chhatra League men. Salam was optimistic, however: 'We will get rid of this motherfucker ... He has lots of money but we have lots of people, so we will see how long he can continue with his money.' Pumped up by the thought of the fight Salam told me they had 500 men, exaggerating, and that if anyone gets near him he will take out his *machine* (gun) and *bang bang*, though I was quite sure he did not have a gun.

I struggled to find any of the group for the next few days, but as I was leaving one day I bumped into Abul, a slightly older member of the group, who took me to the opposite side of the bazaar and then up a small staircase where there was a remote tea stall. Rubel was there with a few of the group looking downcast. Offering me tea and a cigarette, he explained that after the strike, Dulal had in fact offered them 3.5 lakh taka to give him the territory back but they refused, and so Dulal had brought in the 'killer[s]' as he put it, paying them 2 lakh to fight the *jhupri* labourers. 'But what can you do now?' I asked. 'I know one person at a higher level,' replied Rubel, 'but it won't work.' 'Taka taka taka,' Abul chipped in. Not only had the Chhatra League called in the police to push off the *jhupri* group, but Dulal *sardar* had a further card to play: He filed police cases (*mumla*) against key *jhupri* members at the Tejgaon police station.

As Rubel put it, 'he had a chargesheet made against us that we pressured him and took away the goods from him' (a seemingly quite accurate picture of what happened, regardless of their grievances). The point of primary contention had been the unloading of the carrot trucks. Dulal *sardar* filed a case against the three *boro bhai*s, Rubel, Parvez and Azad and eight others. This forced them into semi-hiding. They became *fugitives* (*ferari*) as Rubel put it. 'How can you resolve this?' I repeated. 'With money it can be solved ... David *bhai*, you don't know anyone who can help do you? ...' Rubel asked. 'I know no one like this, I am just a student,' was my formulaic but honest response. Before I left, I heard them plan their next move. Rubel instructed: 'We will attack them again after *azan*. So we need to buy some "monkey tupee" [balaclava].'

Returning a few days later after celebrating Christmas, I found Rubel back outside WASA sitting on one of his rickshaw vans behind the parked buses. He had evidently found a way to resolve the situation, at least for himself, and brushed off my question about how he had managed it. He explained that two of those with cases against them were in prison (including Azad), while the rest had got bail (*jamin*). Though released they remained *fugitives*. 'Why?' I asked. Because they used to do BNP. Their party doesn't have any power now. Parvez does BNP as well,' Rubel explained. An undertone to these events, but one not made explicit at the time to me, was the group's BNP connections. I noticed how Rubel had begun to soften his portrayal of his political affiliation. At the post-fight tea stall, he had been adamant in telling me that 'we aren't BNP, we aren't Awami, we are workers (*sramik*).' On this occasion he told me that 'I'm both BNP and Awami. I do both, it depends on the situation. They are the same.'

Dulal meanwhile managed to maintain his status through continued payments to the Chhatra League. As one labourer explained: 'Dulal *sardar* doesn't have a good situation but he still has lots of money – so he can pay his people to come and protect him.' Others told me that if Dulal *sardar* did not continue to pay he would have to flee the market. The situation returned to how it was prior to the strike, but resting on an uneasy peace. Dulal reclaimed his trucks but was too cautious to return to the bazaar, managing everything through his men. Rubel and the *jhupri* group retained theirs, and Parvez continued running his *samiti*, turning up infrequently at the bazaar, but only staying a short while and mostly coming during the daytime. Life seemed to settle down, only for it to become far more serious for Parvez and Rubel.

Bombing Your Way to Power

> All of us in the *jhupri* group support [the] BNP because ... This government isn't able to provide security ... Now poor people are going to the police station and giving their complaints but there's no justice for them. The rich people are capturing poor people's children. Nowadays we see that one kilo of rice is 50 taka, so how can people who have big families survive? The richest people in society are keeping the poor people under pressure, and that's why the poor people don't like the Awami League ... This is a country of democracy, it's not a country of kings. When a king dies his son comes to power. It's not like this here. It shouldn't be like those kings, so we should vote.
>
> —Rubel, *jhupri boro bhai*

The conflict with Dulal *sardar*, the Chhatra League and the police took place during a highly unsettled period in the recent history of Bangladesh.

The controversial general election of early 2014 had been directly administered by the incumbent Awami League after the caretaker government system had been repealed through a constitutional amendment in 2011. *Hartal*s, the typical tool of Bangladeshi politics used for decades by opposition parties to pressure the government, were largely stifled. Only a few years previously the call for a *hartal* had closed down cities, led to shuttered shops, buses stowed away in parking lots and a serious threat of violence and unrest against those in power. By this point the net was closing in on the BNP. Political commentators and the BNP's own members were speculating that the decision to boycott had been a mistake. Unlike 1996, when the Awami League had mobilised a mass movement, there seemed to be insufficient appetite among the public or wider apparatus of the state, perhaps in part remembering back to the corruption and excesses of the early 2000s. Khaleda Zia meanwhile was put under effective house arrest (though in her office) and the BNP's wider attempts to organise blockades or rallies had little success.

Public appetite was not the only problem. The BNP was becoming widely recognised as a diminished force, failing under the weight of pressure inflicted through the security agencies. Ten or so years prior, the party would have looked to the likes of Picchi Hannan to orchestrate violence and maximise pressure on the government, but times had changed. Under their own hand these *santrashi* figures had been killed off, depriving them of the type of muscle they needed to compete, as leaders across the party would later lament to me.[6] After failing to mobilise a mass movement against the government, the BNP appeared to resort to more desperate and extreme measures to demonstrate their capability for violence and publicly question the ability of the ruling Awami League to maintain order. Between 5 January and 24 February 2015 there were approximately 119 deaths due to political violence in the country, including ruling party and opposition activists, as well as many civilians targeted in cocktail blasts in public spaces and petrol bombs on buses.[7]

The bombings that were marking Dhaka city were increasingly the topic of conversation among the *jhupri* labourers and myself. The CNG rides I took to and from the bazaar took on a different meaning when public spaces were being bombed. Newspaper reports gave opaque descriptions of the perpetrators behind such events, and each party pointed fingers at the other. For the Awami League, these were clearly the BNP's attempts to destabilise the country, and for the BNP they were an example of the Awami League's cunning, bombing their own streets to frame them. One of the *jhupri* van drivers portrayed the mechanics behind such bombings to me:

It's not people like you or me who throw these bombs. Why? I want to develop myself. I don't want to throw a bomb. I don't need to be listed in a police diary and go to jail. I have a family, I have a child. But if someone's sleeping in the corner, the *rasta-kangali-oshohi* [road-destitute-helpless], they will go to them, ask them if they want to work, and start convincing them. There will be a 'contract' of 10,000–20,000 taka, and they will give seven, eight, nine 'cocktail[s].' For him, he has no future. If you have a really bad situation, you don't have money, you can't eat three times a day, and then someone comes and asks you 'will you work?' then of course you will say yes. Their hunger is their greatest desire. Maybe he will hit a car, or maybe a 'meeting', and instead he will get 20,000 or 50,000 taka. Or maybe he will give you a gun and 1 lakh, saying you should take it, it will be helpful for you. You're thinking now you're starving, but if you get 1 lakh it will be good fortune. You just kill someone to get the money. He's a *kangali*. He needs money, and after throwing the bomb, if a person dies or a dog dies, it's not his problem.

At the end of December, I expressed fear to Rubel about continuing to come down to Kawran Bazaar. Not only did the group's *boro bhai*s have cases against them due to the conflict with Dulal, but 5 January 2015 had been lined up as a showdown, the one-year anniversary of the 2014 general elections, which the BNP had boycotted and the Awami League had therefore won by a landslide. Rubel agreed, 'there could be problems. It will be everywhere. There will be fighting, shooting, bombs, stabbings.' 'So maybe I shouldn't come down?' I suggested. He responded:

There won't be any problems because you're friends with the boys who would be doing it. And the main thing is that their target is the Awami League. In the fighting people can see from your face that you are a foreigner. But if someone gets inside the fight then what can be done? Otherwise we know you well, you can come, no problem.

My suspicions about their involvement had been sparked off by his comments, but others in the group seemed to express genuine fear about the spate of mysterious cocktail blasts and fires at Kawran Bazaar over the next month or so. These targeted buses, the police and the underpass beneath Kazi Nazrul Islam Avenue. On at least one occasion they made national news.[8] The report describes 'miscreants' throwing 'at least two crude bombs' at a bus in the north of the bazaar, hurting the driver. By this time, I had expanded my research sites southwards in the city, and only visited Kawran Bazaar a couple of times a week. In early February the intensity of buses and CNGs targeted as well as the occasional sound of cocktail bombs going off at my new research location by Dhaka University persuaded me to lay low and write for a couple of weeks, as well as spend time at the National Archives.

I returned to Kawran Bazaar on 23 February to find that the fates of Parvez and Rubel had changed quite dramatically. Around 10 February, Parvez was (so the *jhupri* group allege) suddenly taken by the RAB. A younger labourer in the group who witnessed the incident, described the informer Sajid walking along with the RAB who were dressed in 'white clothes' (civilian clothes). Pointing out Parvez, they allegedly grabbed him, and took him down to near WASA where, according to others, they tied him to Shumon's rickshaw van and 'crushed' or 'smashed' his hands and feet before arresting him. The night before I arrived (22 February), the RAB had reportedly returned around 7:30 pm taking Rubel, and he was at that point in Dhaka Central Jail.

The charges – which all the labourers in the *jhupri* group agreed were true – were that they had been 'doing BNP politics,' orchestrating the local bombings. They had been paying younger children associated with the *jhupri* group (and often the nearby NGO centres) to torch buses, start fires and throw Molotov cocktails.[9] Here it was not the group's connection to Ahsan that mattered, but upwards to the Swechasebek Dal, who others in the group later claimed had paid them to act. Not only had Rubel and Parvez been arrested, but other younger children in the group had similarly been detained, pointed out by the RAB source and reportedly charged with vandalising a car under BNP instructions. When I interviewed a younger member of the group, he expressed his anger that his own younger brother had been arrested, and described how the *boro bhai*s had pressured the younger children associated with the group:

> They [Rubel, Parvez, Azad] make them throw bombs. They put pressure on them. Like today I've come here to the centre, and if they ask me to clean the floor then I will do it, because otherwise I won't be able to come here tomorrow. So, it's like this. It's mandatory.

For some in the group, these arrests were a continuation of the consequences of their conflict with the *sardar*, though other (more informed and older members) were far sharper with the difference. Liton, for example, was adamant that this was entirely separate. In his own words:

> This time it is a political problem, but that time it wasn't political. That time he was taken by the police and charged. But this time he was captured by the RAB. And you know the RAB only captures those who do big crimes. If there

is a case placed then the police come to get you. But the RAB come with the law (section 54) that they just have doubt. They take [them] with 54, then beat them and get information.[10]

Liton's adamance that the previous conflict was not a *political* (*rajnatik*) problem is interesting given the clear involvement of the Chhatra League and the BNP, and Rubel's explanation of how problematic their BNP ties were at that stage. What it implies is that although that conflict involved political actors it concerned territory for work and personal rivalries, whereas the political violence here was at the behest of the BNP and focused on establishing the dominance of the BNP as a political force and coalition.

Members of the group described how now that Parvez and Rubel had been caught they would be beaten and information would be extracted from them, and that the RAB had a long list of people they would take one by one. First Rubel would be beaten, then another would be taken and so on. A number of the group reflected that Rubel would get out but would have to pay huge amounts of money. 'Maybe when he gets out, he will kill the source,' one said. By the time I caught up with events Parvez had been released on bail, having paid 50,000 taka.[11] His hands and feet were fractured and though he could walk, he could not work. He was staying with family on the outskirts of Dhaka and visited the bazaar occasionally by day, though his *samiti* had broken up and he therefore no longer received the daily 700 taka. As we walked slightly away from the bazaar towards Tejgaon station and therefore completely out of earshot, Liton told me how Parvez had got out of the situation, claiming that he had now become a *former*. They had beaten him and convinced him, saying he would get paid. 'He's really proud now. He thinks he's a big person again, saying that he's now an RAB person. He still has the BNP links, but they are quiet now.'

When later reflecting on events with younger rickshaw van drivers who were either within the *jhupri* group or worked nearby under different *sardar*s, I tried to steer conversations around to the tricky subject of Rubel and Parvez. By this point they had both been taken by the RAB, Parvez was out and Rubel in Dhaka Central Jail. I asked two younger labourers in the group Mamun and Salman about why – given all these problems – they did BNP politics. Mamun replied straight-faced and bluntly:

> Love. As you love your Labour Party,[12] they love their party ... If you like the Awami League then of course you will support them and never the BNP. If you support the BNP you will not like the Awami League.

The sense that they were motivated by *love* or conviction is also indicated in the passionate speech Rubel had given me, quoted at the beginning of this section. A younger labourer whose brother had been arrested reflected differently on their involvement, however, saying 'they get different opportunities from different political parties.' He continued,

> You know what the latest system is? It is to think about opportunities, then you just do the party which has power then you will get the opportunities. They are opportunists [*shubidabadi*]. I'm also an opportunist.

Liton had a similar analysis of their involvement: 'They do BNP because they think when they [the BNP] get into power, they will become very rich men.' For Parvez, Rubel and by extension the wider group, demonstrating a willingness to take risks was done with the hope of new opportunities. It was a speculation, a risky calculation that the opposition could gain power and they would be rewarded for the degree of their support. The hope was that they could gain more work, gain control of syndicates at the bazaar and find new political opportunities through the connection. Rubel's passionate speech to me in favour of the BNP (quoted at the beginning of this section) sat alongside him purposefully distancing himself from them when needed or disregarding any difference between the BNP and the Awami League. Labourers within the group described the relationship in terms of opportunities. As it turned out, it was not the wisest of calculations, but instead a source of disquiet and anxiety in the group. For months one particular member of the *jhupri* group Liton had been highly critical of their alignment to the BNP, not for any ideological reasons, but because he saw it as a futile political calculation. Indeed, he had very different plans for the group.

Notes

1. This can be when a ruling party body 'invites' them to a political event, so too when Rubel or Parvez invite *coolie*s to do politics. As Rubel put it: 'The *minti*s don't do politics like us. But when we do one of the parties then I know lots of *minti*s so I take them with us. When we make an offer to them they can't reject it, but they're not actually involved in any particular party.'
2. At the same time it should also be recognised that labourers sometimes move between *sardar*s, rickshaw van owners and areas, for example. Jibon once told me 'if you don't go to the [political] meeting then the *boro bhai* will get angry. You won't be able to keep a good relationship with him.' I asked him what's the

problem with that? He replied, 'It's not always a problem because I can find another *boro bhai*, there are so many. But everyone needs a *boro bhai*, they won't rent you a van otherwise so you can't work here.' In reality, however, these ties are formed over many years and decades, and the decision to leave the *jhupri* group would be a very difficult one for these labourers.

3. Retrospectively people's descriptions of Rubel's interests differed slightly. Salman's interpretation of Rubel's interests, for example, was: 'Rubel wants to split the work with the *sardar*, for 6 months he will take the orders, then the other 6 months the *sardar* will take them.'
4. The reference to old people from the group was to people who had previously been in the *jhupri* group but had moved on to more senior positions elsewhere.
5. As we saw earlier in the case of Picchi Hannan's affiliates, 'killer' is a common way of referring to hired muscle, and here means the Chhatra League.
6. Jackman (2023).
7. Bergman (2015).
8. *Daily Star* (2015).
9. Some of these children were the younger siblings of labourers within the *jhupri* group and others were scavengers and thieves at the market who associated with the *jhupri* group. As discussed, the *jhupri* group are a common entry point for young 'street children' seeking work or affiliation, due to the shared background, with most of the group having grown up at the bazaar.
10. Section 54 of the Code of Criminal Procedure empowers the authorities to arrest someone under suspicion of a crime.
11. It was unclear whom this was paid to, however. Some said it was to a lawyer while others said it was to the RAB.
12. I had been interrogated about my political affiliations in the United Kingdom, and word had evidently spread. Both English words, Labour and Party, have strong resonance in Bangla, and people had interpreted it as a positive sign about my potential involvement with the *jhupri* group.

6

(Not So) Friendly Societies

> For these twenty boys I've given four years of my life. I taught them honestly.
> With these twenty boys I will fight. If you want you can join us ...
> —Liton, speaking to me about his *samiti*

Parvez's *samiti* had seemed for much of my time with the *jhupri* group little more than a harmless side act to his role as a *boro bhai*. I knew that at least ostensibly the *samiti* was a savings group, where each of the seventy labourers deposited 10 taka daily, which he in principle would keep safe for them. I was aware, however, that Rubel, who had similarly run a *samiti* in the past, had been known to have in fact kept most of the capital. It was also clear that Parvez, unlike Rubel, did not own rickshaw vans apart from his own and did not hence receive income from renting them, nor did he work during the night, instead monitoring activities by the side and fielding questions from the labourers. I sensed then that Parvez was perhaps living on the *samiti* funds day to day. At times the money given to him was portrayed by the labourers less as a savings system and more as a tribute. When asked why they gave to the *samiti*, younger labourers in particular would often reply along the lines of: 'He is our *boro bhai*, that's why we give it.' The way it was spoken of was as *chanda*, with the complexity this word entails. The *samiti* then seemed to stand alongside the other ways Parvez earned: money from rounding up the boys to attend rallies, some from more dangerous acts of political violence, some from a short-lived syndicate, some from the thieving of vegetable sacks and some from the labourers themselves.

What then also appeared clear was that while larger bodies such as the Van Workers' Union were intertwined with party politics, whatever this *samiti* was, it appeared far less meaningful politically than the rallies the group attended or the bombings they orchestrated. A common portrayal of similar societies in academic literature[1] is furthermore as mutual aid associations understood within a 'development' paradigm, seen as a way of overcoming short-term horizons or mobilising groups in a 'civic' manner to better negotiate with the state. When events with the Chhatra League, the police and eventually the RAB were unfolding, the significance such *samiti*s can take was, however, revealed through the manoeuvrings of Liton, one of Parvez and Rubel's strongest critics from within the *jhupri* group. In Chapter 5 we saw how *boro bhai*s attempt to become bigger. Here we look one step further down the chain, to how labourers envisage becoming *boro bhai*s.

Liton's *Samiti*

> You know how Liton *bhai* looks. He looks like a bad guy from a new film at the cinema. He looks like the villain.
>
> —Hassan, *jhupri* labourer

Liton never expected to find himself sleeping at the side of a road. Growing up in Dhaka in the 1980s, the city's streets had been a playground, where he would roam with friends after school and play cricket in nearby fields, before returning to the comfort of his lower middle-class home.[2] At the time the city was a far calmer, greener place. Patches of jungle still dotted the city centre, alongside open fields and waterways, with less of the generic apartment blocks which today plaster most of the metropolis. By the time Liton entered his teenage years, however, the significance of the city's streets in his life had changed. Protests were mounting against Ershad's military rule, and Liton himself remembers burning an effigy of Ershad in front of the Press Club while only a school student and the pride in seeing his photo in newspapers the next day. At the same time, he saw *santrashi*s rise to power in his neighbourhood, figures he described fearing. In response, he found the 'shelter' of a *boro bhai*, as he put it, in this instance a prominent local politician and industrialist, who was known to have patronised a rival gangster to the one who ruled his neighbourhood. Through such relationships Liton not only sought political status but also work, and leveraged such contacts as a 'contractor', specialising in commercial decorating.

And so began a career in the opaque world of political muscle. In later years he would find himself close not to the Awami League, but the BNP, mobilising a group of forty young men behind the party rebels who sought to challenge the party chief Khaleda Zia in the mid-2000s. He described paying 1 lakh taka every week to provide the *yaba* that his group enjoyed, and which had started to become popular at the time. As he described it: 'I did different politics. I mixed with everyone. BNP, Awami League. I have lots of *boro bhai*s who will save me if I need it.' Liton was thus connected to senior politicians in Dhaka and was able to mobilise dozens of men on the streets as needed. This, he claimed, had brought him a degree of notoriety. He had been armed ('I used to carry a gun that was as long as my leg,' he said) and had scars from what he claimed were bullet wounds from clashes.

In the early 2010s, however, life took an unexpected turn. Around the time this research began, Liton fell from life as a political cadre, with a home, wife and young child, to life on the streets. He always kept the precise story well-guarded but this transition was connected at different times to bad luck, to the fact his wife had died, to suffering from mental health problems and to 'politics', said as if the word itself provided sufficient explanation of his circumstances. In his teenage years one of his haunts had been Kawran Bazaar which he used to visit with friends not to buy vegetables, but the cheap locally brewed alcohol that was sold from the railway *basti* for 10 taka a bottle. It was here, now in his late thirties with a young son being looked after by his sister, that he returned.

At first, Liton found work through Dulal *sardar*, unloading vegetables in the *jhupri* lane, but aggrieved by the cut he took, joined the *jhupri* van drivers. The days of work took their toll. As a decorator he had managed the contracts, not the paint. Here he had to sleep in the racket of the bazaar, being pestered by mosquitoes and the fear of being pickpocketed. Despite living and being friends with the *jhupri* labourers, he was distinct. He had not grown up on the streets. He wore jeans rather than a *lunghi*, kept his money in a wallet not wrapped up and as a friend who met him would later tell me, his spoken Bangla suggested an educated middle-class background. He would pepper our conversations with details of the historic figures and events he knew and was fascinated in particular by European dictators.

Amongst most of the *jhupri* group, dissatisfaction with the *boro bhai*s was rarely articulated in my presence. For younger labourers, the appearance of loyalty and deference to Rubel and Parvez was crucial, and only those at the fringes of the group could risk avoiding their demands to come to political rallies or conflicts. For well-established labourers, these figures may not have been perfect, but they were one of them, people they had grown up alongside and knew they could depend upon. Liton, by contrast, had seen the world beyond the *jhupri* lane. He claimed various mid-ranking leaders in the city chapters of the Awami League, BNP and their affiliates as 'friends' and that an 'aunt' figure

(Not So) Friendly Societies

and others close to him had been members of parliament (MPs; though people questioned the strength of such ties given his presence at the bazaar). He himself had once been a businessman and contractor, lived briefly in Singapore and led a group of forty young drug-fuelled men on the losing side of the infighting seen in the BNP during the caretaker government period.

Part of Liton's grievances with the *jhupri boro bhai*s were then driven by the sense that it was he who had a rightful place at the top. His background, sense of class superiority, education and the hierarchy that comes with age and greater political experience all logically meant that his natural place within the group was as a *boro bhai* giving orders, not taking them from men ten years his junior. But his grievances also stemmed from specific criticisms waged against Rubel and Parvez, and anger at the direction the group was heading in under their control: 'I hate them. They said they would develop everyone but they just developed themselves and their families,' he described to me. In the brief period that the *jhupri boro bhai*s controlled new goods to unload, Rubel had allocated these to his syndicate rather than the group as a whole. Although they had been mobilised to take control from the rival *sardar* on the basis of class discourse and promises about all benefitting, in practice it appeared that the group's leadership were consolidating control and building their political power to the detriment of some ordinary members. Liton's claim then was that Rubel – like the *sardar* – was taking, or going to take, an unfair cut from the fee given to the group for conveying the goods, as well as mediating access to work within the group unfairly. With his authority extended he had greater power over the *jhupri* van drivers. But Rubel was not just being unjust, he had a bad character:

> Rubel is no good. He has his beard to show people he is pious but actually he isn't. Inside he is evil. Do you know how he is? Just one year ago he used to sleep on top of the water tank at WASA with a prostitute. How could he manage to sleep at night with a prostitute like this? He has his wife, son and daughter.

This anger extended to Parvez because of his *samiti* – 'he's dangerous, he is a trouble for everyone. He's not thinking in the right way, not for the development of everyone. He just thinks about himself.' In practice Liton claimed that Parvez was simply taking the 700 taka a day collected from the *samiti* and resting, not bothering to drive his van but sitting at the side drinking tea. Rather than treating the money deposited as savings, it was taken as income. Around 70,000 taka had been given, allowing Parvez to 'go home and eat well.' These *boro bhai*s, he claimed, had 'been given' a responsibility, power and role by the group, which they had misused.

Parvez's *samiti* was not seen as problematic simply because the money was being embezzled rather than being kept safe, but because for Liton, it was associated with the affiliation the group had developed with the BNP. Liton hence described Parvez's act of starting the *samiti* as 'doing politics' and associated it with the group's affiliation to the Sweshasebek Dal leader Muzaffar. Parvez has only been doing politics for six months he would insist, 'I've been doing it since birth, is he really that senior to me? Rubel treats me like he's my senior. He sometimes orders me around. But I'm his senior.' In the build-up to events with the Chhatra League, police and RAB, Liton would reiterate to me over tea and cigarettes how risky the alignment with the BNP was and how it jeopardised the safety of them all.

When tension built among the *jhupri* labourers of Kawran Bazaar in late 2014, Liton hence decided to break away from the group, and found work delivering goods around Dhaka by night, learning how to ride a rickshaw van with chains and brakes. He nonetheless still kept close to many in the group, would socialise with and sleep near others on their vans or on the benches under the lane's *jhupri*s. The work earned him the equivalent of his old *jhupri* income, but crucially meant both that he had not been involved in the fighting with the Chhatra League, and that he did not rely day to day on Parvez or Rubel for access to work in the *jhupri* lane. It therefore brought a distance from these *boro bhai*s, a freedom and ability to survive without relying on the work they mediated access to. He later explained it:

> Rubel and Parvez have been working on the BNP's side. They've been vandalising, torching, throwing bombs ... that's why I gave up being with them because I knew I would be blamed and captured like them. If I stayed with them the RAB would also capture me. But I realised a long time ago so I slowly left them ... and I'm fine now.

Distancing himself from the group was, in his mind, his first strategic step to controlling the group. Out of this situation, Liton attempted to craft a new role for himself within the *jhupri* group, not as a lowly labourer, but as a *boro bhai*, a leader. The problem for Liton, however, was that he was relatively new to the area: 'How could I have become a leader four years ago? No one knew me, no one could trust me. Parvez and Rubel have grown up here, they know everyone.'

It was only now, after years of spending time together that he was sufficiently known to be able to gain the trust of the other labourers.

Liton's plan for his future began with forming a *samiti*. Using Shumon, his most trusted friend, he began signing labourers up for the *samiti* in early January 2015, carrying a small notebook to record transactions and keeping the funds in Shumon's locked wooden box next to a nearby government building ('What will you do if Shumon loses the money from his trunk,' I once asked. 'I will make him sell his rickshaw van!'). Every day he would ponder on the name he should give the *samiti*, frustrated that he could not think of an appropriate identity. Rather than a *samiti* that would end at some fixed point, he wanted to create a fund that would be 'for life'. Labourers therefore deposited daily (30 taka or more if they could give it), and from the collective fund it was planned that people would eventually be able to borrow (rather than be returned) money, without paying interest. Within the next two or three months he thought he could help between two and five of the members. Within one year he would have 1 or 2 lakh taka. 'What can people do with it?' I asked. 'With this money you can buy your own rickshaw van, you can buy goods in the evening and sell them in the morning, give me back the capital and walk away with the profits.' Liton often described how people could buy better clothes and change how they were perceived at the bazaar.

As Liton attempted to build this role for himself, he also began acting like a leader, appearing strong, wise and reliable, smoking less marijuana and giving advice more confidently to the labourers in his *samiti*. He began openly carrying his notebook, which he kept in the breast pocket of his shirt and in which he detailed who was in the group, the deposits made and the total *samiti* fund. This symbolic indicator of status was particularly impressive for those of the group who could not read and write and was similar to how labour leaders and other figures of authority would carry notebooks. His education and manner of speaking also brought a respect from others at the bazaar. He would help people fill in government forms when needed (some were applying for government identity documents [IDs]) and chat to women on the Facebook app on mobile phones. But Liton's appeal was not only his perceived dependability, or the financial benefits of the *samiti*, nor were his ambitions confined to the *samiti* itself. Why people joined his *samiti* was also his vision for what it would become and enable them to do politically at Kawran Bazaar. The *samiti* then, was only the first step.

A Political Vision and Failure

> Liton wants to become a leader, he's the *samiti* 'cashier,' but people won't cooperate with him.
>
> —Rakib, *jhupri* labourer

Over the course of a couple of months Liton detailed his plan to me, stage by stage. The first step, as we saw, was to establish a *samiti* of thirty men from among the *jhupri* labourers. The second step (which never came to fruition) was then to align the *samiti* with a local branch of an affiliate body of the Awami League. In particular he had the Krishak League in mind. The next step, he explained to me, was to use the group to contest the roles of both Dulal *sardar* and the *jhupri boro bhai*s Parvez and Rubel and take hold of the *jhupri* lane. The final step was for the *samiti* to expand. He imagined how as a '*samiti* for life', it would eventually become a 'limited company'. They would buy land or rent their own office and this would have a *karam* (carrom) board and television (TV). Members would also have their own 'visiting cards'. Later on, this 'limited company' was framed as an NGO, and Liton suggested I could be the 'chairman'.

The significance of the case is not whether much of this happened, but that this was how Liton envisaged taking power, how he understood the significance of the *samiti* and how he marketed it to potential members. The first step in Liton's plan can be understood as a way of binding other labourers around interdependencies weighted in his favour.[3] Being capital poor, few labourers have the thousands of taka needed to invest in small business opportunities at the bazaar.[4] The *samiti* would create real material opportunities and therefore a solid base, which Liton as their leader and the *samiti* cashier, would provide for them.

In Liton's mind the *samiti* would also establish him as a leader in the wider world of the bazaar. The presence of a strong and functioning *samiti* with Liton at the head was a declaration of intentions, and therefore of symbolic significance when viewed from the outside. It demonstrated that he, Liton, was the clear leader of a group of labourers, who were bound to him and committed to his leadership. When Liton hence promoted his *samiti* to potential members, he would openly discuss not only his plans for loans and business, but more importantly his plans about the rival *sardar*, about Rubel and Parvez, about the Krishak League and about who they as a group could be within the bazaar. Critical to how he positioned himself and the *samiti* were his connections to political leaders. When Liton attempted to recruit a labourer (whose younger brother was later detained for his involvement with the bombings), for example, he described the advantages of joining his *samiti*:

> I know the metropolitan Jubo League chairperson, X *bhai*, Y the organisational secretary, they are my friends. He has lots of power. He does north city politics. He manages the whole north side of the city and I'm with him. Do you know what this means? If he makes a call to Saad [the Jubo League leader] or anyone else here so that people don't put a case at the police station, or even if he calls the police station – even if they have committed murder – it's no problem for him. Don't you understand? Their party is ruling now. So if the police don't listen to him who will they listen to? They are my friends from my childhood, I can call them and there won't be a problem any time.

Liton's daily collections from the labourers were thus being made when Rubel and Parvez were in a tight spot. They, it seemed, had brought trouble onto the doorstep, while Liton was claiming to offer an alternative course. Parvez and Rubel's links, he would argue, had clearly become a liability for the group, based on an unrealistic calculation that the BNP could gain power, while signing with the Awami League provided security and opportunities. This of course angered Rubel who became for a period frosty with me, trying to slight me in public (for example, by using the informal pronoun for you [*tumi*] instead of the formal [*apni*]). This was not helped by Shumon's public insistence that I was with Liton, for example by shouting in the bazaar for everyone to hear that 'there's only one Liton, and one David at Kawran Bazaar!'

Political affiliation for Liton had very little to do with ideas or ideology. He claimed to have been a BNP leader elsewhere in Dhaka but insisted that in Kawran Bazaar it did not matter because he did not have a BNP 'signpost'. Indeed, when I asked him what he would do if the BNP got into power, he would nonchalantly say 'I will do BNP,' as if it were a silly question. Such links were flaunted to potential recruits. They were made more believable by Liton's class background, the fact he said hello to certain leaders when they passed through the area, as well as by the 'visiting cards' of local politicians that he would ceremoniously retrieve from his wallet, as if proving his connections and establishing his claims of friendships to *boro bhai*s in power.[5] These gestures gave the sense that Liton was closer to the world of tenders, *chanda*, motorcycles and power that these figures represented.

Liton's *samiti* was then understood in context not as a neutral mutual-aid association, but as an attempt to manoeuvre within the political order.

'What will your relationship with the Krishak League be like?' I once enquired of Liton: 'I won't need to give them money, they will give me money. If I take money then they will use me. Nothing else is required – they need manpower and we have people.' Liton imagined keeping five people around him at all times as his *bodyguard*, and after registering with the Krishak League, would challenge the rival *sardar* in the way Rubel failed.

> First I will register [the *samiti*] then I will fight Dulal [the rival] *sardar*. Maybe I will take an AK47. I will solve the situation. He has money, he has many *goonda*s, *mastan*s, he can make all of them come. No problem we can also call many *mastan*s. We have many *mastan*s. He is senior so he has had his turn but now we want to do it ...[6]

In forming a *samiti* and attempting to mobilise labourers under him, Liton's intentions were high risk. As he said to me once, 'I have to take a big risk, because I need to get married again. I have to take care of my son, so won't I take the risk now?' Liton had come to the point where he felt confident enough that he knew people, knew how things worked and that he had built up sufficient respect as a potential leader to take the risk. And at the same time, he also felt he had wasted so many years, he was getting older, the work was getting physically harder and he needed to move on with his life and become something more.

Liton's vision and formation of his *samiti* provoked diverging reactions. Although some gave him their confidence and began depositing in his *samiti*, many did not. Liton was able to attract twenty members, but not the thirty he had intended. Some labourers questioned and even ridiculed him. The key issue was trust. From the perspective of the *choto bhai*s they wanted to know whether Liton could be trusted with their loyalty, their labour and their futures. Shumon only half-jokingly called him their *guru* while others outside the *samiti* called him the 'educated crazy man'. People, however, questioned his family situation and ability to care: 'He doesn't go to see his son often, does he really care for him?' a young potential recruit to the *samiti* asked me when considering whether to join. They described him as sometimes doing things that 'are beyond explanation'. They questioned his ability to show respect for, 'love' and 'adore' his *choto bhai*s. Salam, a *jhupri* labourer, explained his view on Liton's *samiti*:

> If he doesn't give importance to the people who will make him leader then how will he become a leader one day? If you take ten people and want to become a

leader but don't 'adore' them, then how will you become a leader? Will people love you? He has thirty people. He wants to take twenty people to do politics and manage the area with ten people. He wants to be a big person, do politics, keep a pistol with him and get a big name.

Liton's ambitions were then to control the contracts at the time under Dulal like a labour leader and control a side of the bazaar as a political leader. But 'he lays his hands on us [hits, slaps], gets angry, how can we make him our leader?' another labourer Hassan asked me rhetorically. People did not trust him with their money; they feared he would run away once the *samiti* was large enough, as *samiti* leaders often do. Not everyone was therefore won over. Salam reflected further on Liton's *samiti*: 'It's bad, in Bangladesh no one believes anyone, a brother doesn't believe a brother, so how can I trust him [enough] to give him my money? If I gave him my money now when the situation at the bazaar is so unstable, what will happen to it?' Some, like Salam, made fun of him too much to take him seriously as a leader. His actions directly challenged Parvez and Rubel's leadership, and for a period tension openly rose between him and these leaders. Though attracting some members, most of the *jhupri* group remained loyal to Parvez and Rubel. Tension built and talk of 'throwing him out' of the bazaar became common. As another labourer put it: 'I will make Liton leave this place, this guy isn't good, he wants to become a leader but won't be able to. I will throw him out. I will throw everyone who is educated out.'

By the time I left Dhaka in April 2015 after my main stretch with the *jhupri* labourers, Liton's *samiti* had collapsed. Rather than end in confrontation, people seemed to simply not trust him enough for it to continue, with members leaving the *samiti* one by one as their confidence in him ebbed. Shumon, his once close friend and follower, had aligned himself with a low-level Awami League leader elsewhere in the bazaar who was 'using him,' as Liton put it. Liton was left resentful, describing Shumon as not thinking in the right way, as being stupid, and the others as being too uneducated to make the *samiti* work. Meanwhile Parvez's *samiti* had also collapsed after he had been arrested and beaten by the RAB. Liton was renting a van from a young van owner in another part of Kawran Bazaar. He seemed to be integrating himself with that group, though he appeared again frustrated to be ordered around by someone a couple of decades younger than him.

Hossain's Street Vendor *Samiti*

> I've seen the hardship they go through, that's why I can't take money from them.
> —Hossain, hawkers' *samiti* chairman and ward-level Awami League Vice-president

Liton's *samiti* was not an eccentric and unusual idea, but arguably a common path to status and authority among the working classes. Around 100 metres south of where Liton hatched his plans, is an example of someone who took a similar path more successfully. The Jubo League leaders of Kawran Bazaar, Kazi and Saad, may have a strong hold on the *chandabaji* networks that invisibly carve up Kawran Bazaar, however, their authority is not total. Around the edges are other sources of intermediation. To the south of the bazaar we find the imposing figure of Hossain, whose long white *panjabi* houses a stocky frame, a deep voice that booms across the bazaar and who towers physically over most, including myself. His demeanour commands respect, and he is given plenty as a ward-level Awami League leader, covering half of Kawran Bazaar. His business card testifies to this status, having styled himself 'Prince' Hossain.

Hossain's journey to leadership is a convoluted one by his own description, having been a restaurant and shop owner in a century-old brothel in nearby Narayanganj that was demolished decades ago as part of a political dispute between the notorious ruling Awami League MP and a rival from the BNP. When in business, the 5,000 sex workers and 24-hour brothels had given his restaurant steady custom, but without it, he could not even pay his chefs. Six months after the last sex workers had left, he closed down, and tried to migrate abroad, but the firm he paid failed to process his visa and tried to steal his money, prompting him to go and 'slap the manager in the face,' as he now casts events. With few opportunities, he moved to central Dhaka demoted in status and beginning a new life as a petty hawker selling clothes on the streets adjacent to Kawran Bazaar, near the five-star Sonargaon hotel. Living in a *basti* within walking distance, he worked here 'under the sun and rain, suffering all sorts of challenges in the open air,' as he portrayed it.

At the time, the hawkers on this stretch of pavement had little unity, and none among them was 'strong' as he put it. When the police came, their shops were regularly destroyed, and they faced exactions from 'extortionists' and 'terrorists' like Picchi Hannan's group. On one occasion he fainted from the heat and exhaustion, yet no one took him to hospital out of fear that they would have to pay the medical costs. And so Hossain decided to take action:

(Not So) Friendly Societies

I thought it can't continue like this. So I built relationships with the police and mixed with the *santrashi* types. I became familiar to them. I told them [Picchi Hannan's group] 'I am an unemployed man, I am poor, If you allow me to, I can survive here somehow. There are lots like me, we are helpless, where can we go if people disturb us?'

Hossain described his attempts to unify the hawkers as 'grouping', meaning that 'if anyone quarrels with one of us, or tries to take anything from us, then all of us will come to resist them.' In order to help the hawkers lead a better life and help them raise their children, he united them by forming a *samiti*, of which he is the 'chairman'. At the same time, he also built relationships with the police and the *santrashi*s. All of this was cast to me as an act of self-sacrifice, or as he put it: 'I didn't want to be involved in politics, but I got involved for them, to see if I could bring them some benefits.'

Hossain's *samiti* incorporates all the hawkers along this particular stretch of pavement, most of whom sell colourful men's clothes. These forty hawkers each contribute 100 taka a day to the *samiti*, which is kept in a bank account under Hossain's control. The *samiti* has multiple functions and in the jargon of savings and credit is both a ROSCA and an ASCA. Part of the 100-taka contribution is taken as savings, distributed to the hawkers on a yearly basis at Eid. Another part is used for the general *samiti* fund, from which they give a number of benefits. Hawkers have few options to get small loans but can take up to 20,000 taka from the *samiti* fund, with a repayment of 200 taka per day including interest. The fund also covers the costs of monthly meetings among the hawkers led by Hossain in which they discuss challenges, how business is going and potential new members. If someone wants to join the *samiti*, they get to know them and watch their business for a year before they are allowed entry. If a hawker dies then they give 5,000 taka to their family and collectively pay for an air-conditioned car to take the body back to their home village.

Although unregistered, the *samiti* has a name, individual ID cards, stationery and a slogan. The demand of the *samiti* in seeking registration is that they are 'rehabilitated' – given space where they can open shops formally. This is central to their identity and part of the *samiti* mantra: 'Save your money and make a market.' The *samiti* has even started to collect funds from the members (2,000 taka per person) as a form of down payment on their space, which, Hossain insisted, they would get back after they have moved to the market. When discussing the *samiti* with me Hossain is clear that this is a service he gives to the hawkers. As such it differs in his view from how street hawkers are typically managed, as he described it:

> Inside the market there is another system, that is for the party. They take 100–150 [taka] from each hawker. The people involved in the party take the money. Here I could take the money, but I don't, because I have suffered here, I can tell how bitter the suffering was.

Although Hossain's narrative of the *samiti* is that it is essentially an act of self-sacrifice and loyalty to the hawkers on his part, he is also candid that it helps him politically. It is important to remember here that for Hossain, starting the *samiti* was associated with 'doing politics'. And it seems to have served him well. When we first met, he was a member of the ward chapter of the Awami League, and in later meetings he had become the vice-president (and acting president on account of the president's illness). Others in the *samiti* are also involved in politics, and collectively these forty men 'helped me a lot to become vice-president. They came to all the meetings and events with me.' Hossain is proud of the photos on his mobile phone with the local MP and home minister whom he described as being close to. This has also enabled him to improve his personal life (his son studies at college and he has built a two-storeyed house in T&T colony, which he has painted and which 'is only possible because I am in politics').

*Samiti*s such as that run by Hossain are a common form of intermediation among street vendors in Dhaka (although in others you have to pay more per day, Hossain insisted). Elsewhere in Dhaka it is common to hear of the *samiti*s that have started and shut, the money that has been lost and the distrust they have bred. Looking at such arrangements from above, *samiti*s can often be conceptualised alongside the *linemen* and other pockets that are filled by *chanda*. A left-wing hawker leader aligned to the Awami League described how if 100 taka is split between the party and the police: 'Fifty will go to the police, 25 to the "political elites" and 25 to the "hawker leaders" ... like the *linemen*, *samiti*s, the leaders in the hawkers' *samiti*.' A crime journalist sketched out to me the place of such *samiti*s in relation to the system of *linemen*:

> *Samiti*s are like an umbrella. Say there are five shopkeepers here, they form a body, they go under a *samiti*, the *samiti* will protect them. They give money to the *samiti*, and the *samiti* distributes the money to the police and the party. They preserve the relationship. They protect their interests ... Those who represent the hawkers' *samiti*, they represent the hawkers, but they are not hawkers.

They are dominated by political leaders, who give shelter to the illegal hawkers. The situation of *linemen* depends. They can sometimes be recruited by the hawkers' *samiti*, but where there is no *samiti*, they are working as the middlemen [*dalal*s]. The hawkers *samiti*s are on the big footpaths. But where there are no *samiti*s, there are *linemen*.

These perspectives then suggest that although *samiti*s can often be framed in normative terms (both by wider literature and in context), in practice they sit alongside other forms of intermediation orchestrated by actors within the ruling party and state. In the case of Hossain, not only did his *samiti* help his political career, but equally his political career has helped his *samiti*: 'There are lots of advantages [to being in politics]. I can talk directly to the OC [officer in-charge of the police station] or even the minister.' Day-to-day life for these hawkers presents all sorts of problems, being in effect surrounded by economically powerful actors who do not want them there. On one side there is the five-star hotel intent on clearing the pavement and wanting higher end shops to attract their guests. On the other side offices complain of the mess and inability to even walk on the pavement. 'We're up against all of these challenges, but we are doing business by keeping good relations with all the political people.'

The relationship with the local thana is crucial to sustaining these businesses. On a monthly basis the hawkers face a 'mobile court' which is directed through the local thana and for which they are given warning: 'The day before it happens, we are told by the police to be ready. We have a man at the thana, who comes to us,' allowing them to pack up all their goods and stalls with time to spare. This relationship is facilitated by a 'lineman', but unlike the *linemen* described within Kawran Bazaar, he is 'our man', appointed by Hossain to collect and distribute the rate agreed upon with the local police. This *lineman* manages Hossain's local gas business, and 'informs me of everything that happens here. He stays with me. He is very good, he prays five times a day.' The money the *lineman* gives to the police (which he described as a small amount while squeezing his thumb and index finger together) then goes, Hossain described, to a number of the police – the duty policeman, the patrol police, the local sub-inspector in the nearby police box and then the OC – 'each is given according to their status.' Similarly when new police are posted in the area Hossain is one of the men they turn to for orientating themselves. When new plain-clothed Special Branch police are posted to the area they 'ask me to inform them if there is a procession or rally [from the opposition]'.[7]

Hossain's status and contacts also protect the hawkers from other *linemen* and *chamcha*s operating under different Awami League bodies nearby. During my research, for example, some cadres of the Jubo League began forcing hawkers to give them 20 taka each. One of the hawkers called Hossain, and he contacted the cadre, telling them (as he put it):

> I am the leader here. You can't take anything without informing me. You must stop. They said that the *boro bhai* has sent us to do these things … I told them I understand, but without talking to me, you can't do it.

For the hawkers then, Hossain is their anchor on the pavement, the figure they turn to for problems little and large and who must navigate the city on their behalf, while utilising the status gained from his *samiti* to solidify himself as a local political leader. In representing the hawkers through his small *samiti*, Hossain is also situated in relation to a wider network of societies and bodies that are organised in this sector. The 'Workers Party', for example, claims eighteen smaller organisations as part of their movement for hawkers' rights and looks to small *samiti*s such as Hossain's to gain traction on the streets ('I'm busy, I don't have time to attend their programmes' Hossain said of them). Other bodies such as the Chinnamul Hawkers' Samiti (rootless hawkers association), which is the oldest of the hawkers' groups, had a strong presence in the past, although at the time of the research appeared to be politically out of favour. A body associated with the Awami League – the 'Hawkers League' – are present elsewhere in Dhaka but not here ('They are opportunists, they have bad intentions, so we don't get involved with them,' Hossain described).

The next step for Hossain's *samiti* is government registration. Although all of his members carry identity cards, these only give the impression of an official, legal status. In practice they are an imitation of officialdom, carrying the weight that Hossain is accorded by virtue of his Awami League designation and the contacts that he sustains. Hossain's hopes for registration were that it would enable them to find permanent and secure spaces for their businesses, and that with registration, the government would help them manage the election of a secretary, chairman and executive committee from among their members. Attempts to register the group have so far been unsuccessful. In a meeting with an inspector of the cooperatives department (under the Ministry of Local Government, Rural Development and Co-operatives), Hossain was disheartened to be told that his *samiti* was too small, and that they needed at least

100 members to register. He put the difficulty in gaining more members down to the fact that time invested with the *samiti* would lead his other businesses to suffer. A more critical reading, however, would point to the fact that adjacent street vendors fall under the authority of the Jubo League's *linemen*, and any attempts to expand would likely lead to direct political confrontation with Saad and Kazi, some of the most powerful local leaders at Kawran Bazaar.

Notes

1. Appadurai (2002); Archer (2012); d'Cruz and Mudimu (2012).
2. Liton described how his father had arrived in Dhaka dressed in a veil, fleeing from his home district of Khulna, where his uncle had murdered the assistant of a local government official in a dispute, and he, as the eldest of the family, had been implicated. He later spent a lot of money and managed to be acquitted. His family was associated with the radical politics of the left, the Sarbahara Party (Proletariat Party) once led by Siraj Shikder.
3. Writing in a different context anthropologist Lawrence Rosen (2010: 3) argues that 'figures of authority, then, must build up their constellations of indebtedness in order for people to begin to attribute to them the qualities of someone who will share benefits with his dependents and not (in the local idiom) "eat" everything himself'. This was the role the *samiti* played in Liton's plans.
4. With around 5,000–7,000 taka the labourers explained they would be able to buy and sell on some goods from the *arotdar*s and, if all went to plan, make around 500–800 taka over the course of a day.
5. It is very common for low-level or aspiring leaders to keep small piles of slightly frayed cards in their wallets. These are proudly brought out and paraded and then delicately replaced as one would a valuable document in a safe. I found street-corner party-affiliated leaders with cards of not only local political leaders, but even those of MPs and ministers.
6. The term *mastan* is used here in the same way as *goonda* or 'killer', to indicate a for-hire fighter. Liton previously spoke of the *jhupri* group itself as *goonda*s.
7. Anjaria (2011) similarly references a 'union' in his analysis of hawkers in Mumbai, noting that it provided a degree of protection for hawkers in the face of the police. The account also contains an evocative description of the collaboration between a hawkers' union leader and the police in orchestrating his very visible arrest as a means for the police to demonstrate their efficacy in cleaning up the streets, and the union leader his commitment to suffer for the union's cause.

7
When Crime Is Order

Syndicates in Bangladesh are felt in many ways. They are felt in the higher prices when the supply of goods is manipulated. They are seen in the shoddy quality of public infrastructure when contractors skim contracts and skip on inputs. They are felt in the hefty sums demanded for jobs in the public sector. They are felt in the violence and conflicts between rival political leaders and their followers when they compete for dominance. But perhaps most pressingly, they also felt in the relationships that people sustain to get by in everyday life. The core argument developed here has been that behind many of the diverse dependencies that people rely upon to get work, seek security, find opportunities and other resources, lie syndicates. Syndicates are the coercive control that a particular group or network exercises over a resource to their advantage. Many syndicates are embodied by individuals sustaining that coercive hold on a resource and mediating access to it. Many intermediaries are thus racketeers.

For some, the syndicates that carve up the lanes of Kawran Bazaar could be seen as somehow peripheral to life in the city, distant from where the real capital or authority lies. These dirty streets feel much like the city's other creases and crevices such as the *basti*s, transport terminals, parks or footpaths where the lower classes live and work. Similarly, when syndicates come to public light, we could easily get the impression that these are a scattered phenomenon, examples of particularly egregious politicians or officials. In drawing together odd combinations of actors such as the leader of an Awami League affiliate body and opaque *lineman*, as well as a very wide range of sectors, they seem idiosyncratic. Others might also characterise the politics we find here as that at the 'margins' of the state.[1] Yet the story told here is that syndicates should be seen as fundamental to Bangladeshi politics. Though the labourers may be poor, and the streets may be dirty, there is nothing marginal about the politics we find here.

This is the lifeblood of the nation's politics in microcosm. This is the core, the unstable bedrock on which politicians build and parties rest. Syndicates are not merely the whims of greedy people in power but serve to sustain the authority of political leaders. They not only enrich them, but help keep groups of cadres on their side, help them win elections, control their territories and confront rivals both within and outside their own party. This is the pool of labour from which rallies are filled, status is won and spectacular acts of violence orchestrated.[2]

The formal apparatus of the state (such as the security agencies) is deeply embroiled in the hierarchies we find here. Local party leaders maintain close relationships with the local officer in-charge (OC) and other security agencies, often dividing up the income from lucrative local syndicates, each getting their cut. For state employees such syndicates appear crucial for those who can and wish to leverage their authority to create and control them, in part because of the extraordinary sums some state officials seem to pay to obtain their jobs, transfers and promotions.[3] Below party leaders it is also partly through the cast of different intermediaries that security agencies exercise control on the streets, such as through *source*s and leaders like Parvez who are informers on the side. This then is often what the state means on the streets. Ultimately, syndicates help sustain the party and state muscle needed to maintain political authority and to dominate rivals. It is in this sense that syndicates are crucial to how political order is sustained in society.

Across the Indian border in West Bengal, the media speaks of the 'Syndicate Raj', where 'goons' run rackets at the behest of politicians, demanding protection money from a range of businesses: property developers to restaurant owners. In academia and the wider media, similar terms are deployed to describe diverse contexts, such as 'mafia states', 'gangster states', 'protection racket states' or as a recent book describes much of South Asia, 'Mafia Raj'. The point of all such labels is that in certain contexts crime appears so entrenched in or inseparable from a nation's politics, that it has come to define political life. The story told here from the lanes of Kawran Bazaar has interrogated what this looks and feels like in everyday life, thereby illuminating how deep the nexus of crime and politics runs. In so doing it also advances a way of approaching this theoretically by positing a relationship between intermediation, syndicates and political order, which will hopefully have resonance far beyond Bangladesh. But this story also raises broader questions concerning how the relationship between crime and order changes over time. This calls us to carefully consider the ways in which intermediaries change, but also to look beyond these changes to recognise the underlying consistency that draws together hundreds of years of history, thereby suggesting that in essence syndicates are far from unique to contemporary politics. This concluding chapter expands on the core arguments developed thus far to reflect on three themes concerning the relationship between political order and crime: history, form and change.

Twenty-first Century Revenue Farmers

> The monopoly of force as the prohibition to use violence unless sanctioned by the ruler was closely connected to the fiscal monopoly, the ruler's exclusive right to collect protection tribute and other levies or to control the local economy.
>
> —Vadim Volkov (2002: 161)

Much like the notion of a 'Syndicate Raj', syndicates in Bangladesh are lambasted in newspaper reports and everyday conversations alike, shaming mostly low-ranking political leaders and officials who have been found to have implausible wealth. One recent case that came to public light revealed how the driver of a senior government officer had for over a decade orchestrated the appointments and promotions of civil servants to that department, amassing multi-storied buildings in Dhaka, a cattle farm and forming a drivers' association as a front.[4] In practice, as we have seen, the term syndicate can be applied to a very wide variety of phenomena, from enforced monopolies to brokered work, the provision of security, control over carrots and the manipulation of tenders. It is not then clear cut and sits alongside a range of evocative English terms that have drifted into the vernacular including godfather and mafia, which have no dictionary definition and are not always used consistently. To use the word is to know that something is not as it should be, that coercion is at play and that powerful people are manipulating something to their advantage. In these ways it approximates the meanings of 'racket' and 'syndicates' in English, with a degree of opacity and fluidity in usage.

Though to the outside ear 'syndicates' may conjure images of 'organised crime' standing in opposition to the state, what they often denote in fact is crime organised by actors in office and extending downwards. Much recent literature from other contexts demarcates criminal actors and examines how they exist in collusion or dependency with officials and politicians.[5] By contrast here such distinctions confuse matters. As we saw in the lanes of Kawran Bazaar, though authority is crafted entrepreneurially bottom–up, it needs to be legitimised top–down from people with official designations. The OC of a police thana, the secretary of a party wing and so on look down to an array of cadres, *lineman*, informers, labour leaders and others who mediate access to resources in a manner that enriches and supports the chains of authority they sit within. Unlike the era of Picchi Hannan, any hazy distinction between crime and the ruling party and state has been eroded. The *lineman*, *samiti*s and street muscle of the *jhupri* labourers and Ahsan on the railway line may be the visible protagonists, but behind them stand not gangsters or the mafia but politicians and officials. One advantage to deploying the term syndicate to capture this as opposed to say mafia, is that it is not wedded to a particular embodiment of authority, and therefore can admit the plethora of actors and characters found to run syndicates in practice.

This perspective is an important compliment and corrective to the dominant way in which Bangladeshi politics has been framed through notions of clientelism and factionalism, in which politics is a world of vertical ties and horizontal competition. The idea of a syndicate points attention to horizontal ties, the 'nexus' between different sources of authority, for example between a local political leader and police chief, or between Rubel and the railway muscle Ahsan, relationships in which hierarchy may be shifting and unobvious. At a macro scale too, similar ties have been observed, yet understudied. In the early 2000s Alam and Teicher for example argue that 'state power had been captured by a nexus of politicians, former civil and military bureaucrats and businessmen'.[6] Similarly, it has been maintained that a serious obstacle to tax reform is the 'informal groups that cut across hierarchy, cadre, and political party' and which 'have enjoyed high level political support'.[7] The point then is that political authority and power in Bangladesh are wielded by opaque horizontal ties that cut across sectors, and which the notion of a syndicate draws our attention to.

The discourse of 'syndicate' or 'racket' evokes twentieth-century notions of organised crime and thus implies that it captures something relatively new. By historicising the forms of intermediation seen in Dhaka and the wider region, however, it has been suggested here that underlying such discourse are familiar forms of authority. De facto authority has long been 'decentralised' with the political centre relying on a wide array of intermediaries to both constitute their power by maintaining local order and operate as conduits for taxation. Such roles were distributed on differing bases and were a realm in which positions of authority were at times inherited, at other times appointed and at yet others bought and sold, but also fought for and won. Violent, coercive intermediaries have thus long existed in varying forms, and can be seen as a fundamental feature of politics and the way in which many aspects of life are mediated. The authority of such intermediaries is constituted and sustained through a variety of other qualities and skills. This has long been an entrepreneurial realm, seen perhaps most obviously in the moments when straightforward tax or revenue farmers bought positions for fixed periods, thereafter attempting to extract the necessary tribute to recoup their investment and profit on top of this.

The argument then is that in important respects today's syndicates and intermediaries are not much different from those of the past. Rather than view syndicates in relation to the history of crime, we need to turn this on its head and view them in relation to the state, systems of taxation and order. The majority of the varied intermediaries and syndicates described on these pages have no formal designation. Where formal arrangements exist (such as the leases emanating from the Dhaka City Corporation [DCC]), these are seen as having been corrupted and usurped by other arrangements and negotiations. In essence, however, these patchworks of different local monopolies and protection rackets accrue payments that feed upwards through the political ladder and, perhaps more importantly, are instrumental in other ways in sustaining the authority of the political centre. They feed local political muscle and it is this muscle which is useful to political elites and parties in their attempts to sustain power. The consistency of payments in the form of *chanda* or *dasturi* across ostensibly dramatically different historical periods highlights how similar logics of tribute persist. The tributes paid locally may not reach the heights of the central government, but they feed local forms of authority on which those at the political centre are dependent. These are not of course legitimised officially by the ruling party and state, yet they are the unspoken benefits of those in power, and part of the de facto arrangements that sustain their authority.

To be clear, however, this is not to try and relegate the very many ideals and values that animate political life in Bangladesh or elsewhere. Any of the people discussed here can of course be driven by desires to bring development, to protect the poor, to see Bangladesh succeed and to take pride in it. These pages should not be read as a dismissal of how genuine such intentions are. Parvez can simultaneously feel love for and loyalty to his fellow brothers in the *jhupri* group whilst also manoeuvring for status within the BNP and orchestrating local bombings. 'Prince' Hossain can desire to protect his *samiti* street vendors whilst also accruing status (and likely capital) on their back. There are no contradictions here. Syndicates may be crucial to sustaining the loyalty and coherence of a party and their wings, but that does not mean that all leaders and officials engage in such rackets, profit from them or wish to sustain them.

In the estimation of many, tax farming has almost or entirely disappeared. Mick Moore for example writes of how 'the image of the greedy, oppressive tax farmer has thoroughly penetrated public consciousness, and the practice has almost disappeared from the modern world.'[8] At times what we have heard about at Kawran Bazaar, however, gets close to a de facto system of revenue farming, particularly the systems of leasing and sub-leasing of toll collection. In the realm of formal political authority (those with designations in party wings or elected positions in government), the consistency with periods of revenue farming is more obvious, as it is widely known that many candidates have to buy their party ticket from seniors at huge expense, investments that need to be recouped (often through syndicates) when in office.[9] Many positions in the civil service are also bought, in part because of the opportunities for accruing wealth they bring.[10] Syndicates are thus contradictory. On the one hand they are constitutive of how order is created and how politicians and parties accrue power, yet on the other, they are also a weakness if they are uncontrolled or extended too far, potentially fatal to a party and leader, if they undermine the other facets on which their authority rests, or unleash powers that they cannot control, such as seen in Dhaka during the 1990s and early 2000s. Syndicates help form the muscular base on which the strength of parties in Bangladesh in part rests, yet can also undermine their legitimacy in the public eye, much in the same way as the 'oppressive tax farmer' was long a source of serious anger in everyday life across a large part of the world.

Saving Money and Flexing Muscle

> Savings ... [have] a profound ideological, even salvational, status.
> —Arjun Appadurai (2002: 33)

The morning I met Rubel when walking around Kawran Bazaar I was with a field officer from a local non-governmental organisation (NGO) which had attempted unsuccessfully in the preceding years to mobilise people living at the bazaar and on surrounding pavements into small savings groups. The savings they were trying to collect were the remnants of that system. Elsewhere I heard of various groups scattered across Dhaka, where NGOs had attempted to unite people, but members could barely remember who else was in their group or the name it went by. The local NGO (and international NGO funding it) had been inspired in particular by Slum/Shack Dwellers International, a network of federations representing poor urban people in dozens of countries across the world, built on small savings groups.[11] A founding body of this federation describes how small groups of women saving regularly together has been the key 'tool for mobilization',[12] and across the alliance, the practice of savings is seen as the 'bedrock' that underpins a wider vision: 'the idea of individuals and families self-organizing as members of a political collective to pool resources, organize lobbying, provide mutual risk-management devices, and confront opponents, where necessary'.[13] The logic of this model is portrayed as simple and unequivocal – without savings there is no federation and without a federation they cannot 'enact change'.[14] The act of saving money then is much more than simply saving money, argued to represent 'moral discipline'.[15]

Collective mobilisation among the poor and working classes is often imagined to embody a particular set of values. In recent development discourse such savings groups have been portrayed in an almost salvific light, as offering a route for the poor to join together to pursue collective aims and negotiate their relationship to the state. Since the 1980s there have been efforts to introduce and promote variations of accumulating savings groups across the world, most often among women in poor and rural communities. Prominent examples include 'self-help groups' in India, the 'village savings and loan associations' model and the 'village banking' model.[16] The diverse roles that savings groups can play have long been recognised. Bouman highlights dispute settlement, helping migrants, providing welfare, supporting the construction of infrastructure and paying teachers to name a few.[17] Alongside their proliferation has been an escalation of the rhetoric around their pro-poor qualities. Conferences are now organised solely to share experiences of savings groups and promote their potential. Part of a recent book title by prominent practitioners reads 'how savings groups are revolutionizing development'.[18] Some claim that savings groups bring not only better financial security to members, but also 'social empowerment' and 'civic engagement'. For NGOs savings groups have been understood as '"entry points" for social and political development',[19] the logic being that regular group savings establishes trust and improves relationships among members. This for some represents 'social capital', creating 'a bond'[20] that forms the basis for collective action; and a 'camaraderie [that] is both empowering and comforting'.[21] As one academic in this field writes, 'finance is a tool, a means to an end, not the end in itself.'[22]

The story told here in part resonates with and in part challenges such narratives. It may be true that savings are a key 'to unlocking community potential,'[23] but we cannot frame this potential narrowly. The politics of savings is not inherently pro-poor or pro-development in the normative sense imagined. Savings may – to adopt the vocabulary often found in some discourse – build the 'social capital' of and 'empower' a group, and may furthermore enable 'vertical social capital'. However, this may not necessarily have the 'civic' qualities that it has been understood to have within such discourse. It may instead be violent, criminal and party political. As Joe Devine has argued, *samiti*s can be the basis on which NGOs attempt to compete locally for access to land, and function to support the explicitly political ambitions of NGO leaders.[24] As such, the decision to join a *samiti* can be a very serious one, indicating loyalty and commitment to a political vision. The fact that savings group leaders often make money from such groups is already acknowledged in the literature. Bouman notes that 'clever presidents demand interest and hence become moneylenders in disguise.'[25] In Dhaka, Stuart Rutherford writes that 'it is well established that managers get a fixed sum, often fifty or 100 taka, from each member at the successful closing of a "fund" *samity*'.[26]

Collectives, unions, savings groups, cooperatives and so on must then be read not in relation to imagined political values, but within the political environment in which they operate. As we saw in Chapter 4 in this volume, the hierarchies embodied by trade unions in the context of Bengal and the wider subcontinent have often aligned closely with the 'traditional' labour leader. While the broader political significance of such *samiti*s is not then commonly recognised within contemporary literature, it is clearer when we look at a period in which savings groups proliferated and have been studied in greater detail. The 'friendly societies' which emerged most notably in the eighteenth and nineteenth centuries in England for example played multifaceted and at times politically charged roles in the lives of their members.[27] With trade unions outlawed, friendly societies provided a cover for union activities, social movements and other political projects, representing a means for mobilising workers, funding political activities and helping supporters. One historian writes that 'virtually every political campaign of the first half of the nineteenth century appealed to or formed its own friendly societies for assistance.'[28] Trade unions, which were then illegal, hence actively disguised themselves as friendly societies meeting in local pubs, while radical movements such as the Chartists formed such societies to promote their agendas.

It is pertinent to remember that in early twentieth-century Bengal, *samiti*s were often seen within public discourse as denoting an explicitly political, violent and even revolutionary group, even if these *samiti*s were clearly different in type. As with the 'secret societies' deemed a threat to the colonial state, the present-day *samiti*s are small associations rooted in mutual aid and a political vision, intimately associated with the physical capacity for violence. A century ago, such *samiti*s fostered political entrepreneurialism in a society in which there was little scope for it to be utilised except for revolution. Today, by contrast, groups of younger men forming a society have a landscape in which that collective action can be directed and used to seek status. Although these older *samiti*s did not, to my knowledge, include savings groups, some *samiti*s did collect funds for the mutual support of members. Members of the Dacca Anushilan Samiti for example reportedly agreed to follow the principle that any money they obtained was to be held in common. The boundaries between societies, crime and politics were also porous. Not only were many *samiti*s 'criminal' by the standards of the state in that they had revolutionary intent and turned to dacoity and robbery to fund their activities, but others also branched more broadly into crime. Secret societies such as the Dacca Anushilan Samiti, established with political intentions, then engaged in criminal activity as a means of supporting the organisation, but arguably also morphed into more 'purely' criminal activities, forming 'gangs'.[29]

The argument then is that here the accrual of savings in *samiti*s often in fact supports rather than challenges the dependencies that people sustain on violent, coercive intermediaries. This is not to suggest that savings groups everywhere operate in this manner; however, this view is corroborated by scattered references within literature from elsewhere in South Asia and beyond.[30] In the coalmines of Dhanbad for example the infamous labour and political leader Surajdeo Singh maintained labour bonded to him yet organised in 'so-called cooperatives'.[31] Labourers were obliged to join certain unions and pay unreasonably high dues,[32] and paid 'chandan' (translated by the author as 'collection, subscription, extortion') to contractors for festivals or in the name of charity.[33] In West Bengal 'chit funds' are regularly identified as part of the so-called 'Syndicate Raj', serving to enrich party leaders. One opposition politician reportedly said '[t]here are four pillars on which [the] Trinamool Congress is standing, bribes, extortion, syndicates and chit funds. Using these they came [to] power, using the same they want to stay in power.'[34] In other contexts we even find that collective savings are inherent to the functioning of criminal groups. The 'vory-v-zakone', the traditional Russian criminal fraternities of the twentieth century, for example held a 'communal fund' used to care for sick thieves, support the families of imprisoned members and bribe officials.[35] In Sicily, the mafia have a long history of creating cooperatives, such as the peasant cooperatives established by the mafia boss Don Calo Vizzini in the 1940s,[36] and even in recent decades it has been argued that cooperatives have coexisted with the mafia, sometimes serving as a means by which the mafia built legitimacy locally.[37]

The basic point then is that at times, collective action can conceal syndicates, and membership of such a body must be understood in that light. Often, the act of contributing to a *samiti* and the act of starting or leading a *samiti* cannot be disentangled from muscle politics, from the influence of the ruling party in everyday life and from the ways in which crime can create order. A *samiti* represents a tool for harnessing the few resources that a poor aspiring leader has available: the small amounts of capital they and others can accumulate and more importantly, their collective strength honed through years of manual labour and a tough life. *Samiti*s can in certain circumstances therefore be seen as tools or platforms, used by ambitious leaders to pursue a political agenda in the hope of power and status. Capital is instrumental and symbolic. From the perspective of members, the decision to join such a *samiti* similarly needs to be read in light of the political roles *samiti*s are intended to play, as is explicit in how Liton promoted his *samiti* to potential members. The capital collected may be of interest to the leader directly, but more importantly may accord him a status socially. Contributing towards a *samiti* is seen as an opportunity, but also positions members politically. This suggests that the act of saving money can itself be demonstrative, indicating allegiance and commitment to a political vision.

In Bangladesh *samiti*s can then be a means through which aspiring leaders seek to establish and control syndicates, but they may also be considered a form of syndicate themselves. At times *samiti*s serve to enrich their leaders who accrue capital in the name of *chanda* as a share of the income of their members. Members in return may get protection, as 'Prince' Hossain offers his street vendors, may have hope for a different future or promises of welfare should the need arise. Syndicates in the form of protection rackets function because they provide a service; they provide access to a resource, to protection and a slice of pavement. Some *samiti*s do exactly the same, but under a different label. In all cases the act of paying contributes to the authority of the racketeer or intermediary, because it solidifies in one's mind and in the mind of the community that this is someone (or a group) deserved of such respect who can provide what they claim. But in the case of the *samiti* this relationship is more intimate; it is the threat of the members themselves that can establish the *samiti* leader as a threat locally, and it is the calibration of the dependency they have on the leader that establishes the authority of that figure. Whether a *samiti* leader is then a racketeer may at times be obvious, but in other instances opaque, ambiguous and a dynamic that emerges over time, only revealed in the fluctuations of the dependencies that people sustain on them.

Boro Bhais Change

> And what is the prize that is to be eventually won? The rebirth of democracy. The glorious prospect of being able one day to choose their rulers from a list of powerful men, most of whose corruptions are generally known and accepted with weary resignation.
>
> —Norman Lewis (1978: 169)

After Rubel and Parvez were arrested by the Rapid Action Battalion (RAB), I interviewed many of the younger *jhupri* van drivers in one of the nearby centres for street children. I wanted to understand not only how events had unfolded from their perspective, but what it meant for their own lives and thoughts for the future. 'Do you want to become a *sardar* one day?' I asked. 'What about a leader?' Their answers were of course shaped by the fact a familiar but foreign older white man was interviewing them in the room of a centre they relied upon. Yet they were adamant about the futility of being involved in local politics. Most wanted to start a business elsewhere, have a small shop, be a bus driver or train to work in a factory. I suggested provocatively that many people seemed to earn lots by taking *chanda* at the bazaar. 'Yes, you will profit,' one responded, but later:

> your party will fall and then people will start beating you. Now it's the Awami League, but if the BNP comes, the person taking the money right now won't be there. He'll hide. If your party isn't ruling, then the public will beat you. They will break your feet and hands.

Referring to the ruling political leaders at Kawran Bazaar, another said that once the BNP comes to power, 'they will pull up their *lunghi*s and run away! Otherwise they will all be shot.' Such severe consequences are not the product of teenage imaginations. Some recalled seeing incidents in their childhood when *santrashi*s of the area were beaten in public, as years of pent-up resentment and fear were released by locals. One described seeing a former 'godfather' (as he put it) being beaten with a weight from measuring scales, then set on fire and running alight around the bazaar.

The syndicates and *boro bhai*s at Kawran Bazaar are always in motion. Nothing is stable or sure. This reflects the machinations of a political system with entrepreneurialism at its core, where political and economic life are very deeply entangled and where political coalitions permeate almost all areas of public life. *Boro bhai*s rise and fall, establish themselves, compete, cultivate groups of supporters and allies and strategise to usurp rivals and sustain their dominance. All the time life is changing, people are growing older, their needs and calculations shifting and the younger generation rising, gaining a reputation or notoriety. This then resonates well with Lucia Michelutti's observation from Western Uttar Pradesh that syndicates are 'flexible, volatile, fragmented and in constant flux'.[38] To study syndicates and those at their helm is then to constantly encounter change. Some of this change reflects the manoeuvres of individual leaders seeking dominance within the system. At other times the change is more profound. Jeffrey Witsoe argues that

> an entire political history could be told by examining the changing role of brokers, and the ways in which this reflects transformations in the relationships between state institutions and the structuring of local power.[39]

To study intermediation is to peer into state–society relations, into political coalitions and into how order itself is sustained.[40] I have attempted to plot this recent history in a small part of Dhaka and have suggested the broader historical lineages we can connect to the intermediaries found on the streets of the city today. I have argued that coercive, at times violent, intermediaries have been a consistent feature over hundreds of years of local political life across much of not only Bangladesh but the wider subcontinent, and a defining feature of how people relate within society and to overarching political authorities. Yet it must also be recognised that not only do the individuals change, but the precise character of local political authorities mediating access to life and resources, too, changes. Dramatic change has been witnessed in the period documented here, with syndicates embodied and controlled no longer by *santrashi*s but by party political leaders and the security agencies.

This points to larger and profound questions about the processes through which the character of intermediaries and dependencies upon them change, and the ways and extent to which syndicates predominate. The view here is that syndicates are often a product of how political dominance is established and sustained by those in power. As already hinted in the book, however, political dominance has many more facets. Domination is not simply premised on rent-seeking: complex goods, benefits and privileges are used to shore up support; legal manoeuvres are used to stymie rivals, repress opposition and induce potential followers and rule is legitimised in a myriad of ways, not least by claims of bringing 'development'.[41] Many syndicates themselves reflect in microcosm the complexity of how domination works, simultaneously providing access to a resource and protection for that, whilst also coercing and ensuring political support. But there are signs that the political advantage of certain forms of syndicate can at times be outweighed by other considerations. This appears to have been the case in Dhaka in the late 1990s with the chaos caused by *santrashi*s and the challenge they often posed to party leaders locally. Understanding how these moments arise and the locus for change within them is crucial, and should be the subject of future research.

A key variable determining the nature of syndicates found in everyday life appears to be the extent to which political authority is associated with a capacity for violence and 'dispersed' throughout society; in other words, the extent to which those in office nationally are dependent upon localised forms of authority. One way of approaching the question of change is to view it in terms of the struggles between more centralised and dispersed forms of authority. Bangladesh's experience of 'democracy' through the 1990s and early 2000s was intimately associated with the rise of local violent entrepreneurs, in part because of the scope and need to build authority from the streets upwards. The transition over the recent decades described here represents an institutionalisation of crime and violence within the apparatus of the state and ruling party, and therefore a greater degree of control by political elites over local leaders. It is easier to control a Jubo League leader than Picchi Hannan.

Might this transition then be part of a 'doorstep condition' towards something better?[42] It is common to contrast such developments with the perceived archetypes of modern states, such as those of Western Europe, where it has been argued that consolidating the means of violence only occurred on the back of 'perpetually lived organizations' and the rule of law.[43] Viewed in this light, the deepening of political control over street-level syndicates does not seem to represent a march towards more liberal and impersonal relationships in society, and also magnifies other challenges, such as the control of the police and other security agencies.[44] Yet we should not underestimate the fact that this transition has brought a degree of stability to the city, and that this is greatly valued. People living and working in places like Kawran Bazaar do not now wake up with the sound of bombs, and murders are not a regular occurrence. One possible, and perhaps charitable, interpretation of this transition is to suggest that consolidating or institutionalising street-level authority in this manner could be part of a broader, messy and difficult process by which the ties between political authority, violence and crime could be undermined from the centre.[45]

At the same time, however, though the city is more stable, syndicates are still ubiquitous and if anything, the authority of today's *boro bhai*s appears more comprehensive, and coercive control over everyday life deeper still. Ultimately then this transition is part of a story about authoritarianism. Elsewhere I have argued that the events described in Chapters 2 and 3 concerning the decline of gangsters and 'politicization of crime' offer a way of understanding how the Awami League has achieved the dominance they enjoy today.[46] Since the Awami League repealed the system of caretaker government, they have successfully fended off the BNP's *hartal*s and attempts to launch a movement to destabilise the government and return their party to power. This success has many facets. It is premised in part on the development achievements so evident over the past decade or so and exemplified in eye-catching infrastructure such as the Padma Bridge or Dhaka city's new Metro Rail (albeit being questioned, as of 2023, by the economic downturn). It is further premised on a pliable military. But it is also premised on events described here. The decline of gangsters at the hands of the BNP arguably deprived the BNP of the muscle they today wish to utilise to disrupt Dhaka and created the vacuum in which the Awami League and apparatus of the state could truly dominate the city's local politics, thereby solidifying their hold on the streets. Changes to the character of local syndicates, intermediation and political muscle, can then reverberate into larger political transitions, perhaps in unforeseen ways.

When we study such transitions, we must also, however, acknowledge the importance of variation. This book has focused on a small, albeit important, part of the capital Dhaka, and one might question the extent to which the dynamics and changes analysed here resonate nationally. Wider literature from elsewhere in Bangladesh hints that syndicates are widespread, even if scholars do not always use the term.[47] My own experiences elsewhere in the country also suggest that other violent entrepreneurs have fallen from strength over recent decades, from the gangsters of Khulna such as Ershad Shikder, to the underground leftists and more recently the pirates of the Sundarbans. And yet we must also recognise that the extent and type of syndicates vary between contexts, and this, as we have seen, is the case even in Kawran Bazaar, and certainly likely across Dhaka, other cities and between rural and urban areas. Understanding variation between micro political economies of crime and order is then a path to better appreciating the variety of factors they are produced by, the relationship between micro and macro political change as well as potential routes to cultivating alternative arrangements, if indeed that type of political engineering is even possible.

As of early 2024 the *jhupri* group are still labouring along the lanes of Kawran Bazaar. Though COVID-19 shut down much of the country periodically over the years 2020–2021, Kawran Bazaar itself was still alive and busy, and the incomes of the *jhupri* labourers in fact improved. They know no one here who became seriously ill from the virus, and its effects were so minimal that for many of them COVID-19 is 'fake', a virus from which 'only the rich get ill' according to Parvez. When I return young boys now have full beards. A girl no older than eight when I first knew her is now a mother with two children, her husband in jail and is selling drugs along the *jhupri* lane to survive. Shumon for a period started a *samiti*, though like Liton's it failed and the Sramik League took over the space where he used to have a *khichuri* stand. His wife eloped with another man, leaving him with their child. The relationship between Rubel and Parvez has also broken down, each dividing the work unloading trucks, and each attempting to establish syndicates. Old friends are today, rivals, Parvez still linked to the Swechasebak Dal and Rubel now to the Jubo League. Liton works once again under Rubel who he described as running a 'one-man syndicate,' acting like a *sardar* and paying the labourers whatever he feels like: 'He acts like a *sardar*, but he has hidden it in a syndicate.' A syndicate is something they together would share in more equally, yet in practice it is Rubel who is benefitting unfairly, he claims. To sustain this, they pay 2,000 taka a day to the Jubo League, a payment Liton termed a 'goondabhata' (payment for *goonda*s). It means that during a period when they would normally earn 200–300 taka each a day, they instead earn 1,500–2,000.

Behind this, however, Liton is still manoeuvring for power. On one occasion I visited he had a group of children whom he was looking after and nurturing under his authority. Aged around ten to twelve, he described how they were not allowed to return to their homes because they had not been able to steal and sell enough vegetables to give to their parents, and so he was supporting them through winter, though 'now it's summer they've forgotten me.' On another visit he claimed that he had agreed with some of his *choto bhai*s in the Jubo Dal that if the BNP get back in power, then Parvez will not be allowed to rise too high through his contacts in the Swechasebek Dal. When we reminisced about his old *samiti*, he was still frustrated he had never found an appropriate name. He continues to be focused on re-marrying and having a career in politics, but fears if he remarries now as a labourer, he won't be able to find a suitable wife. He also thinks opportunities still lie ahead. In his own words:

> Though I am grey, I am not that old. A moment will come. Like a moment came during the Ershad period in 1989. In 2006 there was another moment, when the Awami League brought down the BNP. Again in 1/11 there was a moment. So I am waiting for the next moment. I'm sitting on this van here, but I don't think in the same way as the others. Whatever you think of me now, I will become a leader one day.

Notes

1. Das and Poole (2004).
2. As noted in Chapter 1, much literature from Bangladesh has illuminated the muscular politics found among students. This focus is deserved given the importance of student groups to political parties and at crucial political junctures such as Liberation and the return to parliamentary democracy. Student politics also displays many points of similarity to the form of muscular politics found at the bazaar. In basic, leaders emerge from dormitories or bazaars to dominate campuses or their surroundings, operate syndicates and set their sights on larger political careers. Undoubtedly also, the sense of pressure and coercion felt by students being coaxed into student politics must be similar to that felt by labourers. There are, however, important differences. Needless to say, labourers in general have far fewer prospects than students, they have less resources to fall back on and fewer contacts to rely upon. They are the less glamorous forms of muscle used for the more grizzly forms of violence, and perhaps face higher risks for their involvement. Their livelihoods are on the line, and many will face the sight of hungry children if they are unable to earn. This is not in any way to dismiss the severity or magnitude of student politics, only to suggest that the choices are even more grave in contexts such as this. It is also likely the case that there are more diverse sources and means of establishing political authority in contexts of labour, where, as we have seen, *samiti*s can emerge, and there is

far less immediate disciplining or institutionalised forms of competition as in student elections.
3. Jackman and Maitrot (2022).
4. Although he was perhaps the scapegoat rather than the centre of this syndicate (Alam and Al Amin 2020).
5. Moncada (2013); Cockayne (2016); Barnes (2017); Staniland (2017); Arias (2017).
6. Alam and Teicher (2012: 864).
7. Hassan and Pritchard (2016: 1711).
8. Moore (2008: 41).
9. Jackman and Maitrot (2021).
10. Jackman and Maitrot (2022).
11. A leading part of this network is an alliance between three bodies based in Mumbai, India: the NGO, Society for the Promotion of Area Resource Centres, the National Slum Dwellers Federation (NSDF) and Mahila Milan ('women together') a group of female pavement dwellers. See Appadurai (2002); Archer (2012); d'Cruz and Mudimu (2012); d'Cruz (2014).
12. Appadurai (2002: 33).
13. Ibid., 32.
14. Ibid., 33–34.
15. Ibid., 34.
16. Rutherford (2009).
17. Bouman (1995: 376).
18. Ashe and Neilan (2014).
19. Rutherford (2009: 99).
20. Ibid., 423.
21. d'Cruz et al. (2014: 9).
22. Archer (2012: 439).
23. Ibid.
24. Devine (2002, 2006).
25. Bouman (1995: 378).
26. Rutherford (1997: 363).
27. Cordery (2003).
28. Ibid., 55.
29. In 1914 Hughes-Buller, the Inspector General of Police in Bengal, argued:

> [E]ven if the original object of the institution was 'political' (whatever that term may mean and I venture to remind you that the word is by no means sacrosanct), it has now developed into a gang organized by the habitual commission of offences against the community and the public peace,

namely, dacoity and assassination ... When a 'secret society' becomes a 'gang,' and develops assassination and dacoity on a systematic basis, I submit that it renders itself liable to the law applicable to ordinary dacoits and ordinary gangs of murderers. (Cited in Silvestri 1998: 202)

30. When viewed historically, there is evidence that intermediaries have not only been long-standing conduits of tribute and taxation, but also savings. There is some evidence for example to suggest that caste groups organised savings groups through *panchayat*s in wider north India (Gooptu 2001: 167). There are also hints that one of the many roles long played by *sardar*s was to facilitate savings. Bates and Carter (2017: 476) write of *sardar*s in overseas colonies for example that:

    [I]t was not uncommon for them to retain a portion of the monthly wages of their labourers as a form of saving. This could then be returned when the labourer wished to remit money home or to go back to India, or if a labourer was ill or absent and his wage was docked, that portion of the past [wages] retained by the sirdar would then be used to provide him with support.

31. Heuzé (2009: 162). Elsewhere in India it has been argued self-help groups are looked to by politicians as vote banks, with their leaders mobilising members to political events (Pattenden 2010: 506–508). In Mumbai we find references to social workers running 'chit funds' in a slum, who also broker votes and support to political candidates (Bjorkman 2014: 625–626).
32. Heuzé (2009: 163).
33. Further afield in the context of Filipino dock workers in the late 1980s, a prominent labour union for stevedores grew and sustained its influence through a mixture of coercion (relying on 'goons' to intimidate and even kill strikebreakers and rivals), cultivating political relationships, operating as a 'broker' to labourers and extortion of members in the form of 'strike insurance', which has similarities then to the *samiti*s portrayed here (Sidel 1995).
34. Singh (2019).
35. The fund came from criminal takings and was held in a bank account (Varese 2001: 155).
36. N. Lewis (2003).
37. Rakopoulos (2017).
38. Michelutti (2019: 172).
39. Witsoe (2012: 51).
40. Others have also sketched such histories. Reddy and Haragopal (1985), for example, trace the role of local 'pyraveekars' intermediaries in the context of

Andhra Pradesh as part of the feudal system under the Hyderabad principality, where such intermediaries served to facilitate the collection of land revenue, bridging the linguistic and political gap between the local political centre and villages. Even with the introduction of ostensibly 'modern' administrative institutions, these intermediaries sit alongside the formal functionaries and lawyers in helping the administration function. In Witsoe's (2012) account of village brokers in Bihar he traces the shifts in these structures through preceding generations, describing how the role of *zamindar*s in the revenue collection hierarchies of the British Raj was eroded in the early twentieth century, giving way to upper-caste brokers affiliated with the Congress Party who mediated access to the state, maintaining patron–client relations. By the 1990s and 2000s, however, lower-caste groups had radically grown in strength, reflected in the formation of the Rashtriya Janata Dal and a far higher proportion of elected politicians. This played out at the village level as a diversification away from upper-class brokers, to a plethora of newer figures, at the expense of 'traditional' landed upper-caste groups. State institutions such as the police were politicised, leading to a rapid surge in criminality.

41. Goodfellow and Jackman (2023).
42. North, Wallis and Weingast (2009).
43. Ibid.
44. Jackman and Maitrot (2022).
45. We might view the so-called war on drugs from 2018, the deselection of MPs associated with the drug trade and attempts to reform the Chattra League and Jubo League in this light (Maitrot and Jackman 2023).
46. Jackman (2023).
47. In particular see Ruud (2018, 2019, 2020); Kuttig (2019, 2020) and Jackman and Maitrot (2021, 2022).

Glossary

abwab	illegal tax
akhara	gymnasium
andolan	movement
aparadha jagat	underworld
arot	wholesale market
arotdar	wholesaler
badmash	criminals
bahini	force, militia
bakshish	tip
bari	ancestral home
bashoman	floating person
basti	slum
bepari	middleman (in distribution chain)
bhag niyom	system of division
boro bhai	big brother
cadre	political activist, muscle
chamcha	sycophant
chanda/chaada	toll, contribution, fee, subscription
chandabaji	racketeering
chaudhuri	headman
chauki	toll house
chaukidar	guard or toll collector
cheater	cheater
chhatra	student(s)
chhyachra goonda	petty thug, criminal, gangster
chinomul	rootless people
choto bhai	small, younger brother

chukti	contract
coil	commission collector in a bazaar
coolie	labourer
crore	ten million
crossfire	extrajudicial, unexplained killing
dada	older brother or older male
dadon	advance
dafadar	supervisor
dakat	dacoit, bandit
dal	group, faction
dalal	broker or middleman
dalpati	headman or leader of a *dal*
danda	stick, rod
dandaniti	the rule of *danda*
dar	tax
daroga	local police officer
dasturi	customary commission
dhandebaaz	opportunists
don	don
durniti	corruption
dwee number	illegal (literally, 'number two')
encounter	extrajudicial, unexplained killing
faujdar	military commander
ferari	fugitive
fokir/fakir	ascetic who lives on alms
foot	area/holding space for storing goods
ganjam	violence, trouble
gaza/ganja	marijuana
ghar	area/holding space for storing goods
ghat	boat launch
godfather	godfather
goli	lane
goonda	thug, criminal, gangster
gram sarkar	village government
habshi	East African
hafta	contribution, fee
hartal	public strike
helper	helper, assistant

Glossary

hordar	labour leader
ijara	revenue farming
ijaradar	revenue farmer
jāgīr	domain or area of revenue
jāgīrdar	holder of *jāgīr*
jamin	bail
jhamela	mess
jhupri	shack
jonoshoba	meeting
jubo	youth
kangali	destitute
katra	caravanserai, royal market
khichuri	one-pot dish made with rice and lentils
khidmatgar	personal attendant
killer	killer, assassin
kotwal	city police official
krishak	farmer
kumhar	potter
labour	labour
lakh	one hundred thousand
langra	crippled
lathial	muscleman armed with stick
lineman	intermediary, middleman, extortionist
lunghi	sarong
mafia	criminal, godfather, mafia
mahalla	city quarter or ward
malakar	garland maker
mastan	hoodlum, thug
matbar	[traditional] leader
mehal/mahal	Mughal tax on occupation or commodity
minti	*coolie*, labourer
mofussil	provincial district or area
mul dal	root party
mumla	legal case
murgi	chicken
nadi	river
nar	dancing boy
nazim	ruler of province

neta	leader
operad/aparadh	crime
panchayat	council of five
pantch/patch	tangle
paramanik	headman
peshkash	tribute
petni	[female] ghost, spirit, witch
picchi	small, short, tiny
piker	a type of middleman
pir	saint, holy figure
potho shishu	street children
rajnaitik	political
rangbaj	gangster, thug, criminal
salish	community dispute resolution
samiti	society, association
santrashi	gangster, terrorist
sanyasi	Hindu religious medicant
sardar	labour leader, leader
sayer/sair/s'āir	tax (on transactions and travel)
serial	queue
shelter	[political] support, shelter
shubidhabadi	opportunist
somobay	cooperative
sramik	labourer
subahdar	Mughal governor
swechasebak	volunteers
taka	money, Bangladeshi currency
tenderbaji	tender grabbing
tokai	scavenger
yaba	yabba, a methamphetamine
zamindar	landowner or holder with proprietary rights or right to collect revenue

Bibliography

Ahamed, E. 2004. The military and democracy in Bangladesh. In *The Military and Democracy in Asia and the Pacific*, edited by R. J. May and V. Selochan, 101–118. Canberra, Australia: Australian National University Press.

Ahmed, I. 1998. The Mughal governors of Bihar and their public works. *Proceedings of the Indian History Congress* 59: 383–392.

Ahmed, Imtiaz. 2004. Mastanocracy and chronic poverty. Background paper in *Chronic Poverty in Bangladesh: Tales of Ascent, Descent, Marginality and Persistence*, edited by B. Sen and D. Hulme, 85–122. Dhaka: Bangladesh Institute of Development Studies.

Ahmed, S. U. 1986. *Dacca: A Study in Urban History and Development*. London: SOAS, University of London.

———. 2018. *Dhaka: A Study in Urban History and Development*. London: Routledge.

Alam, H. 2021. Extortion institutionalised. *Daily Star*, 4 April. https://www.thedailystar.net/city/news/extortion-institutionalised-2071717. Accessed 5 February 2024.

Alam, Q. and J. Teicher. 2012. The state of governance in Bangladesh: The capture of state institutions. *South Asia: Journal of South Asian Studies* 35(4): 858–884.

Alam, S. S. and Al Amin. 2020. More names start coming to the fore. *Prothom Alo*, 23 September. https://en.prothomalo.com/bangladesh/more-names-start-coming-out. Accessed 5 February 2024.

Allen, B. C. 1912. *Eastern Bengal District Gazetteers: Dacca*. Allahabad: Pioneer Press.

Andersen, M. K. 2014. The politics of politics: Youth mobilization, aspirations and the threat of violence at Dhaka University. PhD thesis, Roskilde Universitet.

Angel, S., P. Lamson-Hall and Z. G. Blanco. 2021. Anatomy of density: Measurable factors that constitute urban density. *Buildings and Cities* 2(1): 264–282.

Anjaria, J. S. 2011. Everyday corruption and the politics of space in Mumbai. *American Ethnologist* 38(1): 58–72.

Appadurai, A. 2002. Deep democracy: Urban governmentality and the horizon of politics. *Public Culture* 14(1): 21–47.

Archer, D. 2012. Finance as the key to unlocking community potential: Savings, funds and the ACCA programme. *Environment and Urbanization* 24(2): 423–440.

Ardener, S. 1964. The comparative study of rotating credit associations. *Journal of the Royal Anthropological Institute of Great Britain and Ireland* 94(2): 201–229.

Arens, J. and J. van Beurden. 1978. *Jhagrapur: Poor Peasants and Women in a Village in Bangladesh*. Birmingham: Third World Publications.

Arias, E. D. 2017. *Criminal Enterprises and Governance in Latin America and the Caribbean*. New York: Cambridge University Press.

Ashe, J. and K. J. Neilan. 2014. *In Their Own Hands: How Savings Groups Are Revolutionizing Development*. San Francisco: Berrett-Koehler.

Ashraf, H. and R. Prentice. 2019. Beyond factory safety: Labor unions, militant protest, and the accelerated ambitions of Bangladesh's export garment industry. *Dialectical Anthropology* 43: 93–107.

Atkinson-Shepherd, S. 2020. *The Gangs of Bangladesh: Mastaans, Street Gangs and 'Illicit Child Labourers' in Dhaka*. London: Palgrave.

Auyero, J. and K. Sobering. 2019. *The Ambivalent State: Police–Criminal Collusion at the Urban Margins*. Oxford: Oxford University Press.

Azad, M. A. K. and M. R. Khan. 2015. Bugged by beggars: Their number shoots up as Eid draws nearer. *Daily Star*, 7 July. https://www.thedailystar.net/backpage/bugged-beggars-108664. Accessed 5 February 2024.

Azam, K. M. 1990. The panchayats of Dacca. In *The Panchayat System of Dhaka*, edited by K. M. Azam and translated by W. van Schendel, 23–47. Dhaka: Dhaka City Museum.

Baden-Powell, B. H. 1889. *The Origin and Growth of Village Communities in India*. London: Swan Sonnenschein.

Bakken, B. and J. Wang. 2021. The changing forms of corruption in China. *Crime, Law and Social Change* 75: 247–265.

Balachandran, G. 1996. Searching for the sardar: The state, pre-capitalist institutions and human agency in the maritime labour market, Calcutta 1880–1935. In *Institutions and Economic Change in South Asia*, edited by B. Stein and S. Subrahmanyam, 206–236. Delhi: Oxford University Press.

Banerjee, S. 2009. *The Wicked City: Crime and Punishment in Colonial Calcutta*. Delhi: Orient Blackswan.

Bibliography

———. 2017. Crime in Calcutta: From childhood in a colonial metropolis to adulthood in a globalised megalopolis. In *Social Dynamics of the Urban: Studies from India*, edited by N. Jayaram, 99–113. Delhi: Springer.

Bangladesh Bureau of Statistics. 2013. *District Statistics 2011: Dhaka*. Statistics and Information Division, Ministry of Planning, Government of the People's Republic of Bangladesh.

———. 2014. *Preliminary Report on Census of Slum Areas and Floating Population 2014*. Dhaka: Statistics and Informatics Division, Ministry of Planning.

———. 2022. *Population and Housing Census 2022: Preliminary Report*. Statistics and Informatics Division, Ministry of Planning, Government of Bangladesh.

Barnes, N. 2017. Criminal politics: An integrated approach to the study of organized crime, politics, and violence. *Perspectives on Politics* 15(4): 967–987.

Basu, I., J. Devine and G. Wood, eds. 2018. *Politics and Governance in Bangladesh: Uncertain Landscapes*. Oxford: Routledge.

Basu, S. 2004. *Does Class Matter? Colonial Capital and Workers' Resistance in Bengal (1890–1937)*. Delhi: Oxford University Press.

———. 2008. The paradox of peasant worker: Re-conceptualizing workers' politics in Bengal 1890–1939. *Modern Asian Studies* 42(1): 47–74.

Bates, C. and M. Carter. 2017. *Sirdar*s as intermediaries in nineteenth-century Indian Ocean indentured labour migration. *Modern Asian Studies* 51(2): 462–484.

Baxter, C. 1998. *Bangladesh: From a Nation to a State*. Boulder, CO: Westview Press.

Bayly, C. A. 2012. *Rulers, Townsmen and Bazaars: North Indian Society in the Age of British Expansion: 1770–1870*. 3rd ed. New Delhi: Cambridge University Press.

Bdnews24. 2007. RAB nabs Dhanmondi crime boss Nazimuddin Babu. https://bdnews24.com/bangladesh/2007/10/26/rab-nabs-dhanmondi-crime-boss-nazimuddin-babu. Accessed 5 February 2024.

Berenschot, W. 2010. Everyday mediation: The politics of public service delivery in Gujarat, India. *Development and Change* 41(5): 883–905.

Bergman, D. 2015. Political crisis of 2015: Analysis of death. *Bangladesh Politico* (blog), 18 January. http://bangladeshpolitico.blogspot.co.uk/2015/01/political-crisis-2015-analysis-of-deaths.html. Accessed 1 December 2015.

Bertocci, P. J. 1970. Elusive villages: Social structure and community organization in rural East Pakistan. PhD thesis, Michigan State University, Michigan.

———. 1982. Bangladesh in the early 1980s: Praetorian politics in an intermediate regime. *Asian Survey* 22(10): 988–1008.

Bhattacharya, D. 2004. Kolkata 'underworld' in the early 20th century. *Economic and Political Weekly* 39(38): 4276–4282.

Bjorkman, L. 2014. 'You can't buy a vote': Meanings of money in a Mumbai election. *American Ethnologist* 41(4): 617–634.

Blok, A. 1974. *The Mafia of a Sicilian Village*. Oxford: Basil Blackwell.

Boissevain, J. 1969. Patrons as brokers. *Sociologische Gids* 16(6): 379–386.

Bouman, F. J. A. 1995. Rotating and accumulating savings and credit associations: A development perspective. *World Development* 23(3): 371–384.

Bowrey, T. 1701. *A Dictionary: English and Malayo, Malayo and English*. London: Sam Bridge.

———. 1903. *Geographical Account of Countries Round the Bay of Bengal 1669–1679*. AES Reprint: New Delhi.

BRAC. 1983. *The Net: Power Structures in Ten Villages*. Dhaka: BRAC Prokashana.

Bradley-Birt, F. B. 1906. *The Romance of an Eastern Capital*. London: Smith, Elder, & Co.

Brass, P. 2003. *The Production of Hindu–Muslim Violence in Contemporary India*. Washington, DC: University of Washington Press.

Burnett-Hurst, A. R. 1925. *Labour and Housing in Bombay: A Study in the Economic Conditions of the Wage-Earning Classes in Bombay*. London: P. S. King.

Calkins, P. B. 1970. The formation of a regionally oriented ruling group in Bengal, 1700–1740. *Journal of Asian Studies* 29(4): 799–806.

Candland, C. and R. Sil. 1991. The politics of labor in late-industrializing and post-socialist economies: New challenges in a global age. In *The Politics of Labor in a Global Age: Continuity and Change in Late-industrializing and Post-socialist Economies*, edited by C. Candland and R. Sil, 3–28. Oxford: Oxford University Press.

Census of India. 1901. *Census of India: Vol VI: Bengal*. Calcutta: Bengal Secretariat Press.

Chakrabarty, D. 2000 [1989]. *Rethinking Working-Class History: Bengal 1890–1940*. New Jersey: Princeton University Press.

Chakravarty, L. 1978. Emergence of an industrial labour force in a dual economy: British India, 1880–1920. *Indian Economic and Social History Review* 15(3): 249–328.

Chandavarkar, R. 2002. *The Origins of Industrial Capitalism in India: Business Strategies and the Working Classes in Bombay, 1900–1940*. Cambridge: Cambridge University Press.

———. 2008. The decline and fall of the jobber system in the Bombay cotton textile industry, 1870–1955. *Modern Asian Studies* 42(1): 123–210.

Chandpur Times. 2020. একসময়ের শীর্ষ সন্ত্রাসী ফরিদগঞ্জের পিচ্চি হান্নান সম্পর্কে অজানা তথ্য [Unknown facts about the top terror Picchi Hannan of Faridganj]. 25 January. https://chandpurtimes.com/পিচ্চি/হান্নান-. Accessed 5 February 2024.

Chatterjee, K. 1996. *Merchants, Politics and Society in Early Modern India, Bihar: 1733–1820*. Leiden: E. J. Brill.

Chattopadhyay, B. 2000. *Crime and Control in Early Colonial Bengal, 1770–1860*. Calcutta: K. P. Bagchi & Co.

Chibber, V. 2005. From class compromise to class accommodation: Labor's incorporation into the Indian political economy. In *Social Movements in India: Poverty, Power, and Politics*, edited by R. Ray and M. F. Katzenstein, 39–66. Oxford: Rowman & Littlefield.

Chowdhury, M. H. 2003. Violence, politics and the state in Bangladesh. *Conflict, Security and Development* 3(2): 265–276.

Chowdhury, N. S. 2019. *Paradoxes of the Popular: Crowd Politics in Bangladesh*. Stanford: Stanford University Press.

Cockayne, J. 2016. *Hidden Power: The Strategic Logic of Organised Crime*. New York: Oxford University Press.

Codron, J. 2007. Putting factions 'back in' the civil–military relations equation: Genesis, maturation and distortion of the Bangladeshi army. *South Asia Multidisciplinary Academic Journal*. DOI: 10.4000/samaj.230.

Colona, F. and R. Jaffe. 2016. Hybrid governance arrangements. *European Journal of Development Research* 28(2): 175–183.

Comaroff, J. and J. Comaroff. 2016. *The Truth About Crime: Sovereignty, Knowledge, Social Order*. Chicago: University of Chicago Press.

Cordery, S. 2003. *British Friendly Societies, 1750–1914*. Basingstoke: Palgrave MacMillan.

Daily Star. 2004. Picch Hannan to be quizzed today as HC rejects stay. 5 August. https://archive.thedailystar.net/2004/08/05/d40805012626.htm. Accessed 5 January 2024.

———. 2005. Top terror Arman gets life term. 23 September. https://archive.thedailystar.net/2005/09/23/d50923012418.htm. Accessed 5 January 2024.

———. 2010. A hint at legitimising extortion? 15 September. https://www.thedailystar.net/news-detail-154427. Accessed 5 February 2024.

———. 2015. Bus driver hurt in Karwan Bazar crude bomb blast. 25 January. http://www.thedailystar.net/bus-driver-hurt-in-karwan-bazar-crude-bomb-blast-61606. Accessed 10 December 2015.

———. 2016. Rehabilitate beggars: Prime minister asks social welfare ministry. 3 January. https://www.thedailystar.net/city/rehabilitate-beggars-196204. Accessed 5 February 2024.

———. 2018. Extortion rampant in transport sector. 18 July. https://www.thedailystar.net/frontpage/extortion-rampant-transport-sector-1607152. Accessed 5 February 2024.

———. 2019. No extortion now: Home minister. 7 May. https://www.thedailystar.net/country/news/no-extortion-now-home-minister-asaduzzaman-khan-bangladesh-1740088. Accessed 5 February 2024.

———. 2023. Vendor beaten to death for 'skipping rally'. 14 June. https://www.thedailystar.net/news/bangladesh/crime-justice/news/vendor-beaten-death-skipping-rally-3345491. Accessed 5 February 2024.

Das, A. 1985. Jute mill strike of 1928: A case study. *Economic and Political Weekly* 20(4): PE27–PE33.

Das, S. 1990. Communal violence in twentieth century colonial Bengal: An analytical framework. *Social Scientist* 18(6–7): 21–37.

———. 1991. *Communal Riots in Bengal 1905–1947*. Delhi: Oxford University Press.

———. 1994. The 'goondas': Towards a reconstruction of the Calcutta underworld through police records. *Economic and Political Weekly* 29(44): 2877–2883.

Das, V. and D. Poole. 2004. State and its margins: Comparative ethnographies. In *Anthropology in the Margins of the State*, edited by V. Das and D. Poole, 3–33. New Delhi: Oxford University Press.

Das Gupta, R. 1994. A labour history of social security and mutual assistance in India. *Economic and Political Weekly* 29(11): 612–620.

Datta, R. 2000. *Society, Economy and the Market: Commercialization in Rural Bengal, c. 1760–1800*. New Delhi: Manohar.

d'Cruz, C. 2014. Community savings: A basic building block in the work of urban poor federations. Working paper, International Institute for Environment and Development.

d'Cruz, C. and P. Mudimu. 2012. Community savings that mobilize federations, build women's leadership and support slum upgrading. *Environment and Urbanization* 25(1): 31–45.

de Haan, A. 1997. Unsettled settlers: Migrant workers and industrial capitalism in Calcutta. *Modern Asian Studies* 31(4): 919–949.

Demographia. 2023. *Demographia World Urban Areas*. 19th annual report.

Den Hollander, A. N. J. 1990. Social control in a city in Bengal: The 'mahalla sardars' and 'panchayats' of Dacca, East Pakistan. In *The Panchayat System of Dhaka*, edited by K. M. Azam and translated by W. van Schendel, 48–73. Dhaka: Dhaka City Museum.

Denyer, G. W. 2015. *The Killing Consensus: Police, Organized Crime and the Regulation of Life and Death in Urban Brazil*. Oakland, California: University of California Press.

Devine, J. 1999. One foot in each boat: The macro politics and micro sociology of NGOs in Bangladesh. PhD thesis, University of Bath, UK.

———. 2002. Ethnography of a policy process: A case study of land redistribution in Bangladesh. *Public Administration and Development* 22(5): 403–414.

———. 2006. NGOs, politics and grassroots mobilisation: Evidence from Bangladesh. *Journal of South Asian Development* 1(1): 77–101.

Eisenstadt, S. N. and L. Roniger. 1984. *Patrons, Clients and Friends: Interpersonal Relations and the Structure of Trust in Society*. Cambridge: Cambridge University Press.

Elsenhans, H. 2021. Global South: The transition to capitalism against rent. In *Development, Capitalism and Rent: The Political Economy of Hartmut Elsenhans*, edited by H. Warnecke-Berger, 135–171. Switzerland: Springer.

Evans, B. 1997. Cultural context and contractual relations: The Madras planters' labour law and the rise of the plantation maistri, 1904–1927. *Journal of the Royal Asiatic Society* 7(1): 73–92.

Faruqui, M. D. 2012. *The Princes of the Mughal Empire, 1504–1719*. New York: Cambridge University Press.

Foster, W. 1923. *The English Factories in India 1661–64*. Oxford: Clarendon Press.

Franda, M. 1981. Ziaur Rahman and Bangladeshi nationalism. *Economic and Political Weekly* 16(10–12): 357–380.

Gayer, L. 2014. *Karachi: Ordered Disorder and the Struggle for the City*. New York: Oxford University Press.

Geertz, C. 1962. The rotating credit associations: A 'middle rung'. *Economic Development and Cultural Change* 10(3): 241–263.

Ghosh, P. 2000. *Colonialism, Class, and a History of the Calcutta Jute Millhands, 1880–1930*. Hyderabad: Orient Longman.

Gilmartin, D. 2020. Introduction. In *South Asian Sovereignty: the Conundrum of Worldly Power*, edited by D. Gilmartin, P. Price and A. E. Ruud, 1–34. New Delhi: Routledge.

Goldstein, D. M. and E. D. Arias. 2010. *Violent Democracies in Latin America*. Durham: Duke University Press.

Goodfellow, T. and D. Jackman, eds. 2023. *Controlling the Capital: Political Dominance in the Urbanizing World*. Oxford: Oxford University Press.

Gooptu, N. 2001. *The Politics of the Urban Poor in Early Twentieth-century India*. Cambridge: Cambridge University Press.

Goyal, Y. 2018. The coal mine mafia of India: A mirror of corporate power. *American Journal of Economics and Sociology* 77(2): 541–574.

Habib, I. 1963. *The Agrarian System of Mughal India 1556–1707*. New Delhi: Oxford University Press.

Hackenbroch, K. and S. Hossain. 2012. 'The organised encroachment of the powerful': Everyday practices of public space and water supply in Dhaka, Bangladesh. *Planning Theory and Practice* 13(3): 397–420.

Hakim, M. A. 1998. Bangladesh: The beginning of the end of militarised politics? *Contemporary South Asia* 7(3): 283–300.

Hambly, G. 1974. A note on the trade in eunuchs in Mughal Bengal. *Journal of the American Oriental Society* 94(1): 125–130.

———. 1987. Towns and cities: Mughal India. In *The Cambridge Economic History of India*, vol. 1, *c. 1200–1750*, edited by T. Raychaudhuri and I. Habib, 434–451. Cambridge: Cambridge University Press.

Hansen, T. B. 2005. Sovereigns beyond the state: On legality and authority in urban India. In *Sovereign Bodies: Citizens, Migrants, and States in the Postcolonial World*, edited by T. B. Hansen and F. Stepputat, 169–191. Princeton: Princeton University Press.

Harriss-White, B. and L. Michelutti, eds. 2019. *The Wild East: Criminal Political Economies in South Asia*. London: UCL Press.

Hartmann, B. and J. Boyce. 1983. *A Quiet Violence: View from a Bangladeshi Village*. London: Zed Press.

Hassan, M. and W. Prichard. 2016. The political economy of domestic tax reform in Bangladesh: Political settlements, informal institutions and the negotiation of reform. *Journal of Development Studies* 52(12): 1704–1721.

Heehs, P. 1992. The Maniktala secret society: An early Bengal terrorist group. *Indian Economic and Social History Review* 29(3): 349–370.

Heuzé, D. 2009. Bondage in India: Representing the past or the present? The case of the Dhanbad coal belt during the 1980s. In *India's Unfree Workforce: Of Bondage Old and New*, edited by J. Breman, I. Guérin and A. Prakash, 147–169. New Delhi: Oxford University Press.

Hirschfeld, K. 2015. *Gangster States: Organised Crime, Kleptocracy and Political Collapse*. New York: Palgrave Macmillan.

Hoornweg, D. and K. Pope. 2017. Population predictions for the world's largest cities in the 21st century. *Environment and Urbanization* 29(1): 195–216.

Hossain, M. E. 2017. Extortion on by using names of top terrors. *Daily Sun*, 4 August. https://www.daily-sun.com/post/245508/Extortion-on-by-using-names-of-top-terrors. Accessed 5 February 2024.

Hossain, N. 2017. *The Aid Lab: Understanding Bangladesh's Unexpected Success*. Oxford: Oxford University Press.

Hossain, S. 2012. The informal practice of appropriation and social control: Experience from a bosti in Dhaka. *Environment and Urbanization* 25(1): 209–224.

Hunter, W. W. 1886. *The Indian Empire: Its People, History and Products.* 2nd ed. London: Trübner & Co.

Huque, A. S. and M. Y. Akhter. 1989. Militarisation and opposition in Bangladesh: Parliamentary approval and public reaction. *Journal of Commonwealth and Comparative Politics* 27(2): 172–184.

Indian Law Commission (ILC). 1841. *Reports of the Indian Law Commission upon Slavery in India.* Fort William.

Islam, M. M. 1983. Industrial relations in Bangladesh. *Indian Journal of Industrial Relations* 19(2): 161–189.

Islam, S. S. 1984. The state in Bangladesh under Zia (1975–81). *Asian Survey* 24(5): 556–573.

Jack, J. C. 1915. *Final Report on the Survey and Settlement Operations in the Bakarganj District: 1900 to 1908.* Calcutta: Bengal Secretariat Book Depot.

Jackman, D. 2018. The decline of gangsters and politicization of violence in urban Bangladesh. *Development and Change* 50(5): 1214–1238.

———. 2019. Violent intermediaries and political order in Bangladesh. *European Journal of Development Research* 31(4): 705–723.

———. 2021. Students, movements and the threat to authoritarianism in Bangladesh. *Contemporary South Asia* 29(2): 181–197.

———. 2022. Beggar bosses on the streets of Dhaka. *Journal of Contemporary Asia* 54(1): 152–169.

———. 2023. Dominating Dhaka. In *Controlling the Capital: Political Dominance in the Urbanizing World*, edited by T. Goodfellow and D. Jackman, 118–143. Oxford: Oxford University Press.

Jackman, D. and M. Maitrot. 2021. Allies among enemies: Political authority and party (dis)loyalty in Bangladesh. *Modern Asian Studies* 55(6): 2088–2112.

———. 2022. The party–police nexus in Bangladesh. *Journal of Development Studies* 58(8): 1516–1530.

Jaffe, R. 2013. The hybrid state: Crime and citizenship in urban Jamaica. *American Ethnologist* 40(4): 734–748.

Jahan, R. 2018. Political parties, movements, elections and democracy in Bangladesh. Gyantapas Abdur Razzaq Distinguished Lecture, Dhaka University, 27 January.

Jahangir, B. K. 1976. *Differentiation, Polarisation and Confrontation in Rural Bangladesh.* Dhaka: Centre for Social Studies.

James, D. 2011. The return of the broker: Consensus, hierarchy, and choice in South African land reform. *Journal of the Royal Anthropological Institute* 17(2): 318–338.

Jauregui, B. 2016. *Provisional Authority: Police, Order, and Security in India.* Chicago: University of Chicago Press.

Joseph, J. 2016. *A Feast of Vultures: The Hidden Business of Democracy in India.* Delhi: Harper Collins.

Karim, A. 1964. *Dacca, the Mughal Capital.* Dacca: Asiatic Society of Pakistan.

———. 1967. Some inscriptions of Dacca. *Journal of the Asiatic Society of Pakistan* 7(2): 289–233.

Kaylvas, S. N., I. Shapiro and T. Masoud, eds. 2008. *Order, Conflict and Violence.* Bath: Cambridge University Press.

Khan, I. A. 2000. Struggle for survival: Networks and relationships in a Bangladesh slum. PhD thesis, University of Bath, UK.

Khan, M. H. 2010. *Bangladesh: Partitions, Nationalisms, and Legacies for State-building.* London: SOAS.

———. 2017. Anti-corruption in Bangladesh: A political settlements analysis. Anti-corruption Evidence (ACE) (Working Paper 003), SOAS, London.

Khan, Z. R. 1981. Politicization of the Bangladesh military: A response to perceived shortcomings of civilian government. *Asian Survey* 21(5): 551–564.

Khanum, N. 1982. Aspects of the urban history, social, administrative and institutional of Dhaka city, 1921–1947. PhD thesis, School of Oriental and African Studies, University of London.

Klem, B. and B. Suykens. 2018. The politics of order and disturbance: Public authority, sovereignty, and violent contestation in South Asia. *Modern Asian Studies* 52(3): 753–783.

Klenfield, R. 2018. *A Savage Order: How the World's Deadliest Countries Can Forge a Path to Security.* New York: Pantheon Books.

Kooiman, D. 1977. Jobbers and the emergence of trade unions in Bombay. *International Review of Social History* 22(3): 313–328.

Krishna, A. 2011. Gaining access to public services and the democratic state in India: Institutions in the middle. *Studies in Comparative International Development* 46: 98–117.

Kuttig, J. 2019. Urban political machines and student politics in 'middle' Bangladesh: Violent party labor in Rajshahi city. *Critical Asian Studies* 51(3): 403–418.

———. 2020. Labour power and bossing: Local leadership formation and the party-state in 'middle' Bangladesh. *Contributions to Indian Sociology* 54(2): 193–214.

Laskar, R. 2007. City beggars: Not so disorganised! *Daily Star,* 12 February. http://archive.thedailystar.net/2007/02/12/d702122504147.htm. Accessed 5 February 2024.

Lata, L., P. Walters and S. Roitman. 2019. A marriage of convenience: Street vendors' everyday accommodation of power in Dhaka, Bangladesh. *Cities* 84: 143–150.

Levien, M. 2015. Social capital as obstacle to development: Brokering land, norms, and trust in rural India. *World Development* 74: 77–92.

Lewis, D. 1989. Technologies and transactions: A study of the interaction between new technology and agrarian structure in Bangladesh. PhD thesis, University of Bath, UK.

Lewis, D. and W. van Schendel. 2020. Rethinking the Bangladesh state. *Contributions to Indian Sociology* 54(2): 306–323.

Lewis, E. M. 1868. *Principal Heads of the History and Statistics of the Dacca Division*. Calcutta: Central Press Company.

Lewis, N. 1978. *Naples '44: A World War II Diary of Occupied Italy*. New York: Carroll & Graf Publishers.

———. 2003. *The Honoured Society: The Sicilian Mafia Observed*. New York: Eland.

Lifschultz, L. 1979. *Bangladesh: The Unfinished Revolution*. London: Zed Press.

Lindquist, A. 1977. Military and development in Bangladesh. *IDS Bulletin* 9(1): 10–18.

Lucassen, J., T. De Moor and J. L. van Zanden. 2008. The return of the guilds: Towards a global history of the guilds in pre-industrial times. *International Review of Social History* 53 (Supplement 16): 9–18.

Maitrot, M. and D. Jackman. 2018. The 2018 Bangladeshi election. Working paper, Effective States and Inclusive Development Research Centre (ESID), University of Manchester, UK.

———. 2023. Discipline, development and duress: The art of winning an election in Bangladesh. *Critical Asian Studies* 55(3): 424–439.

Malejacq, R. 2016. Warlords, intervention, and state consolidation: A typology of political orders in weak and failed states. *Security Studies* 25(1): 85–110.

Maloney, C. and A. B. S. Ahmed. 1988. *Rural Savings and Credit in Bangladesh*. Dhaka: University Press Limited.

Mamoon, M. 1990. Introduction to *The Panchayat System of Dhaka*, edited by K. M. Azam and translated by W. van Schendel, 1–79. Dhaka: Dhaka City Museum.

Maniruzzaman, T. 1992. The fall of the military dictator: 1991 elections and the prospect of civilian rule in Bangladesh. *Pacific Affairs* 65(2): 203–224.

Maniruzzaman, T. and U. A. B. Razia Akter Basu 1983. Civilian succession and the 1981 presidential election in Bangladesh. In *Transfer and Transformation: Political Institutions in the New Commonwealth*, edited by P. Lyon and J. Manor, 117–142. Leicester: Leicester University Press.

Martin, M. R. 2008. The conqueror's prize: Revenue, information and conflict in British Bengal, 1765–1819. PhD thesis. Yale University, New Haven.

Marx, K. 1953. The British rule in India. *New York Daily Tribune*, June 25.

Mascarenhas, A. 1986. *Bangladesh: A Legacy of Blood*. London: Hodder & Stoughton.

Masselos, J. 1982. Jobs and jobbery: The sweeper in Bombay under the raj. *Indian Economic and Social History Review* 19(2): 101–139.

Mavis, M. 2022. Bangladesh has the lowest tax GDP ratio in South Asia. *Dhaka Tribune*, 20 March. https://www.dhakatribune.com/business/265992/bangladesh-has-the-lowest-tax-gdp-ratio-in-south. Accessed 5 February 2024.

McGregor, J. A. 1989. Towards a better understanding of credit in rural development: The case of Bangladesh—The patron state. *Journal of International Development* 1(4): 467–486.

McLane, J. R. 1993. *Land and Local Kinship in Eighteenth-century Bengal*. Cambridge: Cambridge University Press.

Meagher, K. 2012. The strength of weak states? Non-state security forces and hybrid governance in Africa. *Development and Change* 43(5): 1073–1101.

Meehan, P. and S. L. Dan. 2022. Brokered rule: Militias, drugs, and borderland governance in the Myanmar–China borderlands. *Journal of Contemporary Asia* 53(4): 561–583.

Michelutti, L. 2019. The inter-state criminal life of sand and oil in north India. In *The Wild East: Criminal Political Economies in South Asia*, edited by B. Harriss-White and L. Michelutti, 168–193. London: UCL Press.

Michelutti, L., A. Hoque, N. Martin, D. Picherit, P. Rollier, A. E. Ruud and C. Still. 2018. *Mafia Raj: The Rule of Bosses in South Asia*. Stanford: Stanford University Press.

Mollah, S. and A. Hosen. 2015. Happy extortion. *Daily Star*, 15 July. https://www.thedailystar.net/frontpage/happy-extortion-112597. Accessed 5 February 2024.

Mollah, S. and Z. Islam. 2021. The allure is a free pass to extort. *Daily Star*, 13 June. https://www.thedailystar.net/frontpage/news/the-allure-free-pass-extort-2109641. Accessed 5 February 2024.

Mollah, S. and M. J. Khan. 2019. Extortion on rise ahead of Eid. *Daily Star*, 4 June 2019. https://www.thedailystar.net/frontpage/illegal-money-extortion-rise-ahead-eid-ul-fitr-2019-1753114. Accessed 19 January 2024.

Moncada, E. 2013. The politics of urban violence: Challenges for development in the Global South. *Studies in Comparative International Development* 48: 217–239.

Moore, M. 2008. Between coercion and contract: Competing narratives on taxation and governance. In *Taxation and State-building in Developing Countries: Capacity and Consent*, edited by D. Brautigam, O-H. Fjeldstad and M. Moore, 34–63. Cambridge: Cambridge University Press.

Mortimer, J. 1852. *A Descriptive and Historical Account of the Cotton Manufacture of Dacca, in Bengal*. London: John Mortimer.

Mukherjee, T. 2011. Markets in eighteenth century Bengal economy. *Indian Economic and Social History Review* 48(2): 143–176.

Mukherjee, Tumpa. 2017. Underworld in Calcutta/Kolkata 1946–2002. *Vidyasagar University Journal of History* 6: 32–45.

Municipal Office, Dacca. 1969. Working paper for the special meeting to be held on 22nd March 1969. National Archives of Bangladesh.

Nandi, S. 2010. Constructing the criminal: Politics of social imaginary of the 'goonda'. *Social Scientist* 38(3–4): 37–54.

———. 2016. Respectable anxiety, plebian criminality: Politics of the Goonda Act (1923) of colonial Calcutta. *Crime, History and Societies* 20(2): 1–54.

Naqvi, H. K. 1964. A study of urban centres and industries in the central provinces of the Mughal empire between 1556 and 1803. PhD thesis, SOAS, University of London.

North, D. C., J. J. Wallis and B. R. Weingast. 2009. *Violence and Social Orders: A Conceptual Framework for Interpreting Recorded Human History*. New York: Cambridge University Press.

North, D. C., J. J. Wallis, S. B. Webb and B. R. Weingast, eds. 2013. *In the Shadow of Violence: Politics, Economics, and the Problems of Development*. Cambridge: Cambridge University Press.

Obaidullah, A. T. M. 2019. *Institutionalization of the Parliament in Bangladesh: A Study of Donor Intervention for Reorganization and Development*. Singapore: Palgrave.

Pattenden, J. 2010 A neoliberalisation of civil society? Self-help groups and the labouring class poor in rural south India. *Journal of Peasant Studies* 37(3): 485–512.

———. 2011. Gatekeeping as accumulation and domination: Decentralization and class relations in rural South India. *Journal of Agrarian Change* 11(2): 164–194.

Piliavsky, A., ed. 2014. *Patronage as Politics in South Asia*. Cambridge: Cambridge University Press.

Pope, N. 2023. Militias going rogue: Social dilemmas and coercive brokerage in Rio de Janeiro's urban frontier. *Journal of International Development* 35(3): 478–490.

Prakash, O. 1985. *The Dutch East India Company and the Economy of Bengal, 1630–1720*. Princeton: Princeton University Press.

Raj, J. 2019. Beyond the unions: The Pembillai Orumai women's strike in the south Indian tea belt. *Journal of Agrarian Change* 19(4): 671–689.

Rakopoulos, T. 2017. Façade egalitarianism: Mafia and cooperative in Sicily. *PoLAR: Political and Legal Anthropology Review* 40(1): 104–121.

Rankin, J. T. 1918. Dacca diaries – I. *Dacca Review* 8 (May): 1–33.

———. 1920. Dacca diaries. *Journal of the Asiatic Society of Bengal* 16(1): 91–158.

Ray, A. 2013. Colonial constitutionalism and the case of Bengal Vagrancy Act. http://dx.doi.org/10.2139/ssrn.2361980. Accessed 5 February 2024.

Ray, R. K. 1979. *Urban Roots of Indian Nationalism: Pressure Groups and Conflict of Interests in Calcutta City Politics, 1875–1939*. New Delhi: Vikas.

Raychaudhuri, T. 1982. The Mughal empire. In *The Cambridge Economic History of India*, edited by T. Raychaudhuri and I. Habib, vol. 1: *C.1200–C.1750*. Cambridge: Cambridge University Press.

Reddy, G. R. and G. Haragopal. 1985. The pyraveekar: 'The fixer' in rural India. *Asian Survey* 25(11): 1148–1162.

Reddy, P. C. 2007. Guilds and their administrative powers and functions in mediaeval Andhra desha. *Proceedings of the Indian History Congress* 68(1): 295–302.

Reporters Without Borders. 2005. *Reporters Without Borders Annual Report 2005 – Bangladesh*. https://www.refworld.org/docid/46e690d814.html. Accessed 24 November 2023.

Richards, J. F. 1975. *Mughal Administration in Golconda*. Oxford: Oxford University Press.

Rosen, L. 2010. Understanding corruption. *American Interest* (Spring). https://www.the-american-interest.com/2010/03/01/understanding-corruption/. Accessed 5 February 2024.

Roy, A. 2018. *Making Peace, Making Riots: Communalism and Communal Violence, Bengal 1940–1947*. Cambridge: Cambridge University Press.

Roy, T. 2008a. Sardars, jobbers, kanganies: The labour contractor and Indian economic history. *Modern Asian Studies* 42(5): 971–998.

———. 2008b. The guild in modern South Asia. *International Review of Social History* 53 (Supplement 16): 95–120.

Royal Commission on Labour in India (RCLI). 1931. *Report of the Royal Commission on Labour in India*. Calcutta: Government of India.

Rutherford, S. 1997. Informal financial services in Dhaka's slums. In *Who Needs Credit? Poverty and Finance in Bangladesh*, edited by G. Wood and I. A. Sharif, 351–370. Dhaka: University Press Limited.

———. 2009. *The Poor and Their Money*. Rugby: Practical Action Publishing.

Ruud, A. E. 2012. To create a crowd: Student leaders in Dhaka. In *Power and Influence in India: Bosses, Lords and Captains*, edited by P. Price and A. E. Ruud, 70–95. Delhi: Routledge.

———. 2014. The political bully in Bangladesh. In *Patronage as Politics in South Asia*, edited by A. Piliavsky, 303–325. Cambridge: Cambridge University Press.

———. 2018. The Osman dynasty: The making and unmaking of a political family. *Studies in Indian Politics* 6(2): 209–224.

———. 2019. The politics of contracting in provincial Bangladesh. In *The Wild East: Criminal Political Economies in South Asia*, B. Harriss-White and L. Michelutti, 362–387. London: UCL Press.

———. 2020. The mohol: The hidden power structure of Bangladesh local politics. *Contributions to Indian Sociology* 54(2): 173–192.

Sanchez, A. 2016. *Criminal Capital: Violence, Corruption and Class in Industrial India*. Delhi: Routledge.

Saviano, R. 2011. *Gomorrah*. UK: Pan Macmillan.

Schneider, J. 2018. Fifty years of mafia corruption and anti-mafia reform. *Current Anthropology* 59(18): S16–S27.

Scott, J. 1972. Patron–client politics and political change in Southeast Asia. *American Political Science Review* 66(1): 91–113.

Sen, A. K. 2002. Mode of labour control in colonial India. *Economic and Political Weekly* 37(38): 3956–3966.

Sen, S. 1998. *Empire of Free Trade: The East India Company and the Making of the Colonial Marketplace*. Philadelphia: University of Pennsylvania Press.

Sen, Sumita. 2010. Commercial recruiting and informal intermediation: Debate over the *sardari* system in Assam tea plantations, 1860–1900. *Modern Asian Studies* 44(1): 3–28.

Sengupta, K. M. 2015. Bazaars, landlords and the company government in late eighteenth-century Calcutta. *Indian Economic and Social History Review* 52(2): 121–146.

Shakespear, J. 1834. *A Dictionary: Hindustani and English*. London: J. L. Cox and Son.

Sidel, J. T. 1995. On the waterfront: Labour racketeering in the port of Cebu. *South East Asia Research* 3(1): 3–17.

Silvestri, M. S. 1998. 'The dirty work of empire': Policing, political violence and public order in colonial Bengal, 1905–1947. PhD thesis, Columbia University, New York.

Simeon, D. 1995. *The Politics of Labour under Late Colonialism: Workers, Unions and the State in Chota Nagpur 1928–1939*. Delhi: Manohar.

Singh, N. and B. Harriss-White. 2019. The criminal economics and politics of black coal in Jharkhand. In *The Wild East: Criminal Political Economies in South Asia*, edited by B. Harriss-White and L. Michelutti, 35–67. London: UCL Press.

Singh, S. 2019. India Today report reveals the extent of 'syndicate raj' in TMC-ruled West Bengal. *TFI Post*, 23 January. https://tfipost.com/2019/01/syndicate-raj-bengal-01/. Accessed 5 February 2024.

Sissener, T. K. 2019. The 'land and real estate mafia', West Bengal, east India. In *The Wild East: Criminal Political Economies in South Asia*, edited by B. Harriss-White and L. Michelutti, 215–339. London: UCL Press.

Sobhan, R. 2004. Structural dimensions of malgovernance in Bangladesh. *Economic and Political Weekly* 39(36): 4101–4108.

Spencer, J. 1997. Post-colonialism and the political imagination. *Journal of the Royal Anthropological Institute* 3(1): 1–19.

Staniland, P. 2017. Armed politics and the study of intrastate conflict. *Journal of Peace Research* 54(4): 459–467.

Stovel, K. and L. Shaw. 2012. Brokerage. *Annual Review of Sociology* 38(1): 139–158.

Sud, N. 2014. The men in the middle: A missing dimension in global land deals. *Journal of Peasant Studies* 41(4): 593–612.

Superintendent of Police, Bakarganj. 1943. Letter from the superintendent of police, Bakarganj, to the assistant inspector-general of police, Bengal, 19th October 1943. Letter No. 6575E. National Archives of Bangladesh.

Suykens, B. 2015. The land that disappeared: Forceful occupation, disputes and the negotiation of landlord power in a Bangladeshi *bastee*. *Development and Change* 46(3): 486–507.

———. 2016. Segmentary opposition, vertical integration and the structure of political relations in Bangladesh: A descriptive model. *Journal of Asian and African Studies* 52(8): 1141–1158.

———. 2017. The Bangladesh party-state: A diachronic comparative analysis of party-political regimes. *Commonwealth and Comparative Politics* 55(2): 187–213.

———. 2018. 'A hundred per cent good man cannot do politics': Violent self-sacrifice, student authority, and party-state integration in Bangladesh. *Modern Asian Studies* 52(3): 883–916.

Taher, M. A. 1999. Politicization of trade unions: Issues and challenges in Bangladesh perspective. *Indian Journal of Industrial Relations* 34(4): 403–420.

Taifoor, S. M. 1956. *Glimpses of Old Dhaka*. Dacca: Saogat Press.

Tayeb, T. 2022. Is Dhaka beyond saving? *Daily Star*, 10 March. https://www.thedailystar.net/opinion/closer-look/news/dhaka-beyond-saving-2979391. Accessed 4 January 2024.

Taylor, J. 1840. *A Sketch of the Topography and Statistics of Dacca*. Calcutta: G. H. Huttmann, Military Orphan Press.

Tilly, C. 1985. War making and state making as organized crime. In *Bringing the State Back In*, edited by P. Evans, D. Rueschemeyer and T. Skocpol, 169–191. Cambridge: Cambridge University Press.

United Nations Office on Drugs and Crime. 2019. *Global Study on Homicide.*

Vaishnav, M. 2017. *When Crime Pays: Money and Muscle in Indian Politics.* New Haven: Yale University Press.

Varese, F. 2001. *The Russian Mafia: Private Protection in a New Market Economy.* Oxford: Oxford University Press.

———. 2013. Protection and extortion. In *The Oxford Handbook of Organized Crime*, edited by Letizia Paoli, 343–358. New York: Oxford University Press.

Volkov, V. 2002. *Violent Entrepreneurs: The Use of Force in the Making of Russian Capitalism.* Ithaca: Cornell University Press.

Walters, H. 1832. Census of the city of Dacca. In *Asiatic Researchers; or Transactions of the Society, Instituted in Bengal, for Enquiring into the History, the Antiquities, the Arts and Sciences, and Literature of Asia*, vol. 27, 535–558. Calcutta: Bengal Military Orphan Press.

Warnecke-Berger, E. 2021. Introduction to *Development, Capitalism and Rent: The Political Economy of Hartmut Elsenhans*, edited by H. Warnecke-Berger. Switzerland: Springer.

Wheeler, J. 2014. 'Parallel power' in Rio de Janeiro: Coercive mediators and the fragmentation of citizenship in the favela. In *Mediated Citizenship: The Informal Politics of Speaking for Citizens in the Global South*, edited by B. Von Lieres and L. Piper, 72–89. Basingstoke: Palgrave Macmillan.

White, S. 1988. In the teeth of the crocodile: Class and gender in rural Bangladesh. PhD thesis, University of Bath, UK.

Wise, J. 1883. *Notes on the Races, Castes and Trades of Eastern Bengal.* London: Her Majesty's Printer Harrison and Sons.

Witsoe, J. 2009. Territorial democracy: Caste, dominance and electoral practice in postcolonial India. *PoLAR: Political and Legal Anthropology Review* 32(1): 64–83.

———. 2012. Everyday corruption and the political mediation of the Indian state: An ethnographic exploration of brokers in Bihar. *Economic and Political Weekly* 47(6): 47–54.

Wolf, E. 1956. Aspects of group relations in a complex society: Mexico. *American Anthropologist, New Series* 58(6): 1065–1078.

Wood, G. 1981. Rural class formation in Bangladesh, 1940–80. *Bulletin of Concerned Asian Scholars* 13(4): 2–15.

———. 1994. *Bangladesh: Whose Ideas, Whose Interests?* Dhaka: The University Press.

———. 2003. Staying secure, staying poor: The 'Faustian bargain'. *World Development* 31(3): 455–471.

———. 2010. The security of agency: Towards a sociology of poverty. Paper presented at Promoting Social Inclusion in South Asia: Policies, Pitfalls and the Analysis of Welfare/Insecurity Regimes, 13–14 September, University of Bath.

Yang, A. 1999. *Bazaar India: Markets, Society, and the Colonial State in Bihar.* Berkeley; Los Angeles: University of California Press.

You, J-S. 2013. Transition from a limited access order to an open access order: The case of South Korea. In *In the Shadow of Violence: Politics, Economics, and the Problems of Development*, edited by D. C. North, J. J. Wallis, S. B. Webb and B. R. Weingast, 293–327. New York: Cambridge University Press.

Index

abwab, 89
accumulating savings and credit associations (ASCA), 117, 128*n*100, 161
Aparajeyo Bangladesh, 106, 141
*arotdar*s, 25, 26, 103–105, 118, 123*n*7, 136, 165*n*4
associations, 8, 11, 16, 17, 91–92, 98*n*41, 104, 114–117, 126*n*65, 127*n*89, 150–151, 172, 174
Awami League (AL), 3, 4, 6, 14, 16, 17, 22–23, 30, 34–37, 39–41, 45*n*72, 48–49, 53, 55, 59–61, 65–68, 70–71*n*39, 72*n*46, 74–79, 82, 83, 85–88, 96*n*4, 119, 121, 131–139, 143–145, 147–148, 151–153, 156, 157, 159, 160, 162, 164, 166, 176, 179, 181

Bakarganj, 51–52, 89
Bangladesh Jatiobadi Chhatra Dal (JCD), 38, 62, 133
Bangladesh Nationalist Party (BNP), 3, 16, 17, 22, 38–40, 47, 55, 59, 61, 62, 64, 65, 73, 75, 77, 83, 120, 131–136, 138–140, 143–148, 151–154, 157, 160, 170, 176, 179, 181

Bangladesh Truck and Covered Van Owners Association, 116
'Basket Owners' Society, 116
basti, 1, 3, 4, 23, 27, 28, 31, 33, 40, 41–42*n*8, 46, 49, 50, 53, 56, 62, 67, 84, 108, 110, 116–117, 152, 160, 166
*bepari*s, 25, 99*n*53, 123*n*7, 123*n*11
bhagtiya katra, 32
bKash, 23, 72*n*48
bomb, 3, 17, 26, 27, 29, 46–48, 49–51, 97*n*19, 108, 109, 112, 125*n*52, 132, 133, 143–148, 150–151, 154, 156–157, 170, 179
*boro bhai*s, 12, 104–108
broker, 9, 10, 20*n*53, 20*n*55, 42*n*14, 99*n*53, 109, 112–113, 168, 177, 183–184*n*40, 183*n*31, 183*n*33

Camorra, 14, 47
caretaker government, 39, 40, 45*n*72, 55, 67, 73, 74, 144, 153, 179
carrot syndicate, 136–143
chamcha, 81, 136, 141, 164
chandabaji, 14, 16, 67, 75, 96, 131, 160
chanda/chaada, 14, 56, 60, 62, 73–96, 97*n*19, 100*n*69, 109, 115, 117–118, 120–122, 137, 150, 157, 162, 170, 175, 176

Chattra League, 184n45
Chinomul, 2, 27, 106
coil, 54, 123n7
*coolie*s, 25–26, 33, 50, 51, 54, 57, 60, 69n20, 103, 105, 116, 118, 123n5, 123n11, 140, 148n1
corruption, 5–6, 18n13, 37, 40, 63–64, 66, 73–74, 88, 96n1, 101n78, 109–111, 113–114, 119, 144, 176
crime and politics, 4–8

dalal, 10, 96n17, 99n53, 103, 163
danda
  dandaniti, 94
Dano Mizan, 60–62, 67, 86
dasturi, 108–112, 114, 115, 124n27, 170
Dhaka, 1–3, 7, 8, 14–16, 22–49, 51–55, 62–67, 69n28, 70n33, 70n39, 72n44, 74, 75, 77, 78, 80–85, 87–88, 90–95, 98n37, 99n53, 99n57, 100–101n71, 103, 104, 110, 111, 115–117, 123n5, 129, 133–135, 141, 144, 146, 147, 151, 152, 154, 157, 159, 160, 162, 164, 165n2, 168–171, 173, 177–180
Dhaka City Corporation (DCC), 77, 78, 170
Dhaka South City Corporation (DSCC), 78
Dhanbad, 113, 174

East India Company, 13, 29, 32, 42n12, 49, 68n10, 90, 93, 100–101n71
East Pakistan, 52, 53
eunuch, 30–33, 42n14, 42n15, 130
extortion, 5, 20n54, 50, 54–57, 60, 63, 64, 67–68, 72n48, 79, 81, 86–89, 94, 97n22, 99–100n57, 101n78, 110, 119, 129, 130, 160, 174, 183n33

factionalism, 35, 169
*faujdar*s, 94, 100n68
five-star group, 59–60
Fokinni Bazaar, 2, 96n4

godfather, 3–5, 47, 49, 55–56, 58–60, 64, 70n33, 74, 90, 95, 168, 176–177
Goonda, 48–53, 55, 67, 68–69n13, 68n10, 68n11, 69n17, 69n20, 83, 90, 110, 134, 140, 158, 165n6, 180
gram sarkar, 38, 39

hafta, 89
*hartal*s, 39, 135, 144, 179

Ibrahim, Dawood, 55
Indian National Trade Union Congress (INTUC), 113
informers
  source, 85
intermediaries, 7, 9–11, 15, 16, 19n47, 20n53, 40–41, 51, 69n20, 75, 80–81, 83, 85, 88, 90–96, 98–99n43, 103, 104, 109, 112–114, 122, 166–170, 174–177, 183–184n40, 183n30
intreccio, 5

jagir
  jagirdar, 92
Jatio Rakkhi Bahini (JRB), 37, 39, 65
Jatiya Party, 39, 54, 55, 59–61, 134–135
Jatiya Shangshad, 3
jhupri, 4, 7, 11, 15–17, 17n1, 22–30, 34, 36, 41–42n8, 46, 48, 56–59, 73, 74, 77, 79, 81–84, 102–108, 120–122, 123n9, 124n13, 128n107, 129–148, 146n9, 148–149n2, 149n4, 149n12, 150–154, 156, 158, 159, 165n6, 169, 170, 176, 180

Index

jobbers, 50, 108–114, 119, 124*n*23, 125*n*52, 126*n*65, 129
Jubo Dal, 59, 61, 62, 65, 181
Jubo League, 37, 46–47, 54, 56, 58–61, 66, 77–78, 80, 81, 83, 84 86, 122, 135, 139, 157, 160, 164, 165, 178, 180, 184*n*45

kangali, 27, 145
Karachi, 12
Kawran Bazaar Van Drivers' Union, 24–34, 116
Kazi Nazrul Islam Avenue, 25, 30, 145
Kerala, 113–114
kidnapping, 5, 54, 56, 63, 64, 73, 79
Krishak League, 135, 156, 158

labour conflict, 37, 60
Labour Cooperative Society, 116, 117, 128*n*103
labour leader, 4, 9, 10, 15–17, 50, 78, 81, 102–104, 108–109, 111, 114, 120, 122, 155, 159, 169, 173
lathial, 52, 68*n*12
La Vinci, 24
liberalisation, 13
liberation, 28–29, 33, 34, 36, 37, 52, 53, 119, 181*n*2
lineman, 15, 16, 79–87, 96*n*4, 117–118, 120, 130, 163, 166, 169

mafia, 4, 5, 8–9, 18*n*28, 20*n*54, 47, 55, 90, 96*n*5, 113, 167–169, 175
*mahalla*s, 52, 69*n*22, 90–96, 98*n*37, 100*n*69
mastanocracy, 5
Member of Parliament (MP), 6, 77, 152–153
Mujib Bahini, 36, 37

Mukti Bahini, 36
Murgi Milon, 14
Muslim League, 42*n*12, 51, 55, 113
Myeferosh, 93, 115

Nawab, 51–53, 94
neoliberalism, 13
non-governmental organisation (NGO), 2, 3, 17*n*6, 23, 25, 41*n*3, 47, 102, 106, 117, 130, 146, 156, 171–173, 182*n*11

officer-in-charge (OC), 58, 72*n*44, 163, 167

paiker, 54
panchayat, 91–92, 94
patron, 9, 10, 20*n*55, 35, 41*n*15, 82, 113, 183–184*n*40
'Picchi' Hannan, 14–16, 46, 49, 53–68, 69*n*28, 70*n*33, 71*n*41, 72*n*42, 73–79, 83–86, 90, 97*n*18, 97*n*19, 103, 108, 117, 120, 121, 123*n*7, 128*n*107, 131, 132, 144, 149*n*5, 160, 161, 169, 178
police, 3, 4, 6, 17, 19*n*36, 20*n*54, 38, 39, 41*n*7, 46, 48, 50–54, 57–59, 63–66, 68*n*12, 69*n*17, 69*n*20, 75, 77–81, 83–85, 88, 92, 96*n*5, 96*n*17, 97*n*18, 100*n*58, 101*n*76, 110, 117, 119, 130, 136, 137, 141–147, 151, 154, 157, 160–163, 165*n*7, 168–169, 178–179, 182–183*n*29, 183–184*n*40
political violence, 5, 16–17, 104, 144, 147, 150
President Ershad, 28–29, 38, 39, 55, 70*n*33
Prothom Alo, 2

Rahman, Sheikh Mujibur, 34
Rahman, Ziaur, 36–37, 70n33
Rapid Action Battalion (RAB), 41n8, 63–66, 75, 79, 84, 85, 119, 136, 146, 147, 149n11, 151, 154, 159, 176
rotating savings and credit associations (ROSCA), 117, 128n100, 161

Sahib Ali, 57, 66, 71n41
*samiti*s, 11, 16, 17, 49, 50, 71n40, 104, 107, 114–122, 127n89, 127n90, 127n97, 128n101, 128n103, 130, 136, 143, 147, 150–165, 165n3, 169, 170, 173–176, 180, 181–182n2, 183n33
santrashi, 3, 4, 47–53, 55, 59–61, 63, 64, 67, 70–71n39, 70n37, 72n44, 72n46, 73–75, 79, 83, 85, 122, 136, 144, 151, 161, 176–178, 121
*sardar*s, 16, 51–54, 60, 69n17, 69n22, 91–92, 94, 100n69, 101n74, 103–105, 109–114, 116–118, 121, 122, 122n3, 123n6, 123n9, 123n11, 124n12, 124n13, 125–126n55, 125n35, 128n107, 136–140, 142–144, 146, 147, 148–149n2, 149n3, 152, 153, 156, 158, 176, 180, 183n30
sayer, 90, 98n36
Serai, 22–45, 90
seven-star group, 59–60, 67, 72n45
Shah, Khwaja Ambar, 30–33, 42n15, 42n16
society of syndicates, 87–90
Sonargaon, 24, 33, 57, 160
Sramik Dal, 83, 134, 140

Sramik League, 37, 41n4, 49, 56, 59, 61, 64, 67, 75, 77, 79, 80, 86, 119, 120, 180
Sreemangal, 8
street children, 14, 17, 27, 47, 149n9, 176
street vendors, 7, 11, 14, 17, 54, 57, 77, 80, 83, 89, 103, 160–165, 170, 175
Sundarbans, 8, 180
Swechasebak Dal, 133, 180
Swechasebak League, 77, 81
Sweden Aslam, 14, 54–57, 67, 83

tax farming, 92, 171
tax intermediaries, 16, 90–96
Tejgaon, 31–33, 46, 48–53, 59, 60, 62, 65, 67, 74, 96n4, 117–118, 120, 135, 138, 140, 142, 147
top terror, 5, 47, 58, 64, 65, 67, 79
Transparency International, 5
Truck and Covered Van Association, The, 78, 83, 86, 116–120

unions, 108–114

Village Defence Parties (VDP), 38

war on drugs, 27, 184n45
Water Supply and Sewer (WASA), 24, 26, 47, 56, 135, 142–143, 146, 153
West Bengal, 4, 43–44n32, 55, 167, 174
'Wholesale Owners' Society, 116
Wise, James, 32, 115

yaba, 25, 41–42n8, 44n72, 66, 83, 84, 140, 151–152

*zamindar*s, 13, 49, 93–94, 100–101n71, 100n58, 183–184n40